Critical Acclaim for Liam Clancy and

the mountain
of the women

"Often wry, always witty—a fascinating glimpse of the Big Bang in folk music."
—*Kirkus Reviews*

"Plainspoken, and consistently interesting, with a growing sense of youthful discovery."
—*Palm Beach Post*

"Clancy masterfully recounts more than forty years of acting, singing, and great foolishness . . . at once brilliant, funny, and sad."
—*Publishers Weekly*

"Clancy is a natural storyteller whose adventurous life provides material for a dozen books."
—*Dallas Morning News*

the mountain
of the women

Memoirs of an Irish Troubadour

Liam Clancy

broadway books

new york

broadway books and the Broadway Books colophon are trademarks of
Random House, Inc.

Originally published in hardcover in slightly different form in the United States by
Doubleday, a division of Random House, Inc., New York, in 2002.

Grateful acknowledgment is made for permission to reprint from the following:
"Strange Fruit" words and music by Lewis Allan, copyright © 1939 (Renewed) by
Music Sales Corporation (ASCAP), International Copyright Secured, All Rights
Reserved; "The Countess Cathleen" by William Butler Yeats, from *The Collected Plays
of W. B. Yeats,* Revised Edition, copyright © 1934, 1952 by The Macmillan
Company, copyright renewed in 1962 by Bertha Georgie Yeats and in 1980 by Anne
Yeats, reprinted with the permission of Scribner, a division of Simon & Schuster, Inc.;
Frank O'Connor, excerpts from *Kings, Lords, and Commons: An Anthology from the Irish:
Irish Poems from the Seventh Century to the Nineteenth* (New York: Alfred A. Knopf,
1959), Copyright © 1959 by Frank O'Connor, renewed in 1987 by Harriet
O'Donovan Sheehy, reprinted with the permission of Joan Daves Agency/Writer's
House, Inc., NY, on behalf of the proprietors; "Do Not Go Gentle Into That Good
Night" and "And Death Shall Have No Dominion" by Dylan Thomas, from *The
Poems of Dylan Thomas,* copyright © 1943 by New Directions Publishing Corp.,
reprinted by permission of New Directions Publishing Corp.

Library of Congress Cataloging-in-Publication Data
Clancy, Liam.
The mountain of the women / Liam Clancy.
p. cm.
Includes index.
ISBN 0-385-50204-4
1. Clancy, Liam, 2. Folk singers—Biography. I. title.
ML420.C533 A3 2002
782.42162'9162'0092—dc21
[B]   2001028450

ISBN 978-0-385-52050-8

Book design by Dana Leigh Treglia

First Paperback Edition

146028962

To Liam "Handsome" Hogan—the teacher who told me to take up writing when I was seventeen. It took me forty-three years to heed his advice.

To Kim, who has listened to my nonsense for thirty-something years.

And to the memory of my brothers Paddy and Tom.

Acknowledgments

Thanks go to: Niki Vettel, whose blind faith in my writing abilities led me to Richard Pine, who took another blind leap with me.

To my nephew Robbie O'Connell and his wife, Roxanne, who sat me down at a lap top computer and showed me how to write the word "the."

To my sister-in-law, Moira, who hounded me unmercifully into making a start.

To Bill Patrick and Patricia Mulcahy, who taught me how to crawl, and Bill Thomas, who, with the help of Kendra Harpster, got me up and walking.

To Maeve Binchy who advised me not to think of writing a book as "A big MOUNTAIN that you have to climb. Just write a little word and that will lead you on to a sentence. The next thing you know you have a paragraph and before you know it you've got a book."

To my daughters, Fiona—who gave me sound advice and could type faster than I could think—and Siobhan, who can't type at all but is a wise and thorough critic.

To my sons Eben and Donal, who listened when listening was the last thing in the world they wanted to do—and also for their invaluable help when it came to getting promotional material into shape.

To my friend Jim McKague, who ran rings around New York doing every conceivable thing to help.

To the Carrick poets Michael Coady and Seamus McGrath, fellow drinkers, tale-spinners, and late-night wonderers at the nature of existence. Michael also gave me a very detailed and insightful critique of my manuscript.

To *Irish Times* journalist Eileen Battersby, who, as an interviewer, gave me some idea of the doggedness that is necessary to get the job done.

To my ancient friend, Joe Kennedy, writer and mentor, who went to bat for me times out of mind.

And finally to my late lifelong friend, Kevin O'Driscoll, who, in spite of Job-like afflictions, kept us laughing up until the day he died. He looked forward so much to seeing his name in print in this book, but his body just couldn't wait.

the mountain
of the women

1

Not far from my hometown in Ireland there is a mountain called Slievenamon. It is shaped like a beautiful female breast and on its summit sits a cairn of stones, like a nipple. The name Slievenamon comes from the Gaelic, *Sliabh na mBan,* the mountain of the women. My blood tells me that my origins are there.

Some say the mountain got its name from the profile it presents when seen from Carrick-on-Suir, the town in which I was born. A more intriguing story tells how the legendary giant, Fionn McCool, would need a new wife each year and, be-cause of his mighty demands, would put all the candidates vying for the job to a test. On a certain day of the year they would all race to the top of Slievenamon and back. The winner, he considered, *might* have the stamina to cope with his virility for the next year.

Our town is in the valley of the river Suir at the top of the tide that surges all the way up the estuary from the sea, thirty or so miles to the east. The wooded hills rise up from the river to the south to good farmland that stretches the eight miles or so to the ice-carved Comeragh Mountains. To the north the land rises to a plain that reaches for the beautiful breast of Slievenamon and its foothills, four miles away. The valley to the west is known as the Golden Vale, the land of milk and honey. It is small wonder that wave after wave of invaders wanted to get their hands on this rich land. Just recently, archaeologists have started excavating local tumulus mounds as old as or older than Newgrange, which predates the pyramids of Egypt by some two centuries. Two groups of burial monuments called portal dolmens attest to the fact that humans have settled in this place since the Stone Age. There is something fascinating and humbling, as the Carrick poet Michael Coady dwells on in his writing, about occupying spaces which others have vacated and which we, in turn, will vacate for the next generation. In the nature of things the people of each generation assume, of course, that theirs is the only important one. In time, others will realize that they weren't the first ones here and try, perhaps, to unearth some knowledge of us.

On the south-facing slope of Slievenamon stand the ruins of a castle or great house of the 1700s with the remnants of walled gardens and old outlying walls with gable shapes of long-gone buildings. These ruins speak to us, as a well-known song about the place does, of the time when Cill Cais, the great house, was full of life and industry, of plenty and hospitality. The song also tells of the Great Lady—an Deigh Bhean, as she was called in the Irish—who held sway over this revered and wondrous place.

> An áit úd 'na gcónaiodh an Deigh Bhean,
> Fuair gradam is meidhir thar mná.
>
> —*"Cill Cais" (old song)*

What shall we do for timber?
The last of the woods is down.
Kilcash and the house of its glory
And the bell of the house is gone,
The spot where that lady waited
Who shamed all women for grace
When earls came sailing to greet her
And Mass was said in the place.

—"Kilcash" (translated by Frank O'Connor)

I learned that song at school as a boy in Carrick-on-Suir. Like all songs of past times, it was peopled with what I thought of as mythical figures, but one day I happened on a scene which brought the myth and the reality together before my very eyes. As my kids and I wandered about the ruins of Kilcash, a man who lived in one of the cottages nearby recognized me as one of the Clancys.

"You're one of the singers, aren't you? Liam, isn't it? I knew your father, Bob, from the insurance business. He used to call you by the English version of your name, Willie. Well, now, this is good. Do you see the old church down there below the castle? That's been there since the seventh century and inside that church there's a headstone with your name on it—William Clancy. The Board of Works are trying to save what's left of the early church, and the big stones are pulled back from the underground vault." There was a hint of awe in his voice. "They've cleared away decades of debris. If you go down the steps and let yer eyes get used to the dark, you'll see herself stretched out there, an Deigh Bhean, the Great Lady, Lady Iveagh, with two other skeletons: her husband, a Richard Butler I believe he'd be, and the bishop of the time, whose name I can't recall. Their lead coffins were taken by the IRA to make bullets during the Black and Tan War."

When the three kids and I went down into the chamber of the dead, sure enough, there on the rubble of the vault floor were the bones, red and moldering, of the woman I used to sing about in school. The kids and I gazed a long moment in fascination before beating a retreat back up to daylight.

As with many ruined churches in Ireland, the graves of what I suppose to be the "important people" are inside the church walls, while the lesser folk have to lie outside in the adjoining graveyard. As we made our way up to the main part of the church, an old man wandering from headstone to toppling headstone said, "There's class distinction everywhere, even in the graveyard." Searching through the gravestones within the ruined walls, trying to decipher the weatherworn names, I came upon the one my friend had referred to. Since it was made from hard slate and leaning away from the worst of the weather, it was easy to make out the names.

Among them was one that read: Willm Clancy Died May 11, 1735. He had died two hundred years and nearly four months before I was born. I don't believe in reincarnation, at least not like that, but it did make me stop for a moment and wonder.

Who was he, then? I thought, this namesake of mine. Possibly a brehon lawyer or bard attached to the big house. The Clancys were reputed to be brehon lawyers or bards since medieval times. Lady Iveagh may have been William Clancy's patroness. In my own case it was a wealthy American lady who took me under her patronage and started my career off in the New World. I wanted to know more about the man. Was he a relative? What was life like in his day? I wished he could tell his story, but the grave is a silent place.

The words of the Greek poet Nikos Kazantzakis came to mind: "When [a man] dies, that aspect of the universe which is his own particular vision and the unique play of his mind also crashes in ruins forever."

I hear a challenge in that. So I take up the challenge and tell my story for what it's worth.

Now in my sixties, I live in a house full of joyous activity, a house I'd always dreamed of building in my boyhood, full of family and friends and people I love. But as I start my story, I lie in a hospital bed because my sixtieth birthday party was full of song and food and music and drink. At some point in the night (I learned later it was four in the morning) I saw someone dive into the swimming pool outside, and since it was my birthday, I dressed appropriately, in my birthday suit, and declaimed:

> Do not go gentle into that good night,
> Old age should burn and rave at close of day;
> Rage, rage against the dying of the light.

With that I plunged into the lung-chilling water. Excess, I'm afraid, has always been one of my failings in life.

With a lung full of pneumonia, the oxygen hissing through my mask and the antibiotics coursing through my veins, I ruminate upon it all. Like the overtures of the operas my father would entertain us with when we were children, snatches of song and story weave in and out through my fever. I feel like Jose Ferrer as the dying Toulouse-Lautrec in the film *Moulin Rouge.* All the friends and characters and events of my life come flitting by my bed. Back again comes the "smell of the crowd and the roar of the grease paint," the countless nights on countless stages through forty years of acting, singing, and general foolishness.

In Carnegie Hall a fellow drops his hat from the top balcony to cheers and roars of laughter from the crowd. Tommy Makem shouts up at him, "Aren't you lucky your head isn't in it?"

The cross-eyed girls in Dundee, front row, center aisle at Caird Hall, every time breaking us up with laughter.

The little dancer who joined us on the stage of the Opera House in Chicago, blinded by the lights and dancing closer and closer to the edge of the stage before disappearing into the depths of the orchestra pit.

The great nights when you could do no wrong and the awful nights when, alone onstage, transfixed by thousands of eyes, you're gripped by cold panic and the overwhelming desire to flee.

Here they come now trooping through the door to say their last farewells, the ones I knew in the real world and those I knew only in the realm of imagination. Come one and all. Come round my bed and in delirium we'll sing a chorus.

> And it's no, nay, never *(clap clap clap clap)*
> No, nay, never no more *(clap clap)*

Will I play the wild rover *(clap)*
No, never no more.

The fire in my head becomes an ember. I drift toward sleep, smiling.

Life spreads out like rings on a lake from the place where the stone was dropped. The first rings are mother, father, family, house. Then your street, your town, the characters, the smells, sounds, tastes, the first sense of place. The rings widen to the valley, the hills and mountains, then beyond to the sea, the plains, the next town, the city, and on to the big world. They lose their physical qualities then and become rings of the imagination, of philosophy, religion, spirituality, and creativity, until they dissipate on the far shores of the eternal mysteries.

I think my first memory was of being in a pram outside our door on William Street on a sunny day. I can see the sides of the pram and hear sounds of laughing and fighting coming from inside the door. There is a pipe on the wall beside the pram. Across the street I see a big purple window and, reflected in it, bright houses. Later I put it together that the pipe is a water chute. The big glass window is Verrington's meat shop with the big purple blind pulled down (it must have been Sunday), and the reflections were the houses on our side of the street.

They called me "the old cow's calf," "the shakin's of the bag," eleventh child of Robert Joseph Clancy and Johanna McGrath Clancy, born when she was forty-seven years old. Of the nine surviving children—one had died before I was born, another when I was six months old—I was the afterthought, six years younger than my sister Peg, who, it was supposed, was definitely the last. My mother blamed my conception on a feed of cockles. Cockles! In January?

After I was born my parents must still have shared a bed for a few years at least because—(good God, how it comes back even now!)—dimly, dimly I see it, feel it, a longing, a need, sobbing in the dark, no answer, no comfort, the longing, the need. Then the arms. I'm raised up. Close warmth. Laid down now in the safest of all places, warm and safe in the nest between two bodies. The safest, snuggest, warmest nest I'll ever know, in the middle, between my father and mother in the back room bed. Fear all gone. Here I can snuggle in forever, in the lovely dark.

Gray light out there. Climb over a big body, out on the floorboards, up on tippy-toes, over to the light—the gray light, the dawn world.

How many times, in later life, will I try to see our backyard with the same eyes, capture the same mood of the yard at dawn as I first saw it? But it's useless. Now I know that that's a wall, those are flower beds and vegetable beds. Lilac is the name of that bush and I know the sweet smell of it. Beyond the wall is the nuns' orchard, which I'll be too timid to rob (not like my brother Bobby), the orchard where I'll see and later be part of the May Procession full of blossoms and lovely joyful hymns of May and the little girls in white and the smell of newness off the boys' clothes. No, try as I will, I'll never see that yard again with the first-time eyes of a child at dawn. I have put it all in a bigger context now and its boundaries won't ever retreat.

What I will learn soon, though, is how to manipulate my parents. I'll hear my father say, "Aw, look! The big salty tears." My God! I can taste them now! "Aw, sure come here, boy! Here in the middle for the golden fiddle." The salty tears will be well used, and the first words I'll string together will be "hock bockilly a poor Willie a haboo bed a mammie house." In other words, "a hot bottle (of milk) for poor Willie to go asleep in mammie's bed."

The bottle must not always have been convenient because I believe I was breast-fed until I was about four. Never lost the taste for it, either.

But in that back room, too, I learned fear. Sometimes I would lie awake between the sleeping bodies of my father and mother and there through the open door was a black tunnel up to somewhere I'd never been. I'd lie in a state of panic and wait for something awful to come down the tunnel from the attic. I would spend hours waiting for one of my parents to wake up, but not daring to wake them for the bigger fear, the fear that the salty tears might not work next time.

The attic, or the garret, as we called it, took on a whole new aspect when I got to know it. It became our castle, our hideout, our rainy-day world, a continent of endless adventure. There were nine of us at home still when I was three or four. Lili was the eldest, then Leish and Cait (twins), Paddy, Tom, Bobby and Joan (more twins), Peg, then me. Willie! God how I hated the name! But my mother insisted on calling me after Father Willie Doyle, a chaplain of the First World War and my mother's hero. It wasn't till years later, when I lived in Dublin and had a walk-on part in *The Playboy of the Western World* with Cyril Cusack and Siobhan McKenna, that I shed the name like a festered skin. On the first day of rehearsal on the Gaiety stage Cyril Cusack asked me, "What's your name, lad?"

"Willie Clancy."

"That's a very English-sounding name, isn't it? Willie! Well from now on in this production you'll be *Liam*. A good Irish name. Liam."

And it stuck.

In a small house, on a little street, that garret was a godsend for the parents of nine children. In my memory, it's full of beds, always being moved around. The mortar had long since fallen off the laths inside the slates, and on clear nights you could lie there, two or three to a bed, covered with old coats on top of the threadbare blankets, and watch the stars through the spaces. On rainy nights the beds and buckets were moved according to the vagaries of the wind, the rain, and the drips. In heavy frost I've seen ice on the piss pots under the beds in the morning.

One night when I was still young enough to sleep in the hollow of the old iron bed between my sisters Peg and Joan, they were reading the *The Girl's Crystal* to me aloud. Suddenly they realized I was gazing in transfixed horror at something above the bed. They screamed for help, thinking I was in the throes of some kind of seizure, until they saw the big spider, two inches from my nose, hanging from his web in the rafters.

The wet days were the garret days, and there was no shortage of wet days in Ireland, but on the sunny day, the day when the whole gang would be headed for the swimming place on the bank of the Suir River, the "bank," as we called it, then the garret was a very different place, a place you wouldn't want to be. One hot day in the height of summer I had to run back up there after breakfast to get my swimming togs, while outside on the street the gang were impatient to be off and shouted up to me to hurry on. I looked at the bed I'd recently slept in and thought what a torture it would be to have to get back into it on a sun-filled day like this and miss all the fun. That night, sunburned and weary, that same bed looked so inviting. Later in life it occurred to me that death must be like that bed, so abhorrent in the hot June of youth, so inviting in the dark days of old age.

Bobby had rigged up a swing to one of the sagging beams that held up the roof. It beats me how the whole thing didn't cave in. The beds would be put close together so that blankets could be used to make hideouts between them. These would be dollhouses for the girls. To me they were foxes' dens, soft and dark and safe, the floor, walls, and roof made of soft blankets like earth and leaves. Certain floorboards were removable as hiding places for valuables such as the cow's horn I hid once and never saw again. Recently I even asked Bobby, who still lives in the house, if he had come across it during renovations, but he hadn't. It was precious to me because the tip was cut off with a hacksaw to make it into a hunting horn. I had painted the narrow end with blue and gold paint. After fifty-odd years I still resent losing that horn. It's a bit like my "Rosebud."

There was a loose brick, too, in the chimney flue that was almost undetectable. That was for hiding secret papers. The rest of the walls, apart from the chimney bit, were very thick, probably three feet. Built about three hundred years before, they were made of lime and sand bonded with cow's blood and horsehair. The mortar tasted lovely. Larry Stuart, my neighbor, and myself used to sneak up there with a knife and dig out chunks of mortar to eat. We sucked all the good out of it and spat out the sand and horsehair. It was wartime. There were ration books and shortages. From simple falls, I broke my left arm once and my right one twice. We must have been starved for protein and calcium.

Once, before the rationing, through some inexplicable good fortune I got a bar of chocolate when I was about four. Not that I ever got to eat any of it. Bobby, who was eight years older than me and a hundred years cleverer, managed to get it all, bit by bit, by getting down on all fours and pretending to be a pig. "Feed the little piggie. Feed the little piggie," he'd squeal, and I, delighted, would break off piece after piece and watch his antics as he gobbled it up until it was all gone. To this day he loves that story.

My older brothers used the garret as a pigeon loft. Pigeons could be nasty and bad-tempered if you bothered them when they were roosting. I used to put socks on my hands and try to tame them, like a lion tamer. I felt very brave as they pecked at my well-protected hands. I had to be very quiet about all this because it was done in the twilight world of the garret in the afternoons when the brothers slept and snored, having spent the night making the dough at Henneberry's bakery for the morning's bread. There was something very peaceful and comforting in the combination of the twilight, the soft snoring, and the cooing and shuffling of the pigeons.

One Christmas a farmer's wife, probably looking for a favor from my father in his capacity as an insurance broker, brought a present of a live turkey. We had nowhere outside to keep it, so we put it in the garret behind a door that had been taken off its hinges and set lengthways across a corner to make a pen. It had to be fed and cleaned up after, of course. We cursed it at night for going *gobble, gobble.* Just before Christmas, someone, probably Annie Daniel, my mother's helpmate in all things, especially things that no one else would face, chopped off its head and plucked it. My mother stuffed it then for Christmas dinner.

My abiding memory of the garret was lying in bed on a dark night of wind and rain, listening to the cry of the curlews as they made their lonely way over our house, back to their haunts on the bogs on top of the Comeragh Mountains. I could visualize the black, black mountain lakes of Coumseangan and Crotty's, with the great foreboding cliffs above them and the lonesome bleating of sheep on the windswept ledges. Then I'd think of Willie Crotty, the highwayman for whom the lake was called, huddled in his cave, listening to the curlews just as I was now, and I'd snuggle deeper and deeper into the hollow in the old bed and "cuddly-wuddly," as Bobby would say, into the warm, wonderful treasure of the family den.

2

Waking up from the sleep that has no beginning, I found myself in the little house on William Street in the town of Carrick-on-Suir in the south part of the island of Ireland. I discovered that the street was called after a king, King William of Orange, a Dutchman who had fought a battle with his father-in-law, James, another king, an English one, on the bank of the river Boyne in the northern part of the island sixteen hundred and ninety years after the birth of someone named Jesus Christ way off in the middle east of the world. William and James did not actually fight each other. They got other men to do the hacking and killing for them.

William's gang won that battle, so they traveled to the western part of the island to the city of Limerick, to try and beat someone there, but they failed. They were making their way back to Waterford in the east of the island to take boats back to England when they stopped by the town of Carrick, where I woke up in 1935. William camped a big army outside the walls of the town that had been built by a gang from Normandy in France in 1247, give or take. To make it all more complicated, when I was old enough to know, I was told that I was Irish and had to be very proud of it. Proud of it! I hadn't even done anything.

My playground was the ruins of the Norman castle and the remains of the massive walls the Normans had built around the town to keep the natives out. My playmates had surnames like English, Irish, Walsh (pronounced *welsh,* indicating the national origin); Stuart, which would be Scottish; Fleming, Flemish. Then there were names like Prendergast, Babbington, Verrington, probably English. My neighbor Ned Orange had to be named after King Billy of the Dutch House of Orange. My life was punctuated by the deafening bell of the "Roman" Catholic church just up the street, which was designed after a Florentine church called St. Minato's. Yet all the place-names around me were in the Irish language or corruptions of it. The Garryrue beside Town Wall was a corruption of Garrai Rua, the Red Garden where four hundred defenders of the West Gate who were slaughtered by Oliver Cromwell's gang in November 1649 were buried in a mass grave. The bottom of our street was called Gob na Fola, the Gap of Blood, where the defenders of the New Gate were slain. Through wave after wave of conflict the old Gaelic names had lived on.

My grandfather was a gamekeeper on the sprawling estate of Lord Bessborough near Piltown, County Kilkenny. The Clancys seem to have always been involved with the big houses of the various aristocracies, the Gaelic aristocracy in Cashel of the Kings, the Normans of Carrick and Kilcash, and in the latter half of the 1800s, the Anglo-Irish Ponsonbys of Bessborough. In 1428 a James Butler, known as the White Earl, granted a tract of land called Cregg, outside Carrick-on-Suir, to a Donal Clancy in payment for his services as a lawyer who could interpret both the Norman and brehon laws. His brief would have been to act as intermediary between the Butlers and Powers within the walls of Carrick and the natives, like my mother's people, the McGraths, outside the walls. In time my brother Paddy, without even knowing the history of Cregg, would buy the land back from the Anglo-Irish Beary family. My sisters Joan and Peg would marry a Butler and a Power respectively, long after most of the town walls had been pulled down for more practical peacetime purposes.

The Normans became integrated with the Irish to such an extent that it has been said they became more Irish than the Irish themselves. The Norman *r* can be heard to this day in the speech of the people of the Southeast. Even the old English colonists had adopted the Irish language and Irish ways.

Events in England in 1649 had disastrous consequences for Ireland. King Charles I was beheaded by the English Parliament, and Oliver Cromwell became lord protector of the Commonwealth. He undertook the bloody colonization of Ireland. With his powerful army he took town after town throughout the country, including the town of Carrick, where much blood was spilled.

To the victor go the spoils. Cromwell's general, Ponsonby, was rewarded with the Kildalton estate of several thousand acres in south Kilkenny, four miles from Carrick. According to my father's telling, a marriage was arranged between the daughter of the Dalton family, whose estate was to be confiscated, and Ponsonby. But the marriage never happened. Some say it had never really been arranged, that the Dalton girl, Cathy, was merely infatuated with the general, who was already married (or was about to be). Ponsonby went back to Parliament in England to secure the deeds to Kildalton. When he returned, he had with him his new bride, Elizabeth, Bess, after whom he named his now secured estate, Bessborough. Cathy Dalton lost her mind and roamed about the estate in her white wedding dress until she was found dead, lying on her father's grave. Her ghost was regularly seen at night by gamekeepers and poachers, especially at a place called "Lady's Bridge" on the Pill River. My father used to terrify us at bedtime with stories of these sightings of the "White Lady."

At the turn of the twentieth century, Lord Bessborough was

governor-general of Canada and was rarely in residence on the estate, but when he was, he threw lavish parties for his English cronies from the "gentry" class. The young lords loved cricket. My father remembered those parties from his youth and would describe how his brother Paddy, my uncle, would be called on by his lordship to show the young bucks his prowess as a cricketer. Recalling one spectacular catch, my father told how the young lords were so impressed that they threw money on the cricket pitch for my uncle.

Other "humorous" peasants would be called on to perform tricks for the visitors. There was a hunchback on the estate who had a hunt scene tattooed all over his back. His hump was a hilly field with horses jumping a stone wall. Down his back ran the hounds in full cry while, for a few coppers more, the hunchback would drop his trousers to reveal the fox disappearing into its hole.

Not all the Clancys, though, could take this subservice. My grandfather's father took off for America, leaving a family of twelve children behind. He settled in Florida and married again. Being a good Catholic, he proceeded to start a family of thirteen children with his new wife. He didn't hide anything, either. One of his descendants, Margaret Clancy of New York, later came back to contribute a new stained glass window to his parish church in Piltown. It's there to this day.

After the rebellion of 1916, Lord Bessborough ordered all Catholics, including the Clancys, of course, off the estate. They moved into the town of Carrick, where my grandfather got a job as caretaker of the town park.

In the War of Independence that followed the rebellion, Uncle Peter McGrath, my mother's brother, was in a Flying Column of the IRA with the famous Dan Breen. Dan had a very simple strategy for dealing with the British. He had large sleeves built into his greatcoat, and up these sleeves he kept two revolvers at all times. "If an Englishman in uniform stopped me in my own country," he'd say, "I pulled out the revolvers and shot him dead." I still have a letter big Dan wrote me from the hospice for the dying.

One of the IRA plans was to burn out the landlords and their big houses. There were lively discussions about this in my house, with my mother siding with her brothers Peter and Tommy and cousin Willie Joe Lanigan in favor of burning them out. My father was initially against burning such a beautiful house as Bessborough, with its great library and priceless antique furniture, but he was won over to the rebel side by the revolutionary leader De Valera's vision of Ireland as a Catholic state, independent and militarily neutral. If there was ever any doubt in his mind or anyone else's, the brutality of the Black and Tan atrocities, not only nationally but also on a local level, left no room for sympathy with anything English.

In 1920 a task force of ex-servicemen was sent over to help the Royal Irish Constabulary, the RIC. They were by all accounts a rabble, recruited from the jails and institutions of England. They wore mixed army and RIC uniforms, black-green jackets, and khaki trousers. They were the most despised forces ever sent by Britain to Ireland. One night there was a drunken group of them carousing in my grandmother Ma McGrath's pub.

"Time to pay up now, boys, and back to barracks," she announced. She was a brave and defiant woman. One of the Tans put a gun to her head and said, "What was that you says about payment, Mrs. McGrath?" and cocked the pistol.

Not long afterward Bessborough was burned to the ground.

One of the first orders of business of the new Irish State was to set up a land commission in the early 1920s to divide up the English-held estates and return them to the Irish people. The Bessborough house was rebuilt as a seminary. The grounds became a college of agriculture and science and the mass returned to Kildalton, as the old people always said it would.

My father and mother met at a hooley on the Burkes' farm in Kilonerry, a couple of miles outside Carrick. Those were the days of barn dances, and the Burkes were known to have a great hooley house. This would be about 1910. My mother had been courting a chap named McNamara but dropped him when she met Bob Clancy, a handsome man with jet-black hair and, like herself, a flair for singing and reciting. Like her, he too was an out-and-out romantic. They fell in love and started planning a life together. My mother had a relative in Arlington, outside Boston, who ran a boardinghouse and had written back to Ireland offering a housemaid's job to one of the McGrath girls. It seemed an ideal opportunity for my mother. She would go to America, earn some money to help pay Bob Clancy's passage out, and they would get married and start a new life in Boston like so many others before them. In 1911 she sailed to New York and from there took the train to Boston, where, by all the accounts in the homesick letters, she was miserable. My father never followed her. In 1912 the *Titanic* struck an iceberg and sank with the loss of fifteen hundred lives. This came as no great surprise to Catholic Ireland. The *Titanic* had been built at the Protestant shipyard of Harland and Wolff in Belfast, and it was common knowledge that every rivet had been driven home with a "To hell with the Pope!" or worse behind it. No way was my father going to get on a boat for America. He wrote to Johanna McGrath to come home. What a gentleman! It didn't seem to bother him that *her* ship might sink on the way back. However, from what she used to tell me, she was so homesick that even the prospect of sinking could not have kept her in America.

With a big sunburn blister on one side of her face (she'd fallen asleep on the deck under a bright summer sun), she arrived back in Ireland in the early summer of 1913. She'd often describe the joy of the first sight of the Kerry mountains, standing on deck, a scarf hiding the blister, and reciting:

> Oh Ireland, isn't it grand you look—
> Like a bride in a rich adornin'!
> With all the pent-up love of my heart
> I bid you the top of the mornin'!

She was a passionate and intensely emotional woman. She and my father were well met. He would recite Gray's "Elegy" and Thomas Moore's *Lalla Rookh* with such emotion that he'd have to hold back the tears. Even in old age they would sing to each other.

> "What will you do, love, when I am going
> With white sails flowing, the seas beyond
> What will you do, love, when waves divide us
> And friends may chide us for being fond?

"Tho waves divide us and friends be chiding,
In faith abiding, I'll still be true!
And I'll pray for you on the stormy ocean,
In deep devotion that's what I'll do!"

Holding hands and singing, they'd gaze into each other's eyes like young lovers.

They were married in 1913. Their first child, May, was born in 1914 and sister Alice, or Lally as she was called, followed in 1915. Neither one survived. Lally died at the age of two, of pneumonia. She was madly devoted to my father and would wait out in the cold for him to come home from work at Cleeves toffee factory. May died in February 1936 at the age of twenty-one, when I was just six months old. She was in the civil service in Dublin. One day she twisted her ankle getting off a tram. A quack doctor set it wrong; tuberculosis developed, then gangrene. My parents never got over it.

But for all the trials of war, the hardships of poverty, and the tragedies of family, their early years as a couple, as I heard them remembered over and over in my childhood, must have been very happy.

One of the things that seemed to keep them going in the face of all adversity was singing. As pals on long walks around the hill above the town, or on Sunday outings in a horse-drawn charabanc to the Comeragh Mountain lakes, at house gatherings, which seemed to start at the drop of a hat, to just working around the house or singing us children to sleep, they sang all the time. Growing up, I thought that everyone sang all the time. You got in a car to go on a journey, you sang all the way till you got to where you were going, and then you had a singsong when you arrived. I was more perplexed than disappointed when I discovered that not everyone sang. Their journeys must have been boring.

A boatload of the "gang," as the extended family was called, were singing their way down the river Suir one day in the summer of 1920 after a picnic on the riverbank, when they heard gunshots in the town a mile or so downriver. A policeman had been shot by the IRA, and the Black and Tans were rampaging through the town. A group of them came running up the path by the river and, seeing the boatload of happy singing people, decided to put some fear into these "bleedin' Hirish."

They aimed their guns and refused to let the boaters come to shore. They were kept out in midstream for hours while total panic set in. My mother always described how my sister May, then a young child, was particularly overcome with terror. What really frightened my mother was the thought that her brother Peter may have been involved in whatever had happened. But it was May's panic that day that my mother would talk of over and over again and that would have repercussions for me later on.

It must have been a very frightening time to try and raise a family in Ireland. My father had gone to night school and learned accountancy after he got married. He was working in Cleeves factory on the outskirts of town in a fairly secure job when the Russian Revolution broke out in 1917. The workers at Cleeves, inspired by Russia, formed a local "soviet" and hoisted the Red flag over the factory. It always seemed to me a humorously incongruous episode, but the practical effect of the new soviet was anything but humorous. The factory closed. My father, with a family to feed, was out of work. Times were desperate.

There was a shoe factory in Waterford city sixteen miles from Carrick. My father would cycle down to the city, purchase two pairs of shoes, tie them to the handlebars and the back carrier of the bike, and cycle the sixteen miles home. Our front window was only big enough to display two pairs of shoes, so the procedure was to sell and replace the shoes in the window as often as possible. The profit-labor ratio, as they say in today's jargon, can't have been great.

After the truce and the signing of the treaty in 1922 that would give Ireland "Free State" status came the civil war between the pro- and anti-treaty factions. At one stage the town of Carrick was in the hands of the pro-treaty Free Staters while the IRA were holding out in the hills above Carrickbeg across the river Suir. To get into the town, my father would have to crawl under the shelter of the hedges and stone walls, rolling the bike and its cargo of four boots while the cross fire of bullets whizzed overhead.

About that time he was offered an office job at the local police barracks, which was temporarily the town's administrative building for the new state. During the interview he noticed that the wall behind the desk he'd be working at was pockmarked with bullet holes. He remarked to the sergeant in charge, "It looks to me like a chap could get himself shot fairly easily here."

"Oh, that's entirely possible," agreed the sergeant. My father turned down the job.

Still, it must have been some comfort to my parents to have their own little house on William Street for a rent of a shilling a week. Their landlord wasn't a formidable Ponsonby but a local solicitor named Verrington whose maiden aunts, Agnes and Ellie, lived across the street from us and were close, if eccentric, neighbors. They, too, were part of the extended family.

Our house originally had a clay floor. There was no toilet, just a dry pit at the bottom of the garden which had to be emptied regularly by the man whose unenviable job it was. But I don't remember any of that. By the time I was growing up there was an outdoor flush toilet, and an outdoor water tap which used to freeze solid in winter. I remember my father lighting papers around it to unfreeze it so we could fill the kettle for the tea on frosty mornings. There was linoleum on the floor and wallpaper on the walls. We had a small piano in what was called the "room" along with a big mahogany sideboard and a great oval mahogany table that was my father's office.

This office was chaos itself. My father was really an old man when I was a child, and it is interesting to contrast my memories of him with those of the older members of the family. He was losing his vibrancy and humor as my emerging memories become more defined. In his insurance agency all his letters were written by hand, in a beautiful copperplate script. Before signing his name to a letter he would poise his pen over the paper, moving it to and fro, preparing for the grand flourish of the signature, *R.J. Clancy.* Yet for all that, there were things about him that remind me now of old Italian peasant men I've seen in art movies. He'd never cut a slice of bread in the normal way but hold the loaf up to his chest and, pulling the knife toward him, cut off uneven *cleips.* A combination of Catholicism and old Gaelic superstition dominated his life, and I often think now of what an arrogant little pup I must have been to feel so critical of that life view. Yet I loved him very much and

I still get a glow of warmth from one of my earliest memories. He took me for a walk one evening up Town Wall and held my hand and gave it a squeeze. Displays of affection must have been rare, since that small transmission of fondness has stayed with me for over fifty years.

In one of the lanes leading down to the river from the town there was a big enamel display advertisement for a sheep-dip called Big Shep. On summer days we would pass it four times or so on our way up to the "bank" for a swim. The ad portrayed a jolly, rosy-cheeked old shepherd with a crooked staff. Although he looked the picture of health and cheerfulness, I knew he was old and must soon die. At night, in bed, his face would float before my closed eyes, and somehow associating him with my father, I would cry salt tears in the dark.

He was a hale and hearty man in his young days, going for a daily swim up until Christmas. True or not, he used to tell me of the times he had to break the ice to take his winter dip. He was also a great believer in herbal cures. He'd often make forays into the countryside and return with what looked to us like a bunch of weeds. These he would dry out and use for various ailments. I have no idea where he picked up his knowledge of herbs, but a lot of people had great faith in him and would come to him for cures. There was a cough medicine he made up which was so tasty it was worth getting a cough for.

The downside of his herbal practice was that every drawer, every desk and cupboard, every nook and cranny around the house had dried herbs in it. He'd forget, most of the time, what these crumbling bunches of dried-up weeds were, but would he throw them out? Not a hope. There they remained year after year.

The bike was his means of transport, and even when he was obviously very ill and ready to "hand in me gun," as he used to say, he would cycle to the doctor's surgery even though by that time the family had progressed to owning a car.

The first bicycle I remember was a huge "high Nellie" on which all the family had learned to cycle, twisted sideways, of course, under the crossbar, like contortionists. To the back axle he had somehow fitted the handle of a strong table fork, which he himself used for mounting the contraption. The reason for this, I learned later, was that he had learned to ride on a "penny-farthing" cycle and could never adjust to getting on a modern bicycle in the regular way. My father was nothing if not a creature of habit.

Later he bought a secondhand bike for the girls. It was a dangerous machine. The saddle had collapsed in the middle and there was a serious risk of losing your virginity if you were a girl or of being castrated if you were a fella. It was parked permanently outside the front door with no fear of it being stolen. Theft was a rarity at the time anyway.

But the unthinkable did happen. The bike *was* stolen. My father reported it to the police. Personally I felt sorry for whomever took it. Not only was the saddle a torturous piece of equipment but the whole contraption reminded me of an old ailing horse who just doesn't want to go. Even going downhill you had to pedal like hell.

Six months after it was stolen a civic guard arrived up at the house pushing the bike, which had two flat tires.

"Would this be the vehicle you reported missing some time ago, Mr. Clancy? It was returned to us by train from Belfast."

"By gor it is. Sure enough. That's the bike. How in the name of God did it find its way all the way from Belfast?"

"There was a note on it, Mr. Clancy: 'Would finder please return to Carrick-on-Suir, County Tipperary.' He was an honest thief, anyway, Mr. Clancy."

"By japers he was. Some poor chap in dire straits, I suppose, trying to get to Belfast to join the British army. But I wouldn't like to have his backside after that trip. Being shot at by the Germans will be like a holiday after that."

3

World War II started when I was four, not that it meant that much to me, being too young to know what was going on. Ireland was a neutral nation in that conflict, of course, so there was no great danger of us being bombed. De Valera, the prime minister, argued that since England was occupying part of Ireland by force, Ireland could not support the enemy in its war with Germany. So while there was no direct threat of invasion in Ireland, precautions of sorts were taken, and I vaguely remember sand barrels being placed in larger fields to prevent German planes from landing. I vividly remember the barrage balloons in the sky over Waterford port when we went to visit my sister Lili and her new husband, Jimmy O'Brien. That was a great treat for a child. There was great excitement, too, when a small plane would fly low over the house and everyone would rush out to see it. Obviously, though, the government people must have realized that if Hitler took a notion to invade Ireland, a little thing like neutrality wasn't going to stop him. Neither were barrage balloons or barrels of sand!

Daily life took on dramatic changes. Imports of things like oil and coal, wheat and fruit, were all stopped. I never saw a banana or an orange until the war was over and never got to eat a whole one all for myself until long after that. Mostly I remember that white flour couldn't be had for love nor money, so we got whole-wheat bread made from Irish flour instead. The people called it black bread, and it was thought of as an awful penance. Because my brothers were working at Henneberry's bakery, our family had no trouble getting "good" white bread. Food was rationed and every family was issued the hated ration books (the very words bring on a flash of depression) with their stamps for sugar and tea, bread, butter, and other basics.

The people of the town started to experiment with all kinds of alternatives to tea. One substitute for the big tea leaves we had then was toasted carrot slivers. We had a cousin around the corner from William Street, Mrs. Walsh, a big, loud woman. I heard her calling her son Jack in for his "tea" one evening when he was out playing on the street. "Jack, come in here for your carrots!" she shouted. The saying caught on all around the town.

Poverty was widespread, especially in the towns. Farmers were used to being self-sufficient and were therefore better off; they had no money, but plenty of food. But then, in 1941, there was a serious outbreak of foot-and-mouth disease, especially in the Southeast, our part of the country. Cattle and to a lesser extent sheep were slaughtered on a large scale. What we did get of fresh beef was so fresh that it was almost inedible. Fried in lard, heart-clogging animal fat, until it was like shoe leather, it was hardly a luxury.

The radio played all the time with bulletins coming in, and my father shushed us as he tried to hear the ebb and flow of battle over the squeaks and squawks of the wireless. Between the bulletins there would be vaudeville-type songs to keep up the hearts of the people. Songs like "Hang out the washing on the Siegfried Line if the Siegfried Line's still there," and Vera Lynn singing "There'll be bluebirds over the white cliffs of Dover, tomorrow just you wait and see." Keeping my sister Peg and me quiet seemed to be my mother's main preoccupation, and she'd put a penny on the mantelpiece as a reward for the one who stayed quiet longest while my father listened to the news.

Since the whole community was in the grip of the war-inflicted depression, there was a great communal closeness, not just among the next-door neighbors but in the whole town, the country itself. Almost every family had somebody involved in the big war, which, with all its horrors, drew the hearts and minds of the Irish people away from the pettiness, the smallness, of its own civil war. People helped each other out.

Plots of land known as allotments could be rented cheaply, and people started growing their own vegetables. These allotments, about a mile or so from the town, became great social centers, and everyone helped weed and tend each other's crops. We didn't have a plot, but our neighbor Paul Stuart, the bicycle mender, did. His daughter Nan was the first girl I ever kissed. It happened when we were playing hide-and-seek with her brother Larry. Nan and I were hiding from him among the greasy bicycle chains under her father's workshop counter when the forbidden, delicious deed occurred. Not the most romantic setting for a first kiss, there amid the rancid detritus of a bicycle shop, but the smell of axle grease always brings back the warm thrill of the first time. That thrill landed me in hot water on many an occasion later on.

I used to help out with the Stuarts' plot, but I'm afraid there was more cavorting and eating done than any real work. The smell of the wet earth was lovely, primal, as you groped around for the big spuds. You could use a sharp stone to peel a turnip for a sweet, pungent snack, and a few scallions or spring onions, cleaned and ready to eat with one deft pull of the outside layer of skin, would make a meal for you.

When we stopped for a break after a few hours' weeding, there was hot tea with sweetened condensed milk from a can. Standing there drinking the tea, we could look out over the valley from the high fields of the allotments to the mountains on the other side of the Suir valley.

That's the setting I always saw in my mind's eye when later in school I read Padraic Colum's poem, "The Plougher":

Sunset and silence! A man: around him earth savage, earth broken;
Beside him two horses-a plough!
Slowly the darkness falls, the broken lands blend with the savage;
The brute-tamer stands by the brutes, a head's breath only above
    them.
A head's breath? Aye, but therein is hell's depth and the height up
    to heaven,
And the thrones of the gods and their halls, their chariots, purples
    and splendors.

But for all that, we must have been undernourished. My bones were so brittle that in a simple child's fall from a park bench, my right arm snapped. While I was still wearing the splints which Dr. Conlon had put on, I tripped on an inch-high step going into my brother-in-law's bakery in Waterford and, on reflex, put out the same arm to save myself, breaking the other bone in it.

At home the girls all learned to make clothes. There was the constant click of knitting needles mingled in with the chat around the fire in the room at night. Upstairs in the front room the girls had set up a miniature dressmaking factory. They also made outfits for me, not the coat, which would have been too complicated and hence had to be made by Mrs. Cullen, the professional seamstress down on New Street, but the short pants, yes. That was easy. I still burn with anger and humiliation when I think of the chorus of laughter I provoked when I demanded that these be real pants with a hole in the front, boys' pants. The girls, being so much older, always got a great kick out of my antics. My brother Paddy, who was nearly fourteen years older than me and remembered when I was born, would ever after tell of a day when I was a baby and my sisters were washing me in the galvanized bath that was always brought into the heat of the kitchen for such occasions. Up sprang this little erection and my sister Leish got such a fit of the giggles that she had to run out of the kitchen. The giggles spread to the other girls, and the more they laughed, the more I wailed.

I wore those pants the first day I went to school, to the nuns. The terror of that morning is vivid in my mind. I had seen these phantoms in black on the street, heard the horror stories from the older ones of the family, seen my sisters imitate them by taking old shoes from the defunct gas stove, lining them up like pupils, and shouting at them and beating them unmercifully with a stick. Now I was to be thrown into the very lair, the taloned clutches of these monstrous creatures. And my mother was participating in this sacrifice, washing me, dressing me up in my best, combing my hair with the fine-tooth comb and cracking the lice.

The nuns ran the girls' school but were entrusted with little boys until they made their first communion at age seven. We were then handed over to the Christian Brothers. The name of the nun I was afflicted with was Mother Teresa. She bore no resemblance to her namesake of Calcutta. She was a terrorist. Today, in a so-called enlightened age, she would be jailed. Her form of abuse was the kind that cut deepest, humiliation! The school was only a few doors from our house, so I was always late. There was an early reader we had, part of which I well remember: "Maura the doll must stay in bed. Her white dress is in the tub. Her new dress is on the line." When I was late, I became Maura the doll. Mother Teresa would make this five-year-old stand at the head of the class, hands over his head until they felt like dropping off, and make the entire class jeer in unison, *"Maura the doll must stay in bed!"*

"Now. What must Maura the doll do?"

"Stay in bed!" And there I'd stand, tears of humiliation spurting from my eyes.

We brought our own lunch to the school yard, hot milk in a bottle with a cork wrapped in greased paper to make it tight, and bread thickly spread with beaded, salty country butter and a sprinkling of coarse sugar. The smell of warm milk always transports me to the little lean-to shed with its wooden bench where we had our lunch. My mother and her sisters had gone to the same school in their time, but the McGrath girls were brought up in a pub on Main Street and they were given ale instead of milk to take to school for lunch. Ale was cheaper and easier (and probably healthier, it didn't carry TB). The nuns couldn't figure out for a long time why the McGrath girls fell asleep on their desks after lunch. Finally one of the nuns noticed the smell.

"Oh my God! The child is drunk!"

A delegation was sent to my grandmother Ma McGrath, who only laughed and said, "Sure, it's good for them. It never did us any harm."

There was a litany in the family of tricks that were used for getting out of trouble or escaping a slapping. One day my sister Cait was late for school and had the hand out for the ruler slaps. Cait pipes up, "My mother had twins." It was true. Bobby and Joan had just been born. However, that was an excuse you couldn't use too often. Two sets of twins in a family were all that credibility would allow.

Cait was endlessly inventive at getting out of trouble. When the whole gang was sleeping up in the garret, it was almost impossible to get them settled at night. My father would often tell of the frustration of quieting them all down (I would have been an infant at the time), and just as he got down to the bottom of the stairs for the umpteenth time, Cait would call out, "We want four breads and three waters."

He'd take off his belt. Every step of the stairs would get an unmerciful slap of the leather that would put the heart crossways in them all— all except Cait, that is. Knowing my father's weakness for poetry, she would say plaintively out of the dark of the garret, "Ah, the shining Suir is ever in my dreams," as if she were dying of thirst. Needless to say, he'd relent and bring them the four breads and three waters.

My mother was very sick when she was pregnant with the twins. She probably had toxemia or something. There was a popular song at the time, "The Isle of Capri." To the day she died, if I started, unconsciously, humming "The Isle of Capri," she would say, "Oh, Willie boy, don't! I can feel that awful sick feeling coming over me every time I hear it!"

She must have also suffered from a calcium deficiency because she took to hiding my father's clay pipes (which were made of chalk, of course), grinding them up, and eating them. She loved the taste of them just as Larry Stuart and I loved the taste of the garret wall. It was years later before my father unraveled the mystery of the missing clay pipes.

No one who's been through the Catholic experience of his or her first confession will remember it without some kind of cringe, and my first time was no exception. The nuns had drilled us thoroughly, of course.

We went to the actual confession box, where a nun would fill in for the priest and go through the ritual so there could be no mistakes. They even told us what sins to tell: stealing sugar, etc. (there was no mention of clay pipes). Alas, the real thing was different. The priest was a frightening figure. Two rows of terrified little seven-year-olds knelt by the benches along the wall at either side of the confession box, taking turns. The empty cavern of the church amplified the voices coming out. Poor Jimmy Wall was first in. Jimmy lived in Ash Park with a woman named Bridgie who had taken him in when he became an orphan. Jimmy had an impediment of speech; he couldn't say r's. One of the sins we had to tell was that we disobeyed our mother, but Jimmy had no mother. All over the chapel you could hear him shout out his first sin, "I disobwayed Bwidgie," in his Ash Park accent.

When my time came to go in, I panicked. I knelt down and looked at the grille. I knew it was supposed to open, but it didn't. I heard the priest's deep voice, "Yes, my child." I started out, "Bless me, Father, for I have sinned. This is my first confession," and blurted out my soul-destroying cargo. When I'd finished, I heard the grille door on the other side of the confession box slide shut and the one on my side slide open. Suddenly there was the big face of the fearful man himself: "Yes, my child."

I felt the wet dribble down the leg of my new short pants, the ones with the hole in front, as I told my awful story again.

A few years later my playmates and I tried all the usual childish things, like trying to milk each other the way we saw Gus Gahan milk Prendergast's cows. The milking sheds were a wondrous world full of hay and cow dung, the smell of warm milk, dust, and old farm implements like the turnip and mangold crusher. In one of the empty sheds we tried an experiment that was doomed to failure, trying to walk and shit at the same time, like a cow.

The first space suits I ever encountered were on the wall of our garret; Tom's flight suits, which he'd bring back when he was on leave from the RAF. From being a baker at age fourteen, my brother Tom, following my brother Paddy, had gone on to join the RAF in 1943. Paddy had been sent to India (big canvas sacks of tea used to arrive regularly with exotic stamps saying "Karachi"), while Tom got the more dangerous job of radio operator on bombing missions over Germany. His flight suits were highly insulated coveralls, complete with a gas mask, which were parts of the equipment of the unheated bombers. These things would hang there like real men on the garret wall. They awed us kids but Tom loved them. To the actor in him they were stage costumes!

He probably didn't know then that the theatrical genes he had inherited would dominate his life and the stage become his destiny. I suppose all of us think that we invent ourselves and glow at our own creativity. Later we discover what our parents and forebears did and we begin to realize—Oh my God! We are just updated repeats!

My grandparents on my mother's side, Ma and Da McGrath, were the models for the whole pantomime that we were heirs to. They ran a pub in the main street of Carrick. At least Ma did. Da ran the local billiard room. Died of a heart attack on the billiard table before I was born.

My brother Tom was destined for the heftiest chunk of the theatrical gene from both sides of the family. But then, we all got our share of it. Daddy Clancy, who definitely had entertainer's blood in his veins, would go through a ritual at parties of taking a stance at the fireplace like it was his stage, glass in hand, his prop, and recite "Kelly's Dream." My brother Bobby recites it still, *It was just a week ago tonight some gentlemen friends of mine invited me to their house to sample their beer and wine,* just like Daddy Clancy, including the right-hand gesture, for emphasis, like screwing in a lightbulb.

Up until the war the opera companies like the D'Oyly Carte and Albert Bowyer company were still touring Ireland. My father knew the plots of all the great operas, and on Saturday nights when the stiff platters of shoe leather from the local tannery were softening in the basin of hot water on the kitchen floor and the shoe-last, hammer, and nails were being set up for the ritual shoe mending, he'd hold us spellbound with the stories and arias from *Maritana* and *La Bohème, Il Trovatore* and *Carmen.* The shoe-last was a great prop for beating out the Anvil Chorus. And when the leather was pliable and the soling and heeling were underway, he would continue to sing "scenes that are brightest may charm a-aha-while" with a mouthful of tacks which we waited for him to swallow. His arias in Italian were a wonder to hear. He'd sing all the parts, tenor, soprano, bass: total gibberish, of course, but he'd have us spellbound.

Other days he'd be in his poetic mood, and if my mother got carried away with her daydreams of fixing up the house, you'd soon hear:

> Let not Ambition mock their useful toil,
> Their homely joys, and destiny obscure;
> Nor Grandeur hear with a disdainful smile
> The short and simple annals of the poor.

And when he was feeling sorry for himself, he'd come out with:

> I never nursed a dear gazelle
> To glad me with its soft blue eye
> But when it came to know me well
> And love me, it was sure to die.

One of the few films, perhaps the only film, he ever saw was *The Great Waltz*. It so captivated his imagination that he could recite the entire script, chapter and verse, until the day he died.

On the McGrath side of the family, Uncle Tommy, a mild-mannered tailor in sobriety, a flamboyant superman in drink, had the same effect on his generation as brother Tom had on ours. With the Shakespearean delivery they both possessed, they could inspire a combination of dismay and pride, delight and terror. Being brought up in a pub, he was fond of the drink. Once, coming out of a binge and still in the limbo between drunkenness and hangover, Uncle Tommy was gingerly making his way from his bed to the kitchen. At the bend of the stairs was a plinth usually reserved for religious statues, but this morning, instead of St. Jude (patron of hopeless cases), Uncle Tommy was confronted by the grisly remains of a pig's head (the pickled head of a pig being a common meal in those days), where it had been left out of devilment to throw a fright into him.

"Alice!" he shouted. That was our Aunt Alice. "Remove this hideous monster!"

Aunt Alice was even more theatrical than Tommy, if that's possible. She played the leads in all the musicals when I was growing up. She was overage and overweight, but that has never stopped divas before. She had the voice. If you closed your eyes when she sang "Dear little Buttercup, sweet little Buttercup," you could visualize a slender young thing singing.

Like Tommy, she never married. Someone said she had gone out with a beau once, never again! Who knows what happened in those puritanical days? Some even wondered if her virginity had been briefly interrupted. They both lived in the family home. The pub was considered too much of a temptation for Tommy so it was converted into a tailor's shop in which they both worked.

The afternoon of the opening night of *H.M.S. Pinafore* at the Castle Cinema in 1944, Aunt Alice's top set of false teeth fell on the floor while she was rehearsing and broke neatly in two. My father, always Mr. Fixit, was called on urgently. His solution to the problem (as to so many other problems) was sealing wax, the red stuff you melted like a candle that hardened in no time, used by kings and potentates in olden times (and by my father) for sealing letters. Although it held the dentures together, Aunt Alice didn't quite trust it; she was terrified the sealing wax would melt if it got too hot. She sang her way through the whole opera trying not to exhale hot air.

It was a time of religious fervor in Ireland. My father had an Irish Sweeps ticket under the Sacred Heart lamp in the room, always praying fervently that he would win. It was the only way he could see up out of the rut. Little did he know that my mother was upstairs at the Blessed Virgin's altar with its night-lights and lilies, praying he *wouldn't* win, thereby destroying the family. Later he discovered what she was up to, and there were days of silence with the word "betrayal" tingling in the air like ice crystals.

My father joined the third order of St. Francis, the bird lover of Assisi, his favorite saint. My mother was fickle with her saints, and, after the Holy Family, she flitted unashamedly from one favorite to another. Then one day, like a new boyfriend, along came Blessed Martín de Porres, and both my mother and Aunt Alice fell for him at the same time. Aunt Alice had his statue installed in the plinth at the turn of the stairs where she had put the pig's head to frighten Uncle Tommy. She cooed to him every time she went up or down the stairs.

The love affair lasted a year or so until she asked him for a special favor; we never found out what it was, but it was urgent. There was a time limit. After three weeks he hadn't delivered and she knew he was a false lover. One morning, coming down the stairs, she passed him with icy indifference. Just after she passed she hissed, loud enough for him to hear, *"Little black bastard!"*

Sometime in the forties, when I was about ten, there was a prolonged drought, believe it or not (it probably lasted for two weeks, in April), and a delegation of farmers went to the Friary Church to beg the intercession of one of the monks, a very saintly man. Cures had been attributed to him. What they didn't realize was that he was also a farmer's son and a pragmatist. He listened to their tale of woe, looked at the sky, stuck a wet finger in the air, and declared, "Me dear men, you might as well be idle as praying for rain when the wind is in that direction."

We were a much more innocent and naive people at that time and so easily manipulated. The Catholic Church had a stranglehold, both politically and spiritually, on the minds of the people. To me, thinking back on it now, organized religions have always been the political wing of spirituality. How incompatible they seem when you think about it, organized religion being made up of rigid rules and the need, sometimes a desperate one, for conformity, for power, for hierarchical structure, contrasting with spirituality, which of its nature is fluid and open, like female sexuality, to the experiment of life.

The church told us we were sheep and we believed them. The church told the government what to do and they did it, by God, or else. All it took was the accusing finger of a bishop to bring down an elected government. Church officials held an uneducated people down with fear and guilt, hell and damnation. If religious belief and spirituality were confused in our childish minds, so were religion and nationalism, the twin dogs of war. The churchmen tore down the natural dignity and nobility of the Celtic nature and made us dirty and unwholesome. Like proselytizers the world over, the priests taught us sin and then persuaded us that we had invented it. The fact is that all our lives, whether we embrace or rebel against them, we are entrapped in the mythologies of our tribe.

Power has always been used to abuse the powerless. One of the Christian Brothers who supposedly taught me was graphically known as Bumsy. He'd put his victims in the back desk of the classroom, where he could put his pudgy fingers up the short trouser leg.

There was a Brother O'Leary who confused teaching and terror. He tried to beat mathematics into us with the rung of a chair. He paralyzed our eight- and nine-year-old minds with fear. On a frosty morning, after a savage beating on the fingertips of both hands, your nails turn purple and you can't hold a pen for the rest of the day, not mind trying to add 2 and 2. You kept your hands in your armpits when you could, but the pain lasted into the night when you were supposed to do homework, sums that may as well have been double Dutch.

They come back to me sometimes at night like torturers coming back to haunt the survivors of the concentration camps. Handsome Brother O'Neill. The girls of the town think he's lovely. Jimmy Fleming is not so impressed. Jimmy is shy. He finds it hard to get out in front of the class. O'Neill knows that. That's why he picks on him at singing class. One day we're all standing "out to the line" around the classroom. The song we learned last week is only vaguely familiar to us.

"Fleming! Out here. Here, I said! In the middle of the floor. Now, Fleming, sing the song we learned last week. Sing it up for the class. You what? Stop mumbling, boy. You what? Can't remember it, sir! What's in that head, Fleming? Cotton wool? Well, let's see what's in it!"

Clatter! Across the side of the head. Jimmy flying across the room, head bashing against the old heating pipes. O'Neill is possessed with purple fury. He goes after him, soutane flying, grabs him by the legs, and pulls him out to the middle of the floor. He picks him up by the ankles and starts pounding his head on the floor.

Oh, yes, singing class with the Christian Brothers is great fun.

But we survived. Maybe not unscathed, but we survived. Certainly we were far more fortunate than some whose stories are emerging now that the floodgates have opened.

But it certainly wasn't *all* bad. Brother Davis, who taught us music (I owe *him* a great debt), was a dedicated teacher—as were many of the brothers who imparted a remarkably rounded education to a backward people at a time when it was desperately needed. For the last hour of the school day we had Brother Ennis, a true teacher. From him we heard the great tales of Fionn McCool and the Fianna, including the story of how Slievenamon got its name, of Ossian in the land of Tir-na-nOg, of Cuchullain and the Red Branch Knights, of Deirdre and the Sons of Ushnach. Tales of battles between good and evil. Tales of love and of betrayal. Epic versions of the stories of our own, small, embattled lives. That last hour of the day with Brother Ennis was a healing hour.

4

When my eldest sister Lili was married in 1939, I was too young to go to the wedding. I have vague memories of the next one, Leish's, I think. I see a hotel dining room and I see colored sparkles on the sherry trifle.

My imagination opens out again to the town, to my fascination and fear of its characters. Michael McGrath, the harmless fool from Chapel Street; Michael, who comes to the front door if it's open, to the window if it's not, and, in mime, begs a cigarette; Michael, who is so proud of his new shoes that he stops everyone he meets on the street and, beaming, looks at them, then at the shoes, then back at the passerby. One day I saw him with his new shoes on, a tortured, frustrated look on his face. The sidewalk was wet and every few steps he'd stop, take out a big handkerchief, and wipe the soles clean.

Then there was Tommy the Fool, who'd shoo us away like chickens, who'd masturbate into old doorways and eat matches constantly. When he ended up in hospital, the surgeon found a veritable forest in his gut.

Ned the Bellman clanged around town nearly every day, as town criers had for centuries: "The water will be off from two to six." Even the dogs on the street knew that newfangled things like water schemes never worked anyway.

On Fridays, Mickey Holloway, the fishmonger, could be heard two streets away—"Fresh mackerel! Fresh mack! Mack-mackerel!"—as he wheeled his wheelbarrow. He used to bring the fish from the fishing pier of Helvic in his ancient Ford lorry, which had no brakes. Mickey wore a perpetually worried look on his face. He had an all-purpose yard out of which he and the wife sold everything from fish to scrap metal. In season they sold berries, rabbits, kid goats, anything that could eke out a living for them. Their big old house was at the end of the steepest street in town, inexplicably called the Level. That created a problem for an old Model T without brakes. The only way he could stop the lorry at his house was if the wife put out a plank of timber on the road in front. When he'd come back with his load of fish on Thursday, he'd first have to make a pass by the house, roaring out the window as he went, "Sarah! Put out the plank!"

His son Joe and I went to school together. One day I was doing homework with Joe at his house when the old Ford roared by. "Sarah, the plank!" shouted Mickey at the top of his voice. Sarah must have been busy out in the backyard skinning rabbits and didn't hear him. Nothing for it but to go around the town again. Then the whine of the antique engine came around again and Mickey roaring like a bull, "Sarah, the plank! The fuckin' plank!"

And there was Pearl Beary, one of the last of the "gentry." Her family were horsey people outside of town. They had trained thoroughbreds for the Aga Khan in their day. All the horses were long gone now, along with all the trappings of privilege. Pearl was reduced to riding into town on an old bike with no brakes. Coming down the steep hill into Carrick, she'd cock her foot up on the front mudguard and press it down on the tire to slow the bicycle down. We schoolboys used to look up under her big flouncy skirt. In this compromised position, completely undaunted, she would doff her big flowery hat to one and all with a big "Hellow! Hellow!"

One St. Stephen's Day, the traditional day for the South Tipperary hunt, when the last of the unspeakable redcoats, with their hounds, bugles, horses, and regalia, were preparing to set off to hunt the uneatable misfortunate fox, Pearl encountered the old stableboy, Mickey Murray, a great horseman in his day, on his odyssey between pubs on the main street of Carrick, still full of Christmas cheer.

"Michael," she said, "have you seen the gentry pawss?" (that was the genteel way of saying "pass").

Michael, who had had enough of the horseshit of the upper classes in his life, rounded on her. "Pearl," he said, "the gentry haven't passed here in the last fifty fuckin' years!"

Another of the town's notorious characters was the Black Prince, whose real name was Nell Bracken, a woman. No one asked why she was called the Black Prince. She was married to Tommy the Tailor and their fights were legendary. They lived in Cooke Lane. She always wore a black shawl, as did so many women of the town, the badge of poverty. The town was divided into classes: the "shawlies," the snobs, and the in-betweens. We were the in-betweens, my mother always trying to get a new foothold up the treacherous slope of respectability. The snobs were the professionals, shopkeepers, teachers, dentists, doctors, and, top of the heap, solicitors. They drank only in the hotel snugs or "gentlemen's clubs." The police and the clergy were outside the system. Or at least they had us believe so.

Family squabbles weren't hidden behind closed doors in a town like Carrick at that time. Family fights in particular got a full public airing, especially when drink was involved. The Black Prince and Tommy the Tailor had a spectacular fight that the whole town turned out for one day. It started in a pub at the West Gate on a Saturday afternoon with strong drink and strong language. It quickly progressed to a skelp on the ear, Tommy's ear, and spilled out onto the street. Down along the main street it gathered momentum. It turned left at New Street, where blood was spilled and the crowd swelled. It was a knockdown, drag-out brawl as it turned up William Street, past our house, to the arena in front of St. Nicholas' Church.

There it turned into high drama. Tommy the Tailor knelt down in the middle of the clearing of spectators, directly in front of the big church door. "Come out! Come out, Kennedy! Come out, you big fat fuckin' frog, if you have the guts!"

Father Kennedy was one of the priests who tried to terrify courting couples on summer nights, prowling the lanes with a big stick. He wasn't about to emerge now from the sanctuary of the church. The scene was like something from an opera at the Metropolitan in New York. Tommy on his knees shouting obscenities at the church gates, the Black Prince a bundle on the ground of black and red. She was bleeding like a stuck pig, moaning in great dramatic groans. The crowd, loving it all but pretending shock, spilled into the side streets.

Suddenly there's a commotion from the William Street direction. The crowd parts to make a path for Sergeant Sullivan, purple in the face, baton drawn, who's finally emerging from the barracks to deal with the situation. No sooner does he grab Tommy the Tailor by the scruff of the neck than the Black Prince makes a remarkable recovery. Throwing off the black shawl, which she'd tied around her waist at the start of the fight to free up her flailing arms, she lifted her long black skirt and produced an iron poker from her stocking. "If you touch a hair on the head of my Tommy, I'll scatter your brains!" she roars at the sergeant.

He backed off fairly smart. Sergeant or not, it would be a brave, or foolish, man who'd get between the Black Prince and Tommy the Tailor, who now gathered themselves up and, arm in arm, like tired old lovers, made their way up Town Wall toward Cooke Lane and home.

Sometimes there would be a crossover between the classes. That was the case with Annie, who had chopped the head off the turkey, who was like part of our family, who helped bring us into the world to begin with and then helped raise us when things got beyond control for my mother. One day when I was about twelve I came home from school to find Annie with the shawl covering her face, huddled in by the fire, crying, and my mother trying to comfort her. Just up the street, outside the church, there was a huge crowd of mourners at a funeral.

Judging by the size of the crowd, it was the funeral of a very prominent person. I had no way of knowing the connection at the time, but years later I would learn that the dead man was Annie's natural father, a publican and one of the wealthiest businessmen in the town. Annie's mother had worked for him as a serving maid, a very attractive one. When she got pregnant, he denied all involvement. Mary, Annie's mother, was at her wit's end. Here she was, penniless, unable to work, undernourished, her milk drying up, while he himself strutted around town with a "who but him" air. One fair day, when the town and the pubs were full of farmers, she could take it no longer. She wrapped the baby, wailing with hunger, in her shawl and made for his pub. His wife threw a fit when she saw the mother and child coming in the door.

"Get out of here, you slut, with that screaming brat of yours!"

Mary plonked the child up on the counter among the farmers' large bottles of Guinness. "Here's your husband's bastard," she said. "I won't have her death of hunger on my conscience." She turned to make her way out the door when the wife shouted at her.

"Come back here! You can't leave the child there. I can't handle her." She put her hand in the till and took out some money. "Here, for God's sake, it's not the poor little child's fault. Take this and come back next week."

Mary came back every week after that. She and Annie were supported on the sly out of his lordship's coffers and he never even knew it.

Annie was a young girl when she discovered who her father was. First she was curious, then fascinated, then, inexplicably, she grew to love him. She knew she was an embarrassment to him, so she would avoid him. If she saw him coming toward her with his rich cronies on Main Street, she'd dodge down a lane to avoid a face-to-face meeting. In a small town of three or four thousand people where everyone knows everyone else, it's very hard to avoid someone all the time, but that's the way she grew up, and that's the way he grew old.

She was a middle-aged woman the day I saw her crying by the fire. Her father was dead and not a single word had ever passed between them.

At the top of the street, beyond the chapel where Tommy the Tailor knelt to make his statement, was Prendergast's dairy. Dick Prendergast was known as Dick the Bull. Mrs. Prendergast was known as Ma Bull. We got our milk there. We also learned a lot about life there. Behind the shop was a yard where my hero, Gus Gahan, who held for me some of the aura of the heroes in cowboy films, milked the cows. He was a Gary Cooper but an Irish, hands-on cowboy, or cowman. He was also a freedom fighter. He had been out on the mountains with Dan Breen during the War of Independence.

In Prendergast's yard, too, was the big hay shed that was our hide-out on winter days. We would tunnel in between the hay and the corrugated roof for about ten feet and then burrow down to make a nest lit by a flashlight hung from a beam. There we'd tell stories while the rain rattled on the roof above us and the smell of dusty hay filled our nostrils. One of the stories was about the banshee, the fairy woman who wailed at a death in certain families. She followed the Prendergast family. The Prendergasts were strong farmers of old Norman stock. Dick the Bull was a man of immense girth who had to have a special coffin when his time came.

I remember well the night he died. Johnny McGettigan, Kevin Driscoll, and myself had hitchhiked to Waterford city that day to buy a book on oil painting that I'd set my heart on. We had stayed too late in Waterford and it was dark by the time we got out on the road to Carrick looking for a lift. Cars were scarce at that time and after dark there was no hope of being picked up, so we had to shank's-mare it the sixteen miles back to Carrick. We arrived in New Street at one o'clock in the morning and were standing in front of Driscoll's shop at the bottom of William Street when we heard the banshee. Never before or since have I heard such a hair-raising cry. It sent shivers through us. We looked at each other aghast, frozen to the spot. Then, without a word, we bolted for our homes and beds. It was the next day we discovered that Dick Prendergast had died, at one o'clock in the morning on the dot.

Mrs. Prendergast was a big woman, too, a big brusque woman.

"I haven't what would color a cup of tea," she'd declaim when she was out of milk.

It was my job to go for the milk every evening, and sometimes I'd have to wait until she'd strained it. It came fresh and warm, of course, from the cows down the yard in the milking shed. To make the milk come faster through the bulging silk strainer, like a cow's full udder, she'd manipulate and stroke it from the bottom, something I found almost embarrassing in its sensuousness and sexual suggestion. Then she'd ladle the milk into your can and finish the ritual with a little extra.

"A tillie for the cat," she called it.

Once or twice I got to drive the cows back up to the fields outside the town where they pastured after they'd been milked. I chickened out of that job when the bull strayed into someone's yard one evening and I had to follow him to get him out.

We young lads spent a lot of time up in those fields helping out with the cows. During a threshing we'd help feed the sheaves into the maw of the big old dinosaur of a threshing machine, or bring tin mugs of strong tea to the sweating men. Big men they were, too. I saw Harry Prendergast, the son, wrestle a full-size bullock to the ground. He must have seen something similar in a cowboy film. He caught the bullock by the horns and held on while the beast leaped and kicked his way around the field three or four times, to the cheers of the farm laborers. When he'd finally bested the beast and let him go, he got down on all fours on the ground while he gasped for breath. Then he started vomiting. What amazed me was that he threw up great cubes of meat just as he'd swallowed them, unchewed. Tough times and tough men.

In the winter of '47 there was a big freeze. The cows' hooves had to be wrapped in sacking before they could be taken up the icy concrete of William Street to be milked. Outside our door the big Clydesdale delivery horse went down in spite of the sackcloth on his shaggy hooves. It seemed like he would knock the little houses on either side of the narrow street in his attempts to get up. I'll never forget the noise and commotion, the rattling of harness and the frightening screams of the big animal as an army of men tried to free him from the shafts of the wagon.

Even the river froze that year, and the snow was so deep at the hairpin bend on the New Line Road over the hill that they had to tunnel under it. My father took us out to Bessborough to slide on the frozen lake where the "toffs" used to skate in style in the old days. Winters like that were so rare in my youth that they were a great novelty and great fun, even for the adults. I believe the police even got something out of it. We kids would pour water down the bottom of William Street to make a slide, and I remember the guards mounting a clever campaign to come at us from all directions simultaneously to catch us in our criminal act. The buggers had nothing else to do.

I think it was that Christmas that the Chinese lanterns started small fires everywhere. Hearn Felice, who was from Malta and had a shop across William Street from us, imported them. They were gorgeous paper things in bright colors and exotic designs. They were flat when you bought them but they pulled out like little concertinas. On top was a wire handle and on the bottom a little stiff cardboard piece for the candle. That was the crux. If the candle burned down, the thing caught fire. If the candle fell over, it caught fire. If you held it in your hand, the candle burned you. If you put it down, it folded up like an accordion and caught fire. They were so pretty that everyone bought them, and little fires broke out all over town. Fortunately none were too serious.

The importer of such exotic things, Hearn Felice, was a cranky, abrasive, talented, innovative little man. He had met his Irish wife in New York, but she was homesick and dragged him back to Ireland, where he spent the rest of his life complaining about the weather and the lazy Irish and just about everything else. He bred gun dogs. I well remember the day he shot his favorite, Bruce, by accident and carried his body home, wailing like the banshee. He also bred little lapdogs with ugly snouts, nasty little things that would take the finger off you. He was good with dogs. I saw him one day throw a bucket of water on two dogs that were still stuck together after their lust was spent. No one else on the street had the guts to go out in public and face the fact of fornicating dogs committing mortal sin in broad daylight.

He was also a painter, a very good one, and made a Christmas crib for the church that was a beautiful piece of work. It was made of painted panels set back in three dimensions like a stage set. Viewed from the front, it led your eye back into the unfolding landscape of Bethlehem. It was our job every year to root it out of the storage room at the canon's house and, under Felice's abusive direction, reconstruct it.

But it was his shop window at Christmas that really enthralled us kids. In one window was a glass fountain with lights and bubbles rising up through a glass tube, a thing of endless fascination. In the other window were toys and games the likes of which were hard to imagine. But there was one thing that I coveted more than anything in the world, an aeroplane. My brothers were in the air force and I had a total fixation on aeroplanes, and this one was a beauty. Two-and-a-half-foot wingspan and every detail exactly right. I wanted it.

A gang of us were gathered around the bright window one evening coming up to Christmas, all of us lusting after this aeroplane, but all realizing that such an expensive, magnificent thing could never be ours. Suddenly there was an adult's voice behind us.

"Are you Willie Clancy?" I was desperately shy and blushed brighter than the toys as I said I was. "I'm your cousin Anna McGrath, from Dublin. You're the image of Da, God bless you. Listen, it's not often I get to Carrick anymore, so let me buy a little present for my cousin. Is there anything in the window you'd like? Anything at all now. Don't be shy. Anything at all."

All eyes were on me, willing me to shout, *"The aeroplane,"* but all full of envy at the same time. I searched the window in confusion and embarrassment, looking at all the common stuff, toy soldiers, windup tin cars, jigsaw puzzles, "Snakes and Ladders," magic sets, cowboy suits with guns and holsters and hats. But I was only seeing one thing and that thing was too much to ask of anyone, even a cousin from Dublin. I looked longingly at the plane, hesitated, and said:

"The ludo set. Please."

In the early nineteenth century, faction fighting was a serious business in our part of the country, two of the best-known factions being the Caravats and the Shanavests. A kind of holdover of tribal warfare, it continued, in a less ferocious form, among the armies of farm laborers that were still needed to work the land before mechanization. Influential farmers who had grievances among themselves would manage, after the harvest was safely in, of course, to settle old differences by setting their laborers against each other like packs of dogs. The fights were not always brawls, however, but formalized battles fought with sticks that had been carefully cut and tested. These pitched battles were usually fought at fairs, but they would often degenerate into bloody brawls after the fair when poteen was consumed.

The faction fights were mostly a memory to us in Carrick when I was growing up, except on Christmas Eve when the pubs would overflow again with old wrongs, blood, vomit, and strong words. One Christmas Eve, I saw the drinking men at Fogarty's pub spill out onto Main Street in front of the post office. I saw a man, already covered in blood, beaten down on the street unconscious. With a crowd gathering, he lay in the street like a dog, his head against the curb. I saw the man who had hit him go into the middle of the street to get a running kick at his face.

Later, at midnight mass, as I stood in line for communion, the man in front of me was so drunk that when the priest came to him with the host *"Corpus Domini nostri Jesu Christi"* he erupted in vomit all over the host, the priest, the paten, the Christmas vestments.

And we young bucks were not immune to the blood-call. Our gang fights started innocently enough, in the autumn. As soon as the chestnuts would burst, like plump brown birds from their prickly shells, and fall, or be felled by our sticks, the faction fights would begin. Coming home from school, we'd have conker fights with the chestnuts on the end of a piece of twine. This would soon progress to pelting each other with the nuts. There would be the odd black eye, someone would go home crying, there would be shouts of "That's not fair!" Alliances would form. Factions were born. It's the same old story since time immemorial.

By the time the chestnut season was over, the bad blood was up and there was no stopping. Stones took over from chestnuts as the weapons. The enemy was now clearly defined. The territories were claimed.

We went head-to-head with the closest neighbors and then teamed up with old enemies to beat back those neighbors into their home ground. We were the William Street gang, and our archenemies were the Main Street gang. Then there were the New Street gang and the Long Lane gang, greatly feared because of their secret weapon. Our theater of war was the park initially, then the Bull's Lough, the Garryrue, the Strand, and the multitude of lanes that led down to the river Suir.

We had our strategies. William Street is near the park, so we had ammunition on hand in the form of chestnuts. When they gave out, we had the County Council stones, used for roadwork, that were kept near the Old Cinema across from the park. We knew better than to pursue the Main Street gang when we'd routed them from our territory. We stuck close to our ammunition source. It was in one of these skirmishes, with my jersey front full of stones, that I fell and broke my left arm. I had to retire from the war for that campaign.

Like big wars, ours were cyclical. The year after my arm was broken, the Great War (among the Carrick gangs) was fought. The Main Street gang had become strong and arrogant. They had the troops, and in the first few forays the William Street gang were beaten back, once in a very cowardly and dirty fashion.

One of the enemy lived in a boardinghouse cum public house behind the wall of one of the lanes. He and his cohorts lay in wait for us behind the wall with the accumulated contents of all the piss pots, collected from all the rooms for days, until we came up the lane chanting, "We won the war! We won the war!" Suddenly there was a shout from behind Butler's wall and a rain of stale piss and worse soaked us head to foot. Fortunately my friend John Ryan had a very understanding grandmother who stripped off all our clothes and dried them in front of the fire before we could venture home. She didn't wash them, mind you, just dried them.

But we took sweet revenge. We enlisted the help of my schoolmate Joe Holloway and his Long Lane gang, who hated the Main Street snobs as much as we did. They joined us for the great final battle at the top of Oven Lane. And they brought their secret weapon.

Joe's father, as I told you, was the fishmonger. He often had boxes of unsold mackerel, which would go rotten. When they did, they swelled up ready to burst. That's when, with a piece of twine tied around the tail, they became a fearsome weapon. When you caught an enemy across the head with this putrid load, it burst, and he was gone from the battle for good!

That was my last campaign, however. All the good went out of it when I discovered, on the day we routed them, that among the Main Street gang were some of my friends and cousins.

When we had driven them back to the river and we held the ruined cottages in the lanes, with all the rubble as our ammunition, we knew we had them beaten. In that moment of triumph I was in a derelict house with no roof when a stone came whizzing in and caught me on the forehead at the hairline. I was knocked on my arse, stunned. The blood covered my hair and clothes. I still have the scar. As I was sitting among the debris holding back the blood oozing through my fingers, I vaguely saw one of the enemy break ranks and run to my aid. It was Seamus McGrath, my mother's nephew, Uncle Peter's son, who came to my rescue and, having washed the blood off my hair at his house, shielded me through the battle, now petering out, back to William Street, home, and mother. Blood, after all, is thicker than water.

5

Were the summers really warmer then? Were the wild strawberries that intensely strawberry? Were the *fraochans* so plump and powder blue in the woods of July? Were the pine trees so dark and fragrant with bubbles of sap so sweet you wanted to eat it as well as smell it? Were my sunburned insteps so sore? My feet so callused that I could run barefoot all summer long through field and wood and stony path and riverbed, through hedges and ditches and lovely oozy river mud, and not a bother on me except the time when my big toe turned septic and Dr. Conlon cut it open with a razor blade and released a half cup of pus with the festering thorns?

That was real. And so were the cuckoo and the corncrake, the meadowlarks, almost all extinct now. And the wild strawberries were real because I tasted them not long ago in Brittany and they were just as luscious as I remember them.

I smell the tar on the salmon fishers' cots on the riverbank blistering in the sun. I taste the sour of sally grass in the field. I inhale the smell of the bundles of new-cut willows on the fresh mud of the sally yards. I feel the quickening of the pulse trying to see the girl boarders sunning themselves on the roof of the convent across the river. I feel the crunch of the fork penetrate the eel's hard muscle behind the head. We'd have stolen the fork from the kitchen and tied it to a stick for stabbing eels. I can taste its sweet flesh fried on a hot slate and the pungent smoke from the dried sally bark and the thrill in the pit of the stomach as your feet left the stones of the old bridge when you finally braved the high dive and saw the far-off water come to meet you and the wonderment of the clear water at high tide with moving meshes of light on the bottom making magic on waving weeds and shoals of minnows called breakeens and eels' heads snaking out from under rocks. All the senses were alive and your feet knew where, under waist-high water at spring tide, the bridge made by a submerged tree forded the deep drainage canal of the sally yards. We knew the land as well as any other wild creatures. Every bird's nest and the color of her eggs and its spots; every rabbit burrow, fox den, and badger set; every undercut of riverbank where hiding trout could be tickled and gilled. We were part of the land.

We called them the sally yards, but the slob lands where the sallies grew stretched for miles down the Suir and supplied the young shoots that were cut by an army of Carrick women employed by the basketmakers, the Shanahans, to be boiled and skinned in the actual sally yards at the bottom of Castle Lane, the heart of the industry of basket-making. In early summer the sally switches would be cut and piled and secured close to the water to wait their turn to be loaded high in cots and paddled up to the processing yard. The gnarled old root stock, trees of great antiquity, stood like regiments of old soldiers, stripped of their bright uniforms, down along the riverbank under the eye of Ormond Castle. This was the place we called the Lades, a short corruption of "the ladies' swimming hole," as it was called in the heyday of the Butler family. Here's where Black Tom Butler had added a beautiful manor house to the old castle, vainly to await the visit of his mistress, Elizabeth I, queen of England. That's where I first became interested in basic architecture, not, I hasten to add, from the castle, but from the fact that the soft ground and the pliant sallies gave endless scope for our hut designs. We stuck the sallies in the mud to make whatever rooms and passageways we dreamed up. Then we tied the tops together for a roof and simply interwove the walls. For a more permanent structure we daubed the woven walls with mud.

The castle was long since derelict, and there were no ladies now to swim in the ladies' swimming hole, so it became our skinny-dipping place, our all-male domain. We never had towels, of course, so after a swim we'd lie back on the hard mud between our huts and let the sun dry us while swarms of flies plagued us until we took shelter in wattle-and-daub structures. Those summer days were paradise. We were kings of our own castles and lords of the flies.

One glorious June morning Mickey Nolan, Tommy Sheehan, and I were reluctantly making our way to school in the monastery. The river was in full spring tide the way we loved it, and the water, looking like a great lucid magnifying glass, was beckoning to us. Another cause for our reluctance was the fact that we were going to an exam, the geometry exam of the summer tests. We didn't take the road to school but the "strand" along by the sally yard and the Lades. The swollen tide was right up to the path, the sally trees nearly submerged. We dawdled. When we came near the school, panic set in. The playground was silent. That meant that the students were inside and the exam had started. We went up the steps in terrified silence and quietly opened the door. There, sure enough, were all the heads down studying the exam paper. There, too, sure enough, was Brother Dugan (Wiggy Dugan, as he was called), glowering at us. He beckoned us outside and closed the door.

"I won't hear any excuses," he said in a voice of deep solemnity. "I want you three to leave here now. Your punishment will be that you are forbidden to sit this exam and you are forbidden to sit this afternoon's exam."

He showed us the gate with accusing finger. We went sheepishly and silently across the deserted school yard, eyes on the ground. A hundred yards down the road, out of earshot of the school, we looked at each other. The sun was hot; the lush hedges of summer in full scent, the birds in full chorus, the river in full tide. A great whoop escaped all three at the same instant.

"Get yer togs quick. I'll meet ye on the old bridge in fifteen minutes. We'll have the bank all to ourselves. Hurry up or we'll miss the full tide. Geometry, feck! Feck feck feck and feck geometry again!"

The river was the life of the town, the very reason for its being, but it also took its toll. The dead house, under the new bridge, had at least one body laid out in it every year.

Paddy Wall was a polesman on one of the sand barges. I remember the day his pole broke and he fell onto the broken shaft. We peeped through the wooden doors of the dead house to look at him laid out, waiting for the hearse.

One day, at the Friars' Rock, young Walsh got into trouble and was swept down by the current. The Friars' Rock was a favorite swimming place but it could be dangerous. The rock itself was in the middle of the river in the deepest part and was named for the indent, shaped like a sandal, on its surface. The print was said to have been made by a friar who was fleeing his Cromwellian pursuers and, trapped at the river, had leaped from the bank to the rock in the middle and from there to the far bank and safety. The mark of his sandal is still on the rock.

Young Walsh was not so lucky. He was swept away and we weaker, younger swimmers watched helplessly as he went under with arms flailing. He came up again, shouting, not prayers but "Fuck ye! Fuck ye! Help me. I'm drownin'. Fuckin' help me!" He went under again. Two big lads on the far side dived in, and one strong swimmer from our bank managed to get to him before he drowned. I couldn't believe the amount of water that came out of him as they laid him out on the grass.

Before we were encapsulated in our homes by television, encapsulated in our heads by Walkmans, encapsulated bodily in the motorcar, before we were isolated from each other and the community around us by mechanical devices, chemical devices, by speed, noise, and the breakdown of family, before all that, there was a telepathy, I believe, that ran through communities, a common consciousness, as when a flock of birds turns together, or a shoal of fish will flash its silver flank. No leader there, no committee decisions. Flash, and the shoal turns.

One day in June, Kevin Driscoll, his cousin Colm, and I were fishing in the Lingaun River, a tributary of the river Suir, at Cregg outside Carrick. A lovely, lazy day, a happy day. Toward evening we walked back to Carrick. Crossing the park at the bottom of New Street, we felt it together. Something was wrong. Something very wrong. There was some kind of gloom over the town. It was in the air, in the sky, in the stones of the houses. As we passed by Driscoll's pub, cousins of the two lads, the mood was overpowering.

Young John Driscoll was never allowed to go swimming with us. He had to work in the pub. He had to bottle the stout out in the bottling shed on summer days when we were all heading out, singing, to the river. He had never learned to swim. But one day he broke the traces. While we were fishing in the Lingaun, he had escaped with his pals to the Suir, to a dangerous part of the river called the Navigation. His pals went swimming while John played football in Johnny Hearn's long field on the bank of the Navigation, a deep channel of cut stone. The ball went toward the river. John ran after it too fast and couldn't stop.

We heard the news at Kevin's house and ran to where they were dragging the river for his body with coils of barbed wire. We got there just as they had snagged his clothing and were pulling this great swollen thing out of the water. It bore no resemblance to the John Driscoll we knew. He was the first contemporary I had ever seen dead.

The burden of mortality weighed a little heavier. God's fishing line tightened.

Maybe that's when the panic attacks started. I had often thought of my mother's story of the day on the river when the Black and Tans, pointing their rifles at them, had prevented their boat from coming ashore. Her description of the panic which my sister May had suffered that day haunted me. I'd had little warning shots before, like when I was lying on the lounge one night alone in the house and I started listening to my heart. It sounded so loud in my ears, I began to think that if it pounded any louder it would stop. Of course the adrenal glands went into action at the thought, and the sound of my heart became an accelerating drumbeat in my head.

I got up and went out to meet the lads and became absorbed in something else. But one day a full-blown panic attack hit me as I was fishing from the quay between the old and new bridges. The river was in flood and the trout were taking earthworms. I was looking at the murky water rushing past when a feeling of unreality came over me. Was this a dream? Who was I? Was I losing control? Was I losing my mind?

I felt the first grip of fear. My heart started racing. "It's going to burst," I thought. Fear was feeding on fear. "I'm going mad. This will never stop. I'm dying, like May. When Daddy told her, she went mad like this. The panic killed her, the panic." I was gasping now for breath and my heart was pounding out of my chest. "I have to escape. I have to escape!"

I threw the fishing rod in the river and jumped on my bike. I fled blindly. Pedaling frantically, I didn't know where to, or why. Speed, speed, the wind, "Get away. Quick. Escape!" But from what? My own mind? My thoughts? My self? My disintegration? My madness? But you can't escape the mind. You can't cycle out of the prison of your head.

I cycled and cycled until the panic spent itself.

It was inevitable—the snap. My eldest sister Lili confided in me one time that she couldn't imagine how I came out so well from the circumstances of my teen years, living like an only child, the rest of the family gone, with parents who should be my grandparents, in a house where old people gathered by the fire at night and the talk was of sickness and death and the past. The past, always the past, and the ones who had died that I'd never known like Aunt Eily and Lally. And then the looks and the silent weeping and the whispers, in case I'd hear, of Mary Jo: "The doctor says, you know, he thinks it's you-know-what! Where? There? Oh, God, sure God help her!"

How could I possibly escape unscathed?

They never talked of my sister May's death when my father and mother were together. But when my mother and I were alone one day, it all came out.

"Oh, she was mad about you. You were only six months old when she died but she used to dote on you. Oh, I can still hear her singing

'The Days of the Kerry Dances' when she'd be running up the stairs in the excitement of going to a dance. Twenty-one, boy, was all she was. Twenty-one. . . . Her whole life . . . her whole lovely young life in front of her. Oh, the joy she had, and singing, always singing:

> O, the days of the Kerry dancing
> O, the ring of the piper's tune!
> O, for one of those hours of gladness,
> Gone, alas! like our youth too soon.

"I was brokenhearted when she went to Dublin. I was delighted, in a way, of course, that she got the job in the civil service. Sure 'twas a real feather in our cap. And she loved it, too, the hustle and bustle of Dublin. But she was homesick. She'd write nearly every day wanting to know every scrap of news from home. Then she wrote one day to say she'd twisted her ankle getting off a tram. Sure we thought nothing of it . . . a sprained ankle. Then another letter saying she felt very bad, could she come home? When we picked her up off the train, boy, I got such a fright. The way she looked. Oh my God, my heart did something awful. I knew immediately she was very sick. We put her to bed and nursed her as best we could, but she wasn't getting any better. The quack doctor in Dublin had made a botch of setting the ankle. Imagine. Sure for a long time we didn't know what was wrong. We didn't know what was wrong, boy. Just kept praying, kept praying, kept praying. And then the day when Conlon came in and I knew by his face when he came out of the back room, that's where she was, I knew by his face there was something awful wrong.

" 'Can I speak privately to you?' says he to me. Oh God, my heart sank, boy.

" 'I want to know the truth, Doctor,' I said. 'I want to know the truth whatever it is.'

" 'I'm afraid it's very bad news,' he said. 'There's TB in the bone and gangrene has set in. It's poisoned her whole system. There's nothing anyone can do. It's in God's hands now. We'd better tell Bob.'

"When he was gone, I said to Daddy, 'God spoke before him. I won't let our lovely May die.'

"I believe in the power of prayer. I set up a little altar out in the landing and we prayed, boy, day and night. The crowd would be kneeling down along the stairs, saying the rosary, begging Our Lady. . . . Don't let her die . . . don't let her die. But it was no good. She got worse and worse. I never slept a wink day or night. Thank God I had Annie there. She took over, fed everyone, looked after you. You were hungry and screaming all the time. The house was pure pandemonium! Trying to keep everyone quiet. Trying to nurse May and keep her hopes up. That was the main thing. Keep her going. I knew that if she lost hope she'd die. That's why I kept talking to her and praying with her all the time. Giving her hope.

"One day when she was very bad Daddy said, 'We'd better call the priest to give her the last rites.' I said, 'If you do she'll give up and die.' But he wouldn't listen to me. He got obsessed with telling her to make her peace with God. Well, if he did, I got just as determined that he wouldn't. It was a nightmare, boy. I had to stay with her all the time 'cause he was waiting, waiting all the time for me to fall asleep or even go to the toilet. I daren't leave her for a minute. Of course I couldn't keep it up. I don't know how anybody could keep the vigil as long as I did, without food, without sleep, praying, praying, a house full of ye neglected, not knowing what was going on. Him trying to get at her. Finally exhaustion got to me and I must have fallen asleep. It could only have been for a minute . . . then I heard the scream . . . and I knew he got to her . . . I knew he got to her."

A great shuddering sigh escaped her then as she relived the whole thing. Her anger came back. There was fire in her eyes.

"I never forgave him. I never will forgive him. He killed her. He thought he had to tell her . . . his duty to tell her . . . to prepare her soul. But he killed her.

"I heard the scream and ran in to her. She was in a state of terror.

" 'Am I, Mammie? Am I dying? Daddy says I'm dying. He wants to get the priest.'

"Well, I looked at him and you know . . . he couldn't look me in the eye. What could I do or say then? The poor love . . . the poor little love. I just held her and hugged her and swayed with her. Eventually I said,

'It wouldn't do any harm to get the priest. It might help you. It might cure you.'

"Suddenly she calmed down. Just this calm came over her. She said, 'If I'm going to die, I want to die right now. I don't need the priest. I'm in the state of grace. Get the blessed candles and we'll pray.'

"I lit the candles and we held one each and started the rosary. Suddenly she stopped. She looked up and this light came into her face and she said, 'Oh, look! Look!' and she smiled and this peace came over her and she reached up her arms and the lighted candle fell on the bed. She said, 'Look!' and a big sigh left her body and she was gone. Gone, boy . . . and you know . . . the candle never burned the bed, not a mark. I think now . . . I know . . . that she saw angels."

What she told me next came as a great shock to a young boy who knew his mother as a devout Catholic. She said, "I cursed God! I cursed Him for taking her. And I cursed your father, God forgive me. But I couldn't accept that it was God's will to take my lovely child. Not only did I curse Him, I went up to the church to curse Him in His own house. That was the madness that came over me, boy. I wouldn't go to mass for a full year. I couldn't say a prayer. I was so full of anger. . . . It nearly killed me. Eventually I couldn't suffer anymore. Daddy finally got me to go to confession, to a very holy man over in the friary. He helped me to become reconciled and I got some kind of peace at last. He told me May was in heaven. She was happy and she wanted me to accept God's will. And sure I've tried, boy. Every day of my life since, I've tried to accept it."

6

One Friday, Wiggy Dugan burst into the classroom, strode furiously up to the blackboard, took a stick of chalk, and started to write a huge "F." The chalk broke with the pressure of his anger. He got another stick and continued U-C-K. F-U-C-K took up the entire blackboard.

Wiggy Dugan had lost all his hair, it was said, to some accident or malady while doing missionary work in China. He now turned his strange, florid face on us. It was shiny and naked: no eyelashes, no eyebrows, no hint or shadow of stubble. His awful wig seemed to float completely free of his scalp, which looked as if it were a continuation of his raw, oiled face. The eyes were hooded and terrible as he fixed us with a stare that withered and shriveled us as we tried to worm ourselves into the grain of the desks and become invisible. His voice, when he got under control, was low and forced.

"What do these letters spell?" He nailed us individually with the hammerblow of his gaze. He waited. He let us squirm!

"What is the word I have written on the blackboard?"

He lowered his voice. He let a hint of sadness creep into it. "Just as I thought. Cowards! All of you, cowards!" Voice down to a growl. Silence. He turned his back on the class. He contemplated the blackboard for a long moment. Then he swung round on us. *"The word is fuck, fuck, fuck."* Each time he said it was like a slap across the face.

"You all knew it yesterday on the hurling pitch! It seemed to be the *only* word you knew! Every Thursday now at sports time I have to suffer the indignity of hearing that word used time and time again. I've tried to make excuses for it. I've tried to ignore it. I've tried to inure myself to the offense of it. But I can no longer ignore it." He got a pointer. "Now, let us examine this word, 'fuck.' What does it mean? Who uses it? And why? First of all it is a word like any other word. Where does any word come from? The words 'the,' 'and,' 'that.' They are simply part of the language that has evolved, the language by which we express ourselves. We can clearly see how some words evolved, like 'good-bye,' which is 'God be with ye' condensed. The way we put words together to communicate complex ideas to each other can be a fascinating process and it can be a very beautiful process. So why use this one word 'fuck' to such excess, such brutal and ugly excess? Because of a failure, through ignorance, or laziness, or both, to *express* ourselves.

"Our whole purpose as teachers is to help you to learn, not only how to express yourselves but how to see the beauty of how others, such as the great poets, the great essayists, the great novelists and theologians, have expressed themselves, thereby enriching our view of the life God gave us, and in so doing perhaps helping some of you to find within yourselves reflections of those lofty visions that ennobled the spirit of man throughout the ages, and the ability to express them. But now what do I find? The word 'fuck.' That pathetic resort of the illiterate! That foul epithet of the most despicable form of soldiery! The most used and abused word in the commonest parlance of the dregs of humanity!

"Boys, it is a sad thing for me to contemplate, that the work I have been trying to do, and that my fellow teachers have been trying to do, in giving to you young men, most of you bright and intelligent young men, the chance of an education, it is sad that it should come to this. The failure is mine."

He slowly picked up the eraser and cleaned the chalk from the blackboard.

"This class is dismissed."

No teacher would have talked to us like that before. We were maturing. An awareness of new ways of looking at life was dawning on us. As well as new vistas opening up, there was the hormonal rush which heightened all the chemistry of my awakening. The year was 1950 and I would turn fifteen in September.

That's when I fell in love with Angela. Like me, she was the youngest in her family. She was five foot three, and soft and warm and so feminine. Also like me, she was painfully shy. She was my first love. Lying in bed at night, I would transport myself to her house, just around the corner, to where she was sleeping, and I'd say fervent prayers for God to keep her safe. My love was a wound that had no healing.

There is an old song called "Donal Og" that goes:

> I saw you first on a Sunday evening
> Before the Easter as I was kneeling.
> It was about Christ's passion
> That I was reading,
> But my eyes were on you
> And my own heart bleeding.

In that song, it was the girl's heart that was bleeding, but well I knew her torment and her obsession. My father used to describe the love he had for a girl in Piltown, his home village, when he was a boy of that age. "I worshiped the very smoke from her chimney," he would tell us. "And, you know, no matter how much you love someone the rest of your life, there's nothing like that first love."

All that summer, when all of us boys and girls would get together for long walks, or swimming adventures out to the millpond in Kilonerry, we would inevitably pair off, or more likely *be* paired off, by the group. Annette was one of the gang, as we called ourselves, and she was the one they paired me off with, to my dismay. "Oh, Willie is caught in a net," they would joke, "Willie is caught in Annette. Haha!" But it was Angela, not Annette, that I was in love with.

From the shy way Angela would look at me I thought, secretly, "They have it all wrong." But I was the one who had it wrong, and the day that Angela got lost among the ferns with Nipper, I slipped home alone by the shortcut through the fields, numb with anguish.

> For you took what's before me
> And what's behind me,
> You took east and west
> When you wouldn't mind me,
> Sun and moon from my sky you've taken,
> And God as well, or I'm much mistaken.

But life is irrepressible at that age and I filled my time with tramping the woods and fly-fishing in the Suir and Lingaun Rivers. Nature became my love because it never let you down. Apart from the woods and the wild, poetry was what I most loved. After that came playing the mandolin and learning songs.

I tried to swallow life in great big gulps. My ambition was to try everything, except for one thing, contact sports, which held no interest for me. Both arms had been broken when I was younger, so I wasn't very strong. On the hurling team they put me in goal (with a good fullback), but on my first day as goalkeeper a dribbling ball came harmlessly toward me. I spread my feet and put the hurley between them to block it. It just slowly rolled between the hurley and my left foot.

They tried me at football but I kept turning an ankle. The only thing I excelled at was the high jump. At a sports meet one day between Carrick and our rivals, Clonmel, I was tipped to win. But the grass was wet as I made my side run for the crucial jump. One leg went over the crossbar but the other slipped on the wet grass. Caught between my knees, the crossbar became a flying javelin and came hurtling with me right into the crotch of the unfortunate Wiggy Dugan, who happened to be in the right wrong place. *I* wasn't hurt but it was mortifying to watch a Christian Brother doubled up in agony and humiliation clutching his crotch.

That was the end of my sporting career. From then on I was given the sports periods, Thursday afternoons, off.

A big metal trunk in the garret was full of my brother Paddy's books. He was off in foreign lands and the trunk was locked. I knew there were treasures in there, so my mother wrote to him for permission to pry it open. When he wrote back giving the okay, we found a magic trove including John Steinbeck's *The Grapes of Wrath, Cannery Row, Of Mice and Men,* and all the others. There was Homer's *Odyssey* and *Iliad,* Samuel Butler's *The Way of All Flesh,* books of poetry and collections of magazines like *The Bell* and *Envoy* with contributors like Sean O'Faolain, Frank O'Connor, Liam O'Flaherty, Louis MacNeice, Patrick Kavanagh. Heady and wonderful stuff for a teenager.

In the pine trees over a beautiful and peaceful little valley called Millvale, just outside Carrick, was a rock that became my reading place on Thursday afternoons. There's where I met Helen and Odysseus and Agamemnon and Zeus and there's where I cried for Hector when Achilles dragged his body around the walls of Troy. I left all the effin' and blindin' behind on the playing pitch.

After the war, Paddy and Tom had emigrated, first to Canada, then on to Cleveland, Ohio, and from there to New York's Greenwich Village. On their rare visits home they would bring treasures with them: ten-inch records of Josh White, the great blues singer, who would later become a friend and coworker as well as a major inspiration in stagecraft, and recordings of Woody Guthrie and Cynthia Gooding and Leadbelly and Uncle Dave Macon from Appalachia. I couldn't get enough of songs like "John Henry" and "Free and Equal Blues." Then there were songs recorded on home tape recorders at Greenwich Village apartment sessions, like "Pirate Jenny" from *The Threepenny Opera.*

In Ireland, too, folk music was getting more of an airing on radio.

I'd never miss *Donagh MacDonagh's Song Bag* on Thursday nights. He'd play an eclectic mix of music from whatever folk recordings came into Radio Eireann studios, mainly American. He was an interesting man with an interesting mind who would become a good friend later. He was a poet and an anthologist as well as a district court judge, a position that put him in touch with people interested in folk music and folklore around the country. He was a son of Thomas MacDonagh, the poet, patriot, and one of the signatories of the Proclamation on Independence in 1916 who was executed along with Pearse and Connolly and the rest.

On a more homespun level there was another popular radio program called *The Ballad Makers' Saturday Night,* which the whole country listened to.

The BBC, particularly their drama department, was also producing some great programming at the time. I loved baby-sitting my sister Joan's kids, the Butlers. On Wednesday nights Christy and Joan would leave me with their children and the BBC Theatre night. That's when the BBC radio ran a series of plays including some by W. B. Yeats. At the Poets Theater at Harvard University, I would later get to play all the leads in the same plays I heard on those nights. I'd get to play Aleel, the poet in *The Countess Cathleen,* and the following year to play in *On Baile's Strand, The King of the Great Clock Tower,* and *Words upon the Windowpane.*

It was a time, for me, of intense spiritual awakening. I had a deep baptismal immersion in the world of poetry, of ideas, music, and writing as well as the joyous upwelling I experienced at the unfolding of the beauty of the world around me. Even organized religion was more spiritual then, at least the ritual, the droned Latin of the mass, the incense, the candles and vestments, the "odor of sanctity," led you into a more meditative place, a place that doesn't exist in modern churches with the jangly guitars and bad folksinging and handshaking and chatty sermons like conversations in a pub.

I sang in the choir for Sunday mass and evening devotions, and on the first Friday of every month, for nine Fridays, I'd often make the supreme effort (for a confirmed sleepyhead) and be up for seven o'clock mass and communion. In school I studied my Thomas Aquinas and my Apologetics, taking it all in "as gospel," so to speak. The "truth" was there to be seen, and it was comforting not to have to question anything.

The choir loft was a special place, particularly for somebody as shy as I was. It was in the back of the church, with dark, narrow stairs winding up to it. Nobody ever had to see you coming or going in church, but you could see everything. It had a smell of old, old wood dust, and the antique organ wheezed and labored, a sound I got to like almost as much as the music. When I first joined the choir the bellows was still hand-operated and I got the job of pumping it up with the big wooden lever that was smooth as silk from the hands of generations. I loved the thumbed hymnbooks and the shape of the Latin script and the square notes of the plain chant. It was all ancient and comforting.

Of course, the choir was also a great vantage point. I could see Angela, who was the organist's daughter, walking up the women's side of the church with that walk that I loved, and could gaze at her, coming back demurely from the communion rail, without fear of other eyes seeing the adoration in mine. Another of my father's quotes was, "Oh, the pangs, the pangs of unrequited love!"

My father in church, now, that was a different matter. I would often be mortified with embarrassment. He had become forgetful with age and he would walk up to the front of the church, center aisle, with an old tea towel or even one of my mother's stockings hanging out of his pocket, in fact anything he'd used to take the hot teapot from the fire. It was his evening ritual to take a nap before the tea, which consisted of two boiled eggs, raw enough to drip down his tie, with a *cleip* of bread, and then the evening devotions. He and my mother never missed the evening devotions, nor did I, of course, since I sang in the choir. On the first clang of the great bell, the bell that dominated our lives, we all responded like Pavlov's dog. It rang for devotions, it rang for mass, it rang the Angelus, eighteen earth-quaking, brain-numbing strokes, three . . . three . . . three . . . then, nine together . . . at six in the morning, twelve noon, six in the evening. It rang for funerals, two clangs for a woman, three for a man.

Joe Shanahan, the basket-maker, was also the bell ringer. We knew Joe well, so he would give us the key to the belfry on occasion and we'd climb up the rickety wooden stairs to the platform where the massive bell itself hung. We called it the Quasimodo loft. It was a messy place from the pigeons, but the view from the top through the granite arches took in the whole valley. Over the top of the Carrickbeg hills you could see a tantalizing glimpse of the peaks of the Comeragh Mountains. I had never been close to them, but ever since the Christmas morning that Colm Driscoll and I had been brought out by Mrs. Jacques, the church organist for the friary, to a little church on top of the hill to sing the Christmas mass and saw the Comeraghs looking so close and magical in the cold dawn light, I had a great longing to go and climb them.

Coming down the Monastery Hill after school one day in early November, Kevin Driscoll and I were looking at the sharp western ridge of the Comeraghs just showing over the wooded hills of Carrickbeg. I said to Kevin, "They're not far, ya know. We could walk to Coumseangan Lake and back before teatime."

"Will we chance it?" he said.

"Why not? We'll give it a go!"

We dumped our school bags and set out at a good march to the mountains. The fact that darkness comes so early in Ireland at that time of year didn't occur to us. It was eight miles on the road to the foot of the mountain, then another two or three miles through the rocky fields and on to the rough land rising up beside the torrent called Uisce Solais, Water of Light, that cascaded down from the mountaintop. Hidden from view in the deep gorge, or "corry," up there was the lake of Coumseangan, which means "the narrow place (or waist) of the ant."

In the deceptive light of a misty, gray November day, it seemed like the lake must be just beyond the first ridge. Above the lake was a sheer rock face that rose straight up for a thousand feet before leveling off to the bogland on the summit. It was a foreboding sight that day with the light fading fast and Kevin and I having second thoughts, but we had walked eight miles and weren't going to quit then.

We followed sheep paths up the ever-steeper slope, around massive boulders that had been dropped by the glacial ice as it retreated at the end of the last ice age. Where we were climbing now had been the southernmost face of the vast ice cap that stretched from this place to the North Pole. I recall reading somewhere that local people found bones of the great woolly mammoth and the sabre-toothed tiger in caves near the Comeraghs, sometime in the 1890s I think it was. The story goes that an anthropologist, traveling by stagecoach through the town of Dungarvan, saw young boys playing on the street with these gigantic bones. Our climb through this glacial landscape was a far cry from the gentle fields and pine woods we were used to in our ramblings. Startled sheep would see us appear around an outcrop and scatter in terror, their bleating, from near at hand, from the middle distance, and from unseen ridges far away echoing back to us from the great wall of the cliff, reflecting in multidimensional sound what we were seeing in the landscape.

Gasping for breath and trying to be heard over the roar of the torrent, Kevin shouted at me, "Can you imagine what it must be like for Lackendarra?" Lackendarra was a hermit who lived in a cave under one of the great boulders somewhere near the route we were taking.

Each ridge we crested we thought must surely be the last, but no, another would unfold above us in the growing gloom. The wind came up. The sheer wall that rose up from the lake in the corry looked close enough to touch. On its black face were narrow green ledges. Small white splotches, like mushrooms, could be seen way up on the ridges, but they were moving: sheep, too distant to be recognizable as such, but the movement of the tiny white mites put the size of the cliff in perspective. They stood out very white now with darkness coming on fast. Finally we clambered over the last ridge and stood awestruck amid the massive boulders. There was the lake, blacker than black, like a floor of polished coal. A sudden downdraft hit us and a fan of white waves rushed across the lake surface. Great fingers of mist and fog came scudding over the summit and were sucked down into the corry. They were sucked in, but they looked like clutching, curving talons of mist, moving incredibly fast, clawing at the black lake as if to tear it out of the mountain. We stood for a moment leaning on the wind, then without a word between us we turned and bolted.

We ran blindly, hurtling down the side of the mountain, jumping from rock to rock, foothold to foothold. At one point Kevin leaped for what looked like a bright green grassy spot and sank waist-deep in ooze covered with green algae. He clawed his way out and sloshed on, whooping, to Uisce Solais as it tumbled down its boulder-strewn path to the road and on to the sea. In almost total darkness we followed the stream until we came to the bridge at the road two miles down from

Coumseangan, what had looked like a few hundred yards that day when we'd started the climb.

Absolute darkness engulfed us now, but we were on the hard surface of the road. We hadn't even bothered to eat before we'd started out after school, it seemed so easy a trek. Now we were dangerously hungry and weak at the knees from the climb and the downhill helter-skelter dash. We couldn't see a thing around us, so we kept stumbling off the hard surface into bramble and hawthorn hedges, cutting our faces and hands. But we were so numbed by exhaustion we didn't feel it, just stumbled on the last eight miles till we saw the lights of the town below us. We had covered twenty miles or more that day.

My mother looked at me in shock when I practically fell in the door. "Oh God, boy, where were you? Look at the mess you're in. You're all scratches and cuts. And look at your clothes! You must be starving! I'll put something on for you." But I couldn't wait for something to get cooked. With my hands weak and shaking I managed to get the lid off a pot of strawberry jam. I devoured the whole pound of jam in one go. To this day I can't look strawberry jam in the eye.

We would climb the Comeraghs many times again and fish in the little lakes, but with a healthy respect now for the dangers and changing moods of the mountains. We got survey maps and spent days at a time hiking and camping and learning the folklore of the area, like the story of Crotty the Robber, the eighteenth-century Robin Hood of our place, how he'd elude the redcoats by turning the shoes of his horse back to front, sending them off in the wrong direction, and how he was betrayed by his friend Norris from Carrickbeg. When he was hanged in Waterford in 1742, his wife composed a lament for him before throwing herself from the cliff into Crotty's Lake. It begins:

> Oh, Willie Crotty, didn't I often tell you
> That David Norris would surely sell you
> That he'd come round you when you were sleeping
> And leave me here alone Ochone! and weeping.

The local historian, J. J. Healy, still had Crotty's brace of pistols when we were kids.

We never did see the hermit Lackendarra, but my brother Bobby and my mother came upon him one day when they had ventured off the main road a bit. He couldn't run away because the arse of his tattered breeches was gone. Seeing a woman, he was ashamed, and just sat down where he was. Bobby had an old box camera and got a photo of him with my mother.

7

The last year at school was a year of discovery. The old system of trying to beat learning into the students with a leather strap was nearly gone: not quite, but nearly. You still got the odd lecture about getting a job with a pension. When I heard "a job with a pension," I could visualize a long, straight road stretching off into the distance, high gray walls on either side, and way, way down at the end of it a kind of crock of gold with a glow around it, the Pension. But just *beyond* the Pension was Death! And I knew that they came as a package deal.

But the terror of going to school was gone. We were young adults and there was a distinct change in the relationship between teacher and pupil. In the winter before our final exams there was a "retreat." The classroom was transformed into a chapel, mass was said each day for three days, and we observed three days of silence while in the classrooms or even on the playing field, which was now used for silent walks. The chapel/schoolroom was open at night and I recall very vividly a night of glistening frost on the ground when Johnny McGettigan and I walked the mile or so up there to spend an hour in silent meditation before the altar. It was such a contrast by candlelight with the classroom we were used to by day. So silent, so peaceful, so evocative, in the moving shadows, of the soul's depths.

We had new enlightened teachers like Spiv Walsh and Handsome Hogan (everyone got a nickname). Liam "Handsome" Hogan and I became particularly good friends with a shared love of poetry and drama. It was a strange relationship. In school I had to call him "sir," and he'd often give me three of the best with the leather for talking in class or some such crime. Then after school we'd walk home together, passionately discussing philosophy or plays and how we would start a drama society. But it was Brother Rossiter who set me on my way to the stage.

"'Ulysses,' page sixty-four," Brother Rossiter said, tapping the leather strap against his palm. "Has everyone got it? This is a poem by Alfred Lord Tennyson. This is going to be a very important poem on the Leaving Certificate papers. Knowing this poem could be the difference between passing and failing. I want you all to learn this poem by heart."

I thought, great! I love it! In third year we had shared a classroom with the older fellows. They had "Ulysses" that year, and since I had delved into Paddy's Indian trunk and found Homer's *Odyssey* and *Iliad,* Greek mythology had become a bit of an obsession with me. Tennyson's "Ulysses" had stirred my youthful imagination as few other poems had. To me it was, and is, a majestic poem, and without realizing I was learning it, I discovered one day that I knew it by heart. But there was a problem.

"What we are going to do," Brother Rossiter was saying, "is take four lines each night, that should be easy for scholars such as yourselves, and recite them for the class the following day. If you can't learn four tonight, you learn eight lines tomorrow night and recite them for the class, et cetera. However, for every four lines not learned there will be four of these!" He brought the leather down on the desktop with an unmerciful slap. We jumped as one man. "Two on each hand. Do we understand each other, gentlemen?"

We understood only too well. But that was not my dilemma. My dilemma was shyness. It would have been easier for me, at that age, to strip naked in front of a flock of nuns than to get up in front of the class and expose, for all to see, the thing I loved so privately inside. The leather didn't frighten me, God knows we were used to that, but I quaked at the thought of reciting even four lines of "Ulysses." Many of my friends who have since shared a late-night jar with me, when I have a tendency to wax poetical, would say, "Jases! I wish he had them misgivins last Saturday night at Mooney's." But that's how it was then.

English class did roll round next day. "Now," Brother Rossiter said, "who's for the first four lines? Mr. Donovan?" Michael stood up, shaky but sound.

> It little profits that an idle king,
> By this still hearth, among these barren crags
> Matched with an aged wife, I mete and dole
> Unequal laws unto a savage race. . . .

He sat down. I finished the sentence for him in my head. Anger should have impelled me to get up then and recite the whole bloody thing, but I couldn't. Teenage shyness, the curse I had to live with.

"Good. Now. Mr. Nolan?" Mickey rattled it off. Eventually my turn came.

"Mr. Clancy." Panic. Heart thumping. Blood rising up to my neck, up my cheeks, my ears.

"Don't have it, Sir."

"Don't have it? Four lines! Didn't open a book, did you, Mr. Clancy? Well, eight lines tomorrow, or else. You know the rules. Two of the best, each hand, every four lines."

If four lines were bad, eight lines were out of the question. Twelve—
no-no-no. Days passed. To get to sixth year, you had to be a half-decent
scholar. So many of us had started out in school together, all those years
ago, with Mother Teresa, thirty-five pupils or so. Now we were six. Six
warriors. Samurai. Six, whose parents were ambitious. No question of
my parents' ambition for me. From the start my father had made sure
to call the insurance company R. J. Clancy *and Sons*. I was one of them.
My mother was the quintessential Irish mother; she wanted a son a
priest. All hope was gone for Paddy, Tom, and Bobby; she had written
them off as confirmed pagans. That left me.

"There are eight lines left. Everyone in the class has learned all the
others except" (pause, walk down steps, stand by desk, slap leather on
desk) "Mr. *Clancy* still will not deign to give us the first four lines. The
first four lines! Coming up to the Leaving Cert. Your future career depending on it! So much to learn and Mr. Clancy" (whispers to the others confidentially) *"cannot, will* not, learn the first four lines of 'Ulysses,'
on which there-will-be-so-many-questions-on-the-paper! Do you realize
how many of these"—*slap*—"are coming to you?"

D-day arrived. The rest of the class had done it. There was no triumph in the faces they turned on me. They seemed to be kind of sad
and wondering. I was wondering, too. Why in hell's name hadn't I done
the first four lines just like the rest of them? Too late now. For me there
was no escape. From the day we are born, they say, we are hooked on
God's great fishing line. Wriggle as we may, we will be drawn in. The
inevitable is inevitable. I stood up. I turned pale, green, red. I swallowed hard and started.

> It little profits that an idle king,
> By this still hearth, among these barren crags,
> Matched with an aged wife, I mete and dole
> Unequal laws unto a savage race,
> That hoard, and sleep, and feed, and know not me.
> I cannot rest from travel; I will drink
> Life to the lees. All times I have enjoyed
> Greatly, have suffered greatly, both with those
> That loved me, and alone; On shore, and when

Through scudding drifts the rainy Hyades
Vexed the dim sea. I am become a name. . . .

The poem took me, like God's fishing line. I neither controlled nor cared. I just tasted blood. The ancestral gene kicked in. I was an actor and I was loving it. I was alone in the poem.

I am a part of all that I have met;
Yet all experience is an arch wherethrough
Gleams the untraveled world whose margin fades
Forever and forever when I move.
How dull it is to pause, to make an end,
To rust unburnished, not to shine in use!
As though to breathe were life! Life piled on life
Were all too little, and of one to me
Little remains. . . .

Riding it now:

There lies the port; the vessel puffs her sail;
There loom the dark, broad seas.

No turning back. Go for it! "Cast all sails out upon the wind":

for my purpose holds
To sail beyond the sunset, and the baths
Of all the western stars, until I die.
It may be that the gulfs will wash us down;
It may be we shall touch the Happy Isles,
And see the great Achilles, whom we knew.
Though much is taken, much abides; and though
We are not now that strength which in old days
Moved earth and heaven, that which we are, we are—
One equal temper of heroic hearts,
Made weak by time and fate, but strong in will
To strive, to seek, to find, and not to yield.

I looked up. Brother Rossiter was now the one to be embarrassed. His eyes were wet. Huskily he said, "Class dismissed. Mr. Clancy, can I talk to you?"

I met him on the street in Dublin sometime in the sixties when the Clancy Brothers and Tommy Makem's songs were sweeping the country. We came toward each other, palms out. "Didn't I tell you?" he said. "Remember? You said your mother wanted you to be a priest and I said, No! Remember that? No! I said, your vocation is on the stage, giving joy to people. Joy of beautiful things. Remember that? Wasn't I right? What? Wasn't I right?"

I grasped him by the hand. "You were right, Brother," I said. "And I thank you for telling me, when no one else believed, not even myself."

My father was dismayed at my lack of interest in the insurance business. I didn't attempt to hide it after Brother Rossiter's words of encouragement.

One day my father asked me straight out, "What is it you want to be, boy?"

"I want to be an actor."

He looked at me over the top of his glasses. "Aren't there enough people in the world acting the goat without you joining them?"

· · ·

We shall not spend a large expense of time
Before we reckon with your several loves,
And make us even with you.

The closing speech from Macbeth, and Tom delivered it, our brother Tom, delivered it majestically and to great public applause, not to mention the pride of the entire assembled family at the Theatre Royal in Waterford for his debut with the Shakespearean company of the great old actor/manager Anew MacMaster. That confirmed something in me what I already knew: I had to be an actor.

Tom had been bitten by the acting bug when he worked in Cleveland, Ohio, after the war. We had an aunt there who sponsored Paddy and Tom into America after they were demobbed [demobilized] from the RAF. He joined the Cleveland Playhouse for a spell, and when he came back to Ireland, he carried the virus with him, first joining Anew MacMaster's troupe and later a group grandly known as Shakespeareana Internationale, ruled over by another actor/manager named Geoffrey Kendall. The company was made up of actors who hadn't a hope of making it on the West End in London, some of them old has-beens who spent their eccentric lives doing what they loved but pretended to hate, touring India in winter, and in summer, Ireland, where the Christian Brothers made them welcome as the flowers of May. Tom ferried back to us cargoes of wonderful tales of the goings-on in a touring "fit-up" company of the dying days of the barnstorming Shakespeareans.

One of the favorite anecdotes he brought back was the story of the night the Geoffrey Kendall group performed *Macbeth* at the Cistercian Abbey, the silent order, at Mount Melleray in county Waterford. The abbot welcomed them just as the king in *Hamlet* welcomed the troupe of actors. From Tom's telling they were delighted to sleep on stone bunks in the cells: the wonder, the theatricality of it all. The whole troupe got up at 4 A.M. to hear the monks chant matins. They were there at masses, nones, and vespers and ready to go onstage at the appointed time of 8 P.M. with a theatrical glow of unreality.

In full makeup and costume they presented themselves at curtain time. They had no way of knowing what their audience might be like, since the monks were sworn to silence and could have no contact with the actors. Only the abbot was allowed that privilege.

At eight o'clock sharp the entire brotherhood filed in. With cowls covering their bowed heads they glided silently on sandaled feet, two by two up the center aisle and into the rows of benches. There was no stage curtain. The actors wondered what the cue for their entrance was. The abbot finally appeared backstage, nodded, and the Weird Sisters started their "Double, double, toil and trouble."

The witches worked their evil spell, and the ambitious Macbeth, spurred on by his even more ambitious Lady Macbeth, played out his fateful destiny to its inevitable deadly conclusion. Tom, playing Malcolm, had the final joyous speech building up to the Shakespearean crescendo designed to bring the audience of the Globe Theatre to its feet shouting, stomping, and clapping.

> So, thanks to all at once, and to each one,
> Whom we invite to see us crown'd at Scone.
> *{Flourish. Exeunt.}*

Dead silence. Nothing. The cast looked at each other uneasily. Macbeth and his lady, back from the dead, came onstage to take their curtain calls. No curtain. No calls. On Geoffrey Kendall's signal the company bowed and stepped back. A long pause, a very long pause, a pause few actors would attempt to sustain followed. Then the abbot, in his own good time, arms in his sleeves and totally ignoring the actors, glided to center stage, faced the rows of bowed, cowled heads before him, and intoned, "My dear brothers in Christ. I would like to speak to you this evening on the futility of ambition."

His soliloquy lasted nearly as long as the play itself, while the actors had little option but to stand like statues behind him and listen. It was only halfway through that it dawned on them that this man had used an entire traveling troupe of players, as well as Shakespeare's great Scottish play, for free, as a preface for his sermon on ambition to these least ambitious of men.

Ambition may be futile, but it's there. All I wanted when I finished school was to be on the stage. Not because I was extroverted. In fact the opposite! The stage was a place where I could hide behind makeup, behind a character. In character I could get away from being me, from the shyness, from the wanting to fade into the wallpaper.

But it was also time to face the reality of the big, bad world where you had to get a job and learn to make a living. As a stopgap I worked with my sister Leish's husband, Lory Kiely, delivering bread (amazing how many of the family were bakers, three brothers and two brothers-in-law). I loved the job with Lory, taking the hot yeasty rows of Carrick loaves from the ovens in the morning and loading them into the little Austin delivery van. The fresh crusts were so sharp we had to wear coats with long tweed sleeves, and even then our forearms were often cut and sore. But making deliveries was what I loved, to all the remote country shops and houses around the Comeraghs and Slievenamon and little townlands I'd heard of in my father's insurance office but had never been to. I felt at home with all the place-names: Crehana, Mothel, Rathgormack, Curraghballintlay, Ninemilehouse, Faugheen, Mullina-hone, Skough, Tullahought, Windgap. Big names for small places.

But soon a major change was planned for me between my father and Edgar M. Deale, head of the Zurich Insurance Company in Dublin.

I really don't know how my father got started as an insurance broker, but he did and it was to be his lifelong occupation. He was a good one; necessity dictated that. There is an old, faded photograph of him and my mother with some posh-looking insurance bigwigs in Dublin on the occasion of the presentation of some award for salesman of the year, not just in Ireland but for England, Scotland, and Wales as well. For a long time he was the only agent in the country who could sign a certificate for car insurance on a weekend, when the company offices were closed, and have it honored by the company. Another reason for his success was his genuine interest in getting the lowest possible rates for his customers. He fretted and worried about it as if he were paying the premium himself instead of collecting the commission.

A crisis arose when our only vet, Tom DeLacy, a very important man, bought the first Volkswagen in town. None of the companies would insure it. Of course it emerged later that the reason for this was that the insurance companies were heavy investors in Ford and wanted no part of this new "Bug."

I recall days of discussion and concern about this issue. In the end my father won out. Then Mr. Deale arrived. He had made visits before but this time was different. He didn't stay in the office, or the "room" as we called it since it was an all-purpose space, but invited my father out for a drink at the hotel bar. When they arrived back, Edgar M. Deale was perplexed. He was saying seriously, "Well, I'll certainly get on to the head office in Switzerland and put it to them. That's all I can do. I'll let you know their answer in due course, but I'm sure they'll be as perplexed as I am, or more so, I dare say, that you don't see fit to accept their very generous offer."

It transpired that the powers-that-be in the head office in Zurich had offered my father and mother an all-expense-paid trip to Switzerland in reward for years of true and faithful service. I later heard my father tell my mother, "I told Deale we were too old for that carry-on. I said if they wanted to honor me in any way, let them give me normal rates on Volkswagens."

And in due course he got it, by God. Tom DeLacy was delighted and the name of R. J. Clancy and Sons became known far and wide, especially by lovers of the Bug. As to the "and Sons," my fate was decided for the time being. It suited me well enough to bide my time, avoid argument, and take up employment in the Zurich Insurance Company on Dawson Street in Dublin as a trainee insurance broker.

8

Arriving in Dublin on a wet November night, I found the lurid yellow streetlights ugly and depressing. The press of people and houses and traffic, mostly bicycle traffic, was confusing and frightening. I had never been to Dublin before, I had never been on a bus, I had never worked in an office or stayed in a rented room. I had never been in a restaurant or ordered food from a menu. For weeks before I was to start the job in Dublin, I'd had a knot of anxiety in my stomach. Now here I was, driving with a stranger who had given me a lift through the rain-drenched yellow suburbs of a hostile-looking city.

"I'll drop you at the North Circular Road," he said. "You can get the No. 7 bus from there to Drumcondra. Where is it you're going to, did you say? St. Patrick's Road? That's easy to find from Drumcondra Bridge."

He might as well have said, "I'll just drop you here on the moon now and you can find the Sea of Tranquillity by yourself, no bother."

Stopping at yet another set of traffic lights, something else I'd never seen before, he said, "No. 7. Good luck!" As he slammed the door and took off, he severed the umbilical cord to all the things I knew.

I found a bus stop. Massive double-deckers were pulling in and leaving every minute or so with great cries of pain from their brakes. That would be the hardest sound I'd have to get used to of all the cacophony in the city. The numbers of the bus routes were written in lighted slots above the drivers' cabs. Finally one came that read No. 7. I got on.

"Where to?" shouted the driver in a nasal twang.

"Drumcondra," I said.

"Ye're goin' the wrong way. This one is goin' to the Pillar. Get the number seven on the other side."

The Pillar, the harsh twang, the shouts of newsboys—"Hearly-mailempirenewsexpressorpeople"—all double Dutch to me. Later I'd learn that they were saying in their singsong accent, *"Herald-or-Mail-Empire News-Express-or-People."* The crowds, the lights, the car horns, the damned wail of the bus brakes: Dante's Inferno.

But finally I got the right bus, the right street, the right row of houses, and the right number, and, clasping my little brown cardboard suitcase, climbed the narrow stairs to a tiny bedroom that was to be home for the next six months. A dim lightbulb hanging from the ceiling shone on a small table with a basin and ewer. Holy pictures were on the wall and a pot was under the bed. The toilet was outside in the backyard. "Not unlike home," I thought as I lay on the little monastic bed. I may have felt like an intruder in the house of a family I didn't know, but I wasn't on the moon. It'd be all right.

Dreaming of all the goings-on at home as I left, the mother's tears; the pals at the pantomime; the pocket money from my good old brother-in-law Christy Butler; the Polonius-like advice from my father; I said some prayers and drifted into the sleep that would close the blinds on one kind of life forever and prepare me for another.

. . .

The Zurich Insurance Company had its office on Dawson Street. I recorded my first song in that office, but quickly shaved it off. Literally. That was my job, shaving yesterday's letters from the wax cylinders of the Dictaphone machines. I had to be there early in the morning, before everyone except the cleaning woman, to prepare the cylinders for the day's dictations. The machines had a kind of built-in lathe to shave off a thin layer of wax. If you took off too much, you got a talking-to for wastage; too little, and a ghost of yesterday's dictation remained. My other job was filing and fetching, finding, taking out, putting away. We had one whole filing cabinet just for film director John Huston. It was mostly for his claims. He lived in Galway in those days, acting out his role as master of hounds for the Galway Blazers. I hope he rode better than he drove, because the accident files grew at an alarming rate. He got a laugh out of that when I got to tell it to him to his face years later when he was making the movie *Casino Royale* in the late sixties and we were both guests at Una Guinness's lodge in the Wicklow Mountains.

The Zurich was one of the more liberal companies at the time. I was the second Catholic to be employed there, apart from the secretaries, who were no threat to Protestant supremacy. They were just females. The other Catholic fellow was only one small step up the ladder from me. His father must also have been an important agent. The Zurich was just around the corner from the Freemason Hall on Molesworth Street. In 1953, Dublin and Belfast were very much Unionist-Mason–controlled. But they weren't alone in the Ireland of the time. Waterford, too, was a loyalist town. King Eddie's visit there in 1904 was still very much remembered in the 1950s. The grip was slipping, however; the ferment had started. In Ireland, as in America, the wasp was losing its sting. In the basement on Dawson Street, I found, among the out-of-date files, a tricolor flag which was brought out for Easter and St. Patrick's Day celebrations, a token to the new order. Business is business.

Coming up to Dublin changed everything for me, but I did drag along some streamers of my other life with me. I had been well brainwashed by the Christian Brothers and still carried my Apologetics. I went to seven o'clock mass every morning at Gardiner Street Church on the north side of the Liffey, which was just as well since I had to be in the office on the south side of the river by 9 A.M. Every day I would walk to mass and then on to Dawson Street. It was in those contemplative times, during the Latin mantra of the ritual of mass, that I would find again the center of the young boy's spiritual connection with the cosmic delight of being.

The buses confused me, the fares, the accents. One thing I admired, though, was the way fellows could get off running before the bus stopped. That held the same kind of wonder for me as I feel now watching surfers duck through a wave tunnel in TV ads. I tried it at the stop in Dawson Street one day, but I stepped off straight out instead of facing forward into a little run. One leg caught the other and I went sprawling on the sidewalk, to the knickers-wetting amusement of the cleaning woman watching my embarrassment from the office window.

The other baggage I brought with me from Carrick was the compulsion to nod hello to everyone, I mean literally everyone I passed on the street. In Carrick it would be unthinkable to pass someone without the sideways nod of the head. Can you imagine trying to do that to every passerby on Grafton Street? If you did that now, you could get more than you bargained for.

I did make the mistake one day of nodding to the big fella beside me at the urinal in Stephen's Green. He was watching me and smiling as we were taking a leak. I thought he was just being friendly. He followed me all round the park, sometimes passing me, then waiting for me with a smile. I thought he was out to murder me. He had the hell scared out of me as I tried to lose him in the crowds on Grafton Street. Finally I made for the College of Art, where I had parked my new bike, chain-locked to the railing. On my way in through the gates I looked around and there he was, coming after me. It was like a bad film. I couldn't find the key for my bicycle lock. He was getting closer. I found the key but couldn't get it into the lock. The sweat was pouring off me. He stopped. His shadow was over me.

He said "Hello" in a soft voice, a killer's voice, just as I unlocked the damn chain. I jumped on the bike and blindly bolted down the steps past him, onto Kildare Street, oblivious to the cars and bicycles whizzing by.

That evening I met Mossy Dwyer, my neighbor from Carrick, and told him the whole story of the fellow trying to kill me. He laughed his head off for half an hour.

"Haven't you ever met a queer before? Jesus, you are green! He wasn't trying to kill you. He was in love with you!"

My pay was one pound, seventeen shillings, and sixpence a week. It was one pound a week for a room. That left seventeen and sixpence to live on. Every night I went to a play or the cinema. That to me was more important than food. It was a shilling to climb up to the "gods" at the Olympia, the Gaiety, and the Abbey (which was moved to the Queens because of fire). I think the Gate and the Theatre Royal were a bit more expensive, but I know that I was lucky if I had ten shillings a week left for food.

Woolworth's cafeteria was the only place where I could afford to eat. Meat was restricted to one day a week, and my main diet was a double order of mashed potatoes and brown paper soup. It was called oxtail soup on the menu but it looked and tasted like boiled brown wrapping paper, and one day I put in my soupspoon and up came a big lump of brown paper. That was my daily diet, that and a glass of milk.

The glass of milk, when I could afford it, gave great relief from the constant pain in my stomach for half an hour or so. I didn't know I had an ulcer at the time. It wasn't until I went to St. Vincent's in New York City years later that I discovered I'd had stomach ulcers since I was a teenager. At home in Carrick I'd lived on bicarbonate of soda. In Dublin I couldn't afford this luxury. Often at night I'd walk back to Drumcondra (that was before I got the bike), up O'Connell Street past Caffolla's and all the cafés and ice cream shops with happy couples sitting at tables laughing and eating, and I'd think that if only I had sixpence for a glass of milk, the pain would stop, even for a little while. But there was nothing for it but to tough it out, to lie in bed with the acid churning and eating the lining of my stomach until sleep came.

The plays were magical. There were always queues then and you never knew until you had the ticket in your fist if you were really going to get in. The lord mayor of Dublin at the time, Alfie Byrne, used to work the queues, walking down the full length of every queue at every theater. He was a dapper little man with a waxed mustache, doffing his hat and smiling benignly for the crowds. They loved it.

And then the excitement when you got the ticket and the cattle charge up the cement flights of stairs, way up to the top balcony that was at a stomach-churning rake of forty-five degrees, to get to the best seat in front, by the grille that kept you from falling into the abyss of the expensive seats below. It really was up there with the gods: you could reach up from the upper seats of the top balcony and touch the frescoes of the Greek deities on the domed ceiling.

When the orchestra would start tuning it was magic time. The lights dimmed and the curtains opened and you got the first glimpse of the stage set. I loved the sets of Michael O'Herlihy at the Abbey. I was disgusted when he went off to Hollywood and became a director of *Hawaii Five-0,* of all things! And of course, the notorious pair, Michael MacLiammor and Hilton Edwards, were at the Gate Theatre. They did wonderful productions onstage, no doubt, but their offstage histrionics made them a Dublin institution. They were the precursors of street theater. With their unabashed homosexuality and flamboyant street makeup, they were loved and jeered in equal part wherever they strutted. The best-known jeer was the one about the two delivery boys shouting to each other on O'Connell Street: "Hey, where was MacLiammor last night?" "He was up to the hilt in Edwards!"

I first saw Shaw's *Saint Joan* at the Gate with Siobhan McKenna enunciating her way through the leading role with Jackie McGowran playing the Dauphin. Then there was Anew MacMaster at the Gaiety, all the O'Casey plays at the Abbey, and, at the Olympia, Alec Guinness and Emlyn Williams and old Wilfred Hyde-White.

At the Astor cinema then you could see all the classic foreign films as well as the best from Britain and America, *Odd Man Out* and *Shane.*

I joined the Brendan Smith acting school and went through the basics two nights a week of elocution, projection, enunciation, and breath control. It was boring but necessary. The other nights I went to plays or films or increasingly to the National Library to vacuum up everything I could find on set design, acting, plays, mythology, poetry, and folklore. One evening I had to be shushed four or five times as I read Eugene O'Neill's play *The Emperor Jones.* There's a drumbeat, like a heartbeat, that starts slowly at the end of the first act and gradually builds up throughout the play, including the intermissions, to an unbearably infectious throb, right up to the climax when the silver bullet hits the heart of the emperor Jones. Time after time I would forget I was in the silent reading room of a library and compulsively start beating out the rhythm on the table.

None of these pursuits were going down well with Edgar M. Deale, who questioned me regularly on my progress in learning the insurance business. My progress in policies and proposal forms and claims was nonexistent. Reginald Renwick, I had remembered seeing the "R.R." of his dictated letters in my father's office, was the one assigned to teach me the details, but try as I may, I couldn't develop an interest, and try as "R.R." may, he couldn't instill it in me. Although at first he seemed very different, very "Protestant" to me, aloof and businesslike, as I got to know him I found he had a humorous, almost childlike streak. We got on very well.

Mr. Deale somehow got to know all about my artistic pursuits and one day called me into the inner office. "Mr. Clancy"—I had to get used to being called "Mister"—"Mr. Clancy, I understand you're enrolled in acting classes, also that you have signed up for art lessons with Mr. Sean Keating at the College of Art. You are also interested, I believe, in music. These are all very admirable pursuits and I wholeheartedly applaud them. I myself have a great interest in music and am quite active with a choral group." (I later discovered that E. M. Deale was a very influential and talented man in Dublin music circles.) "But I would be doing a great disservice to your father if I didn't do my utmost to carry out his wish of giving his son the best possible grounding in this business. Maybe you're too young and inexperienced to realize the number of young people who are interested in the arts in one form or another but how few actually ever make a living at it. My advice to you is to learn the family business that would provide you with a good reliable income and enjoy art and music and theater as the wonderful pastimes that they are."

He went on and on, but my young rebellious mind was not responding. I had a fire in my belly, and the last thing I wanted to hear was practical, sensible advice.

I'm afraid I shocked the whole office—the girls turned white—by slamming the door on the inner sanctum and almost breaking the glass.

I was reassigned to the basement, to a new job, tearing up decaying files, anything over three years old. I draped the Irish flag, the one kept for patriotic show, around me to keep the filth off my clothes, while I sang at the top of my voice:

Wrap the green flag round me, boys—to die were far more sweet
With Erin's noble emblem, boys, to be my winding sheet.

Life at the Zurich became impossible, and by mutual agreement I was out. Just before I left, though, the old wax-cylinder Dictaphones were replaced. The new machines had a disposable loop of red plastic on which to record dictation. The recording quality was great, real hi-fi. A whole new world had revealed itself to me.

Being on the dole in Dublin in the 1950s was depressing and lonely, especially on Sundays, but I filled my days with as many new adventures as I could. Once again my mother had come up trumps and persuaded my father to send me the money to buy the bicycle, the one I thought had saved my life the day the "murderer" stalked me. It seemed like everyone in Dublin rode a bicycle to work at that time. The bicycle traffic made Dublin look like Beijing. It was so dense at rush hour that I remember losing my balance once on O'Connell Street as the traffic light changed and not being able to fall off for lack of space. I got a Raleigh racing bike and it sweetened my life immeasurably. I could now get to films playing in the suburbs, I could speed around the Phoenix Park, and at weekends head for the Dublin mountains and even down to Glendalough. I had freedom, not least of all from the buses and bus fares, which left more money for acting lessons.

I moved from the rented room on St. Patrick's Road to digs on Fitzroy Avenue, where I had the company of other lonely souls and the little fat landlady who made regular meals: meager and greasy, but regular. The ulcers got worse, however, and I was in constant pain.

I now spent all my days at the National Library, and my reading into Irish mythology in particular got deeper and deeper. At nights it was the Brendan Smith Academy or the College of Art. My teacher, Sean

Keating, was a wonderful man. I had admired him as a painter for a long time, particularly his big canvases of the Aran Islanders, and as a teacher he was inspiring. I had no great talent as an artist but he was a man of endless patience, even with a trier like me.

Meantime, good news spread at the acting class. The Cyril Cusack/Siobhan McKenna production of *The Playboy of the Western World* was coming back to Dublin after a brilliant run in Paris. Word was that Jack Arnson, a director from San Francisco, was looking for extras for the Gaiety Theatre production. I was picked as one of the extras. Initially I even had a line, but try as I may I could not get that damn line out. They gave me a whole day to try and get it but to no avail. Of course I know it now and, even if all the other lines in the play should desert me, I will never forget that one. "A flat and three thorned black-thorn that would lick the scholars out of Dublin town!" Cyril Cusack himself even took time out to try and help me say it. No good. That's when he changed my name from Willie to Liam. The line went to Harry Thullier, a friend from acting school who later went on to bigger things.

That production of *The Playboy* was one of the most exciting things happening for me at the time. I had lost my one line but I got to carry Cyril Cusack onto the stage after the race scene every night. The smell of Leichner's 5 and 9 greasepaint became an intoxication to me. Number 5 and number 9 were the color sticks that combined to make skin tones. The feel of the costumes, the camaraderie of the dressing room, the sound of a full house through the fire curtain, like rain on Prendergast's hay shed, the call of "Beginners [Places], please": all these things became part of the long-running buzz.

For the entire run of the play I never left the side of the stage during any performance. I inhaled every nuance of it. I knew every line, every pause, even the precious line that had been mine. Before the curtain went up I'd study the set, the construction of it, the way it was painted. I made up charts of how the play was lit and how the mood changes were accomplished by simple lighting. By the end of the run my plans were well in place as to how I would re-create the whole thing in Carrick, with myself, of course, in the lead and my sister Peg as Pegeen Mike. My teacher Liam Hogan and I would create a drama society in the town that would put the Abbey to shame.

What I couldn't know at the time was that the same Gaiety Theatre would become like a second home for many years in the 1970s and 1980s to a singing duo called Makem and Clancy, and that we would record some of our best material there.

The glimpse of the mountains or the bicycle trips to Sally Gap couldn't satisfy me any longer. I had to get home, home to the lush hedgerows of Tipperary. I had to see Slievenamon and the Comeraghs. One Saturday I was rambling through the Phoenix Park. It was a glorious July evening and I just kept going, out past Kilmainham and on to the Naas Road. My feet took me. I had a half crown in my pocket but I was headed for home and nothing would stop me. I got a lift right away from a traveling salesman who was going through Naas where the road divides.

"I'm branching off here for Portlaoise," he told me. "Do you want to chance your luck on the Waterford Road?" I thought I'd stick with my friend. He was a nice talkative fellow and I mightn't get another like him. So he dropped me in Portlaoise. The sun was still above the horizon, with a long twilight to follow, so I wasn't too concerned. A farmer picked me up and took me about ten miles in his Morris Minor, which leaked fumes and never got over twenty mph. He dropped me in the middle of nowhere.

The roadside hedges were abuzz with summer and the light was still good. I started walking, mile after mile but not a car, not a cart. The world seemed to be empty except for the birds singing their last chorus before settling in for the night. As the twilight came on, I saw in the distance before me an old tramp emerge from a ditch. He started walking in the same direction I was going but I kept my distance. From what I could make out he was a scruffy looking character. I thought of my half crown and the possibility of the old lad having a knife. All kinds of thoughts like that come to you at twilight on a lonely road.

Eventually I saw lights of a village as darkness fell. Sitting on a wall outside the village, I contemplated what to do. There was no traffic. The chance of getting a lift after dark was remote. Of course, I'd stayed in hay barns before and that looked like the only possibility.

Just then the headlights of a van came around the bend and I put out a thumb. It was a bread van that stopped and when I got in I realized how hungry I was and thirsty.

"I'm going to Kilkenny. Any good to you?" He was a young, smiling chap.

"Great," I said. "I'm trying to get to Carrick-on-Suir. Kilkenny's on the way."

He laughed. "You won't get to Carrick tonight, lad. There's not a sinner on the road. How far have you hitched?"

"I left Dublin about six o'clock. But here I am still far from home. Begor, there's a lovely smell from this van. I used to deliver bread in Carrick."

"Did you? With who?"

"Did you ever hear of Kenny and Kiely?"

"In Carrickbeg. Oh begod I did, Paddy Kenny and Lory Kiely, sure I knew Lory well. A big fan of St. Mollerans. I used to meet him at the hurling matches. And sure we're in the same business. Listen, you're starving with the hunger, I bet. There's a few curreny buns back there."

"Do you know anyplace in Kilkenny I could spend the night? I only have half a crown."

He laughed again. "Begod, for that money the only place you'll get in is the louse house."

"I've heard of it," I said. "There's a song about it 'The Kilkenny Louse House.' "

"Ha! I heard it many a time. But that's an old song. The place is not that bad now. Besides, the only other place you'll get for half a crown is a hay barn. And you'll be covered in ticks in the morning."

To my grief, I opted for the louse house.

The tough old battle-axe who ran the house was delighted to get a customer at that late hour on a Saturday night. She took my half crown before she let me in the door, and she made me a cup of tea while she laid down the ground rules. "Breakfast is included. It's at half nine on the dot. Everyone who stays in my house goes to mass of a Sunday, I don't care how drunk he is on Saturday night. Now I'll show you to your bed."

We went up a flight of rickety stairs into a big room. I counted eight beds in the room, all empty. The floor was covered with sheets of newspaper. As usual there was a fifteen-watt lightbulb in the middle of the ceiling. The light switch was at the door.

"The house is full tonight, so you'll have to share the bed with John Joe. He's a big man, so keep well in *be* the wall. This is his bed here. He don't like sharing it, but if you keep quiet he'll be too drunk to notice. If you're lucky," she added ominously.

If I had my half crown back then, I would have gladly fled to the nearest hay shed. But the worst was yet to come.

"Where is everyone now?" I asked. She looked at me like I was soft in the head.

"Where do you think?" she said. "In the pub spending their week's wages getting drunk. Now, I want you in bed and the lights out before they come in." She went out.

Somewhat reluctantly, I took off my pants and hung them on the brass knob at the end of the bed. I felt very vulnerable without them. I didn't even own a pair of underpants in those days, just slept in my shirt.

I switched out the light at the door and made a run across the newspapers for where I gauged the bed to be. Scrunching as close to the wall as I could, I lay there dreading the return of my roommates.

No sooner was the light out than the action started. They must have been in hiding just waiting for lights-out: fleas, millions of them. As the old traditional song went:

> Oh, I jumped into bed and I put out the light
> And in less than five minutes I had to show fight.
> In less than five more sure the story was worse
> For the flays came around me and brought me a curse.
> Laddly fol the diddle eye raddly fol the diddle ero.

> Well I stood up in bed and demanded fair play
> Sayin' if I had a stick I would fight me own way.
> Then the bloody old major gave me such a pick
> That I nearly was losin' the use of me . . . hip!
> Laddly fol the diddle eye raddly fol the diddle ero.

Normally these nippers in their feeding frenzy would have had twelve or sixteen bodies, all oozing alcohol, to choose from. Now the whole army attacked the one, succulent, alcohol-free body in the room, mine. All I could hear was the *ping-ping* of the big, fat fellas as they leaped joyously from every corner of the room, every nook and cranny, from every other bed, to where the warm feast lay waiting for them. When they struck, I was like a man afflicted with St. Vitus' Dance, doing contortions around the bed, trying to get to the spots they were nipping at.

What a night! I almost welcomed the raucous sounds of drunken men stumbling up the stairs and falling into the room. Here at least were some other bodies for the fleas to gnaw on.

Unfortunately, when they turned on the light, John Joe was not so drunk that he didn't spot the body in the bed.

"What the fuck!" he roared. "I'll fuckin' kill that greedy whore. She's after sellin' half me bed again." Obviously this was a common occurrence.

"Push in there, boy!" he roared as he stripped. "And keep your hand on your ha'penny!" he guffawed. Guffaws all round, except from me.

He wasn't a man at all; he was a monster, a great tub of guts and muscle, a hunk of earthmoving equipment, full now of fuel and farts. The stench off him would knock a horse. Fortunately his head no sooner hit the pillow than he was asleep. Then the snores started. From around the room came a cacophony of snores and farts, grunts and groans, and the timpani of the *ping! ping! ping!* all over the newspapers to complete the orchestra. I knew then how the poor servant girl felt who uttered the lines

> Oh the haaat of him and the weeeight of him
> And the smell of stale porter,
> I thought the dawn would never come.

One thing I'll say for the landlady: she put on a great feed of rashers, eggs, sausages, and black puddings in the morning before shushing us out to eleven o'clock mass at the cathedral. My roommates of the night, including my bedfellow, the big one, that is, were as timid as a bunch of schoolgirls headed for first communion. My other roommates of the small jumping kind were probably resting up after their night of gluttony.

Getting a lift home in daylight was no trouble, and I arrived at my own door on William Street in time for Sunday dinner. My mother, when she finally got over the surprise of seeing me, looked me up and down curiously. "Oh, my God, Willie boy, what's wrong with you? Have you got the measles?"

Dublin had given me everything that I wanted or could use at that stage of my life, and now I had to move on, or rather back. I returned there only long enough to tie up loose ends and pack my bike and guitar—I'd picked up a guitar and a Burl Ives songbook for a pittance at a pawnshop—and take the train back to Carrick. All I could think of now was my own production of *The Playboy,* and I wasted no time. The night I arrived home I went to Liam Hogan's house and we plotted and planned into the small hours.

To keep the atmosphere sweet with my father at home, I set about organizing a filing system for the office. Even if I had learned nothing at the Zurich, I had absorbed enough to make some sense out of the chaos of my father's office.

His filing "system" consisted of the mahogany table piled high with layered mounds of policies, proposal forms, certificates, correspondence, and ledgers. They say that a good farmer can take the hay from a haystack with such ease because he remembers where he put each forkful. My father's filing system was based on the same principle. A client would come in, a farmer most likely, since farmers made up the bulk of the business, and my father would say, "Come in, my good man," desperately searching for a name, a clue, an association, the name of a townland, a localized accent, anything to bring this man into focus without letting him know he couldn't remember his name. That was bad business. Maybe the Norman *r* would trigger something: Mothel. Yes. Mansfield! That's it.

"Now, Paddy, is it about the bull?" he'd ask casually, as if there was never a moment when he didn't know this man and all belonging to him.

"No, it's about the house and contents, Mr. Clancy."

"The house and contents, oh yes." In went the hand to the jumble of papers on the table and out would come the policy for Paddy Mansfield's house and contents.

Thinking back on it now, my father's decline started when I came back from Dublin at the age of nineteen with the know-how he had sent me there to acquire. The cross-filing system I set up by name, type, and policy number made him confused and to some extent redundant, and I was too young to grasp the sadness of it. He had understood the chaos. He would never understand a system. But he was delighted to see me apply myself in the office.

In spite of my hatred of the insurance business, there was many a laugh in that office. Once there was a knock at the door. When I opened it, there was no one there. I was about to close it when I looked down and saw a little bald man in a three-piece suit carrying a briefcase. He was a perfect miniature of an insurance man, standing there smiling up at me. "Hello. I'm Mr. Joynt." That was exactly the way we pronounced "giant" in Carrick, and the laugh nearly tumbled out of me and down on his little bald head.

I still laugh to myself when I recall the Monday morning when Mrs. Comerford (not really her name), a great, blustery farmer's wife, arrived in the office with a basket of two dozen eggs.

"A little present for you, Mr. Clancy," she announced with a big smile.

"Come in. Come in, Mrs. Comerford. What can I do for you?"

"Well, I'd like to insure the hay barn, Mr. Clancy, against fire."

"I see. Well, sit down there like a good woman and we'll fill out a proposal form."

Of course he'd have smelled a rat, or maybe a whiff of smoke, by this time, but he couldn't let her know that, so he'd go through the motions.

"Now, full name . . . property of . . . husband's name . . . address . . . value of barn . . . value of hay . . . et cetera. All completed down to the date and signature.

"And today's date is . . ." (pretending not to remember).

"Ah, Mr. Clancy, does the date really matter? Couldn't we put Friday's date on it?"

The hay barn, of course, would have burned down on Sunday night.

Under pressure again to further my career in insurance (and to make money to finance the production of *The Playboy*), I went to work at the Hibernian Insurance Company in Waterford. My boss this time was none other than—Mr. Joynt. He turned out to be a patient and gentle little man. On my Raleigh racing bike I'd cycle the sixteen miles to Waterford every morning and home in the evening, over an hour's hard slog each way. There was no such thing as deodorant at the time, and I'm sure that when I arrived at the office in the morning (always a little late), I must have smelled like a rancid fox. But I never heard a complaint.

Nights and weekends we worked on the play. First we had to get the hall for rehearsal and performance. Big Father Harty arranged that for us. He had the run of the Forester's Hall for his musical society, and he was a great promoter of panto(mime)s and operettas and anything else where he could keep an eye on the young people and protect them from "the Dangerous Occasions of Sin."

So the hall came free. Then there was the cast, which was a task. Very few people in Carrick had any acting experience. Some who had been in the musicals would fit the parts, but it was really a matter of typecasting nonactors and getting a performance out of them.

Needless to say, I cast myself in the leading role of Christy Mahon. My sister Peg was made for the part of Pegeen Mike. In a lovely piece of role reversal Liam Hogan became the father, Old Mahon, whom I got to beat up and lord it over. (It's great to have your old teacher taking directions from you.) I unashamedly cast family and neighbors in most of the parts. In the sniveling, effeminate part of Shawneen Keogh, I cast Pat Power, who was highly insulted when I told him he was perfect for the part. Later he realized I was right but didn't come out of the closet until the 1970s. He was so good in the part that he went on to a professional career in acting. The biggest problem with the rest of the cast was that they would be full of enthusiasm at first until they discovered that getting it right was hard work. We went through three changes of cast before finding people who weren't there just for the laugh.

To get materials for the set, I had to call on the blind faith of the hardware shops and assure them that the play would be a huge success, with piles of money to pay them back at the end of the run. My neighborly suppliers, O'Keeffe's and Johnny Hearnes, came through for me. My friend the carpenter, Pa Casey, built the set. Pa was a meticulous builder and everything he made was built to last. We ended up with the only stage set I've ever seen before or since where nothing shook when you slammed a door—a door, by the way, that always opened and closed properly. The only problem was getting the damn thing broken down when the run of the play was over. The set was more permanent than the hall it was built in.

Rehearsals dragged on for months with numerous cast changes. People asked if this play that all the talk was about was ever going to happen. Finally I had a committed cast who knew their lines! All that remained now was the performance. One night would be fine; on the next, the giggles would set in and the whole thing would fall apart. I got more frantic as the opening night, which was finally set, approached. The set was painted and looked great. All the props were in place. My brother-in-law Christy Butler was an electrician as well as a projectionist at the cinema, so he had a built-in grasp of theatrical lighting. He had set up a dimmer system for the mood changes and the sunlight effect shining through the window. The half door looked realer than real. But something was missing.

A few nights before the opening, it came to me as I lay in bed pondering the problem. Conviction and timing. That's what separates the amateur from the pro. Conviction and timing. The following night at rehearsal I put a stop to giggles and embarrassments. I read the riot act to the cast. I became a little demented. At one point I found myself standing on a barrel whipping a length of rope over their heads. I made them use the pauses. Silences can be more powerful than speech. I even frightened myself but I knew what I wanted and they knew they must give it. Overnight they turned into a serious working group of actors.

There is a point at the end of the play when the Playboy gives his speech: "Ten thousand blessings upon all that's here, for you've turned me a likely gaffer in the end of all, the way I'll go romancing through a romping lifetime from this hour to the dawning of the judgment day."

He makes his final exit. The stage should freeze and the moment sink in before a word is spoken. I felt out the timing in my head over and over again. It always came out the same. Seven seconds. It had to be seven seconds. No more, no less. But I couldn't get the actors to feel that. Frank Driscoll, playing Michael James, the boss of the house, felt the audience would think he forgot his lines and start laughing if he didn't come in on cue. Christy Butler, playing Philly Cullen, one of the customers in the pub, was to stand like a statue, backed against the wall of the pub for the rest of the action until the curtain closed.

"God, Willie, I feel like an awful feckin' eejit standing there all that time doing nothing."

Finally I made Frank do a slow count of seven in his head, a thousand one, a thousand two, until, at the count of seven, he said his line: "By the will of God, we'll have peace now for our drinks. Will you draw the porter, Pegeen?" I told Christy Butler I'd break his arm if he moved.

We had a packed house on opening night. Packed at the Forester's Hall meant perhaps three hundred people. Father Harty had assumed the role of patron and was guest of honor.

The play was a sensation. From the moment the curtain opened, the audience sat in willing suspension of disbelief. Of course, they recognized everyone onstage but suspended that recognition and only saw and heard the characters. We didn't let them down. Peg as Pegeen Mike was riveting and her conviction was contagious. The whole cast became immersed in the play. Even the love scene between Peg and me, not the easiest thing between brother and sister, became totally believable in makeup and costume.

At the end Michael James held the pause, all seven seconds. Philly Cullen never moved a muscle, and when Pegeen Mike gave that last outburst at poor Shawneen Keogh—"Quit my sight! (hitting him a box on the ear) Oh my grief, I've lost him surely. I've lost the only Playboy of the Western World"—what a gasp went up from the audience!

We were so elated backstage that we didn't even hear Father Harty's tirade to the audience against "Pagan Plays and Pagan Playwrights and the Shame of having a Schoolteacher and a boy from a Respectable Family put on Such Filth in Our Town!" It was only the next day we got mad at that, especially when we remembered that the last production

Father Harty had produced was *The Belle of New York,* about a woman of dubious morals from the Bowery. However, no one was going to take that night from us. Over the tea Christy Butler came to me, his eyes full of excitement: "Did you hear it? Did you hear the silence?" Frank Driscoll said, "How did you know 'twas exactly seven seconds? 'Twas magic! Magic!"

The real magic for me was that I'd found a path that could lead me out of the world of Willie Clancy's head into any of the great broad places where the inner, the nameless inner me, wanted to pitch my tent. Behind makeup and stage lighting I could be anything I wanted.

Back in William Street afterward, Aunt Alice presided over the postmortem. "Oh-ah! That strap! Pegeen! 'Tis a good kick she should get for lettin' him off like that! And wasn't that Widow Quin the right trickster?" She then proceeded to tell us the whole plot, with Peg and me listening, as if none of us had seen it except herself.

And of course we hadn't, we hadn't, not with her eyes.

But it was my father's reaction which most surprised and delighted me. He was aglow with pride. He seemed almost eager for me to pursue the career that he had scoffed at a short time before.

When I left for America not long afterward, under circumstances I couldn't possibly have foreseen, all the bills for the production were paid and there was twenty pounds' credit in the bank, a profit not to be sniffed at in those days. Peg and Liam Hogan started on a new production almost immediately. They even ended up buying their own theater, the Brewery Lane Theatre, still going strong forty-some years later. Father Harty apologized profusely to Liam Hogan and myself and said, "I don't know what came over me. I loved every minute of the play." He slipped a ten-pound note into my hand to help me on my way in my American adventure.

9

It is difficult to imagine now how
innocent a twenty-year-old boy could be
in a small town in Ireland in the fifties,
but I had one foot in the twentieth century, the other in the Middle Ages.

All that changed on an evening in
August 1955 when I answered a knock at
our door on William Street. There stood
two American women: one narrow-waisted,
big-bosomed, sallow, and soft-spoken, the
other huge, gaudy, and loud. They were
glaringly American against the drab, gray
backdrop of an Irish town of the time. They
looked to me like two exotic birds that had
been blown off course in some storm and
had come to earth in the wrong place.

The slimmer of the two said in a soft, refined American accent, "Hi, my name is Diane Hamilton and this is my friend Catherine Wright. We're in Ireland collecting folk music. This is the Clancys', isn't it? We were told to come see Mammy Clancy by her sons Paddy and Tom in New York. They said she had some wonderful children's songs."

At the mention of Paddy and Tom my mother emerged from the room, straightening out her cardigan and putting on her great beamy smile reserved for visitors.

"Come in, come in. Ye're welcome."

"Are you sure we're not intruding?"

"Intruding? On what? Sure we were only listening to the old wireless. Come in. Willie boy, put on the kettle. Ye'll have a cup of tea."

It turned into a "night," of course. Bobby and I lugged in the recording equipment. Diane brought in an instrument which she called a mountain dulcimer. She sang and played for us, strumming on the three-stringed dulcimer with a quill. She sang silly little songs, she called them play-party songs: "Go tell Aunt Rhody," "Swing and Turn Jubilee," "There Was a Pig Went out to Dig." She told us about Paddy and Tom in New York and the midnight concerts in the theater in Greenwich Village and all about someone she seemed to look up to as her mentor named Jean Ritchie. She told us about her collecting trip to Nova Scotia with her "friend" Mick Hill. She sang us songs she'd learned in Nova Scotia, "Great Big Sea" and "Lukie's Boat." She gushed on about people and things we had never heard of; the English and Scottish Country Dance Society, Cecil Sharp. She did a little morris dance for us. She wore flat dancing shoes and a folksy plaid dress, and she was so animated and extroverted it was embarrassing to people like us who had to be coaxed for half an hour to give a verse of a song.

"Ah, do go on!"

"No, I couldn't."

"Ah, go on, we'll help you."

The house filled up and the recording gear was put together. The room was a jumble of cables and stands and headphones, boxes of Ampex tape, and all kinds of paraphernalia. Finally it was all set up and my mother started remembering old songs. As she was singing, I looked over at Diane. She had headphones on. The tape reels were going round.

There was a hint of a sad smile just touching the corners of her mouth. But her eyes, her eyes were distant, haunted. Then she did something I'd never seen an adult do before, she put her thumb in her mouth and started to suck it. It was a startling thing to see an adult do that. In time it was a gesture I would get so accustomed to that I would hardly notice, but it made me uneasy that first time. In my youth and innocence I couldn't know what a very, very disturbed and complicated person I was seeing here. My mother sang, Diane listened. In the next couple of years these two intensely driven women would tear me apart.

When the last reel of tape wound down in the small hours, Diane asked my brother Bobby and me if we would like to join them next morning on their trip to Kerry to track down the renowned fiddle player Padraig O'Keefe. "I usually go to half-eleven mass," I told her, "but if I'm up for the ten o'clock, I'll go along." I did get up. And that decision literally changed the course of my life.

At eleven o'clock the next morning we set out for Kerry on the trail of the legendary Padraig O'Keefe. Bobby and I sat in the back of the rented Austin A40, Diane drove, and the weighty Catherine made a fair dent in the front passenger seat. There's an expression in Ireland, "shorten the road." Catherine shortened the road to Kerry for us with her sardonic New York wit and commentary. She didn't exactly say that her trip to Ireland was a disaster, but the litany of complaints implied that the Ireland of the fifties left much to be desired by way of creature comforts. We laughed and sang all the way to Kerry, with Diane's incessant questioning sometimes driving us to distraction. "Have you got a version of this one? It's a play-party song from Kentucky." I didn't know what the hell a play-party song was. Or, "Is there a local version of 'Barbara Allen'?" Soon the mountains of Kerry, a sight I'd never seen before, loomed near.

Finding Padraig O'Keefe was not the easy task one might think. We were told he was a schoolmaster and could be found at his school near Scarthaglen. When we did find the school, it was boarded up. A neighbor wasn't much help. All she could say was, "Ah sure, poor Padraig, poor Padraig" (sigh).

"Oh dear, he's not dead, is he?" Diane asked.

"No, no. Worse!" she said. "He took to the fiddle." Taking to the fiddle and taking to the drink were considered fates worse than death, and Padraig had taken to both.

In time we found him in a pub in the nearby town of Castleisland. He was not well. He certainly was not fit to cope with the overbearing "Yanks." However, he was clever enough to realize that there could be a "cure" in this and maybe more. Stories abound about Padraig and the drink. He once got a weakness and collapsed in his local pub in Scarthaglen. In spite of the fact that he was heavily in debt to the "slate," he was given a large whiskey to revive him. A second one was even put up in front of him when he was strong enough to sit up on a bar stool. Contemplating the amber magic in the glass in front of him, he noticed that a comrade-in-drink was eyeing his whiskey with a greedy glint. Padraig rounded on him. "Would you ever go off," he said, "and have your own weakness!"

There was a small problem when it came to recording him. His fiddle was in "hock" behind the bar at his local in Scart. If we wanted to record him, we'd have to secure its freedom by paying off the ransom. Many adventures later, we set up the recording equipment in the pub.

He was not at his best, but a couple of whiskeys later he looked up slyly and said, "She's purring now." A couple more and he announced, "High purring." The fiddle was always referred to as "she." "The best wife a man ever had," he used to announce. "All you have to do is stroke her belly and she's purring for you." For me, though, the treasure that emerged from the session was the photograph of Padraig with the glass of Guinness in one hand and the fiddle and bow in the other. Look carefully at the bow. See? The strings are held away from the wood by the cork of a porter bottle. Many serious musicians pay thousands of dollars for the right bow to suit them. Vanity!

I saw sights and heard music on that recording trip that I never knew existed on this island. It was to set the cornerstone, for me, of a life of involvement and fascination with the world of traditional music and song.

We traveled through Kerry and Limerick and Clare, up through Galway, Mayo, and Sligo. In Sligo I got to visit the grave of W. B. Yeats. I got to climb Benbulben, the mountain in whose shadow Yeats is buried, and Knocknarea, where Queen Maeve lies under her cairn of stones.

The wind has bundled up the clouds high over Knocknarea
And thrown the thunder on the stones for all that Maeve can say.

Diane sought every opportunity to get me alone. I didn't understand her attentiveness.

One glowing evening in Ballisodare, where she and Catherine stayed at the hotel while Bobby and I had been dispatched across the road to a cheap B&B, she asked me to climb Knocknarea with her. It was there on the uplands, the yellow furze glistening in the setting sun, that I first started getting the long, lingering looks and the teasing, probing jibes from her. "Have you got a girlfriend, then?" I was very shy about those things and my shyness seemed to set her on. She began to call me "Willie" more often. I had never heard of the modern term "come-on." There was the "come-hither look," but I didn't recognize Diane's approach as being the same thing. But that's what it was, and it set off alarm signals in me.

I was just twenty. I'd hardly ever kissed a girl. I was a small-town boy, Catholic, parochial, puritanical, now being given the "come-on" by a Jewish, middle-aged (to me), twice-divorced woman from some exotic world, so foreign to me that she might as well have been from Mars (or is it Venus?). Besides, in our travels up to now, she had continually talked of someone named Mick Hill and their recent collecting trip together in Nova Scotia. He was a psychiatry student at Yale University in New Haven, Connecticut, not far from Deep River, which she also spoke of frequently. Mick was living in her house there right now, she said, the implication being that they were lovers. This came as a shock to my prudish sensibilities and made her flirtations even more confusing.

And yet I was drawn to her, not physically, but to the great broadening vista her conversations were opening up to me. She was so chameleon in her intuition that, when she sensed a change, such as an apprehension in my mood, she could immediately shift the subject and focus to set me at ease.

Catherine, of course, never joined us in any of the forays that involved physical exertion and sweat such as hill climbing. One day she unceremoniously presented Bobby and me with a jar of Mum deodorant. "I'm not traveling another mile in this car with you two until you rub some of this under your 'oxters,' as you put it so quaintly in this country. Gawd, you smell like mountain sheep!"

Speaking of armpits, there was a hotel in Armagh town, just inside the border of the British-dominated Six Counties, where we encamped during the recording sessions at the Makem house in Keady. It was a primitive and dangerous establishment, with narrow, winding timber stairs. I encountered Catherine one morning on a particularly narrow bend where two normal-size people would find it difficult to pass. She was dressed outlandishly in an ankle-length dressing gown of multicolored stripes, yards and yards of it, and carried in her hand a chamber pot covered with newspaper. Completely unabashed, she commanded me to "Make way, young man!"

"Catherine, where are you off to?" I asked.

"Well, I'm not going cycling," she retorted as she crushed by me with her aromatic cargo.

The recording sessions at Makem's house were memorable. Peter, the man of the house, with his pipe and fiddle: "Oh, aye. Oh, begob aye," was all he ever seemed to say; and Jack, his son: "Don't give that man another drop or he won't be able to play at all." Ann Jane Kelly, the neighbor, with a perpetual fag bigger than herself, shouting, "Make the tay, make the tay." Tommy, the youngest son, in the corner nearly as shy as myself (hard to imagine now). And the girls hustling and bustling, making pots of tea and cutting cake with nonstop (and to me, a southerner, completely unintelligible) chatter and they all buzzing around the queen bee herself, Sarah Makem, as she sat placid in the eye of the hurricane.

It was so much like the Clancy household it was uncanny, in our case Mammy Clancy being the queen bee. All that was different were the accents.

Sarah Makem had a vast store of songs which the Clancy Brothers and Tommy Makem would later plunder. Sean O'Boyle, too, the great musical scholar and folklorist, was a regular at the sessions. From him I got the beautiful Gaelic song "Buachaill on Eirne." It was later "Englishized" by a journalist from a Glasgow newspaper and became quite famous as an Irish "folk song" renamed "Come by the Hills."

A mighty day and night, too, were spent with the great Paddy Tunney and his mother in Letterkenny, County Donegal. What a trip that was, with half the town of Keady in the entourage, driving in convoy from Keady to Letterkenny, singing all the way. The singing continued in the hotel lounge in Letterkenny where we set up our recording equipment for the day.

After a session of blinding poetry and song that went on into the early hours, there was an air of growing unease among the Keady contingent at the thought of driving back on the dark winter roads of the North at such an hour. The "B specials" were active and dangerous at the time. They were the Protestant militia, armed civilians really, who patrolled the roads of Northern Ireland. They had shot and killed a young man near Keady the previous year. The province at that time was very much like South Africa under apartheid, the Catholics being the blacks. However, we need not have worried. Coming out of the hotel in Letterkenny, someone had stepped in "doggy doo," as Catherine so delicately put it, and although we were stopped several times by the B specials, they quickly backed off when they got the whiff emanating from the lead car.

The young Tommy Makem and I struck up an instant friendship. Our interests were so similar: girls, theater, and singing, in that order. He was heading for America soon, he told me, to try his luck at acting. We agreed to keep in touch. One night we went to a dance in Newry. The band knew Tommy and invited him up on the stage to sing a song. The hall was mobbed and I thought, "My God, this crowd will never listen." He got onstage and asked for a chair. Putting his right foot up on his left knee, he started making the motions of mending his shoe. He began, "Oh me name is Dick Darby, I'm a cobbler." Those in front started shushing those behind, and before he'd finished the first verse, there was total silence. I was impressed.

Sarah Makem's song "The Month of January" haunted me all the way to Edinburgh. Diane was complaining of a dubious back problem and asked if I would come to Scotland with Catherine and herself to help lug the recording equipment. I was on for adventure and agreed. There were to be adventures, though, that I hadn't bargained for.

In Edinburgh we booked into Mrs. Muir's guesthouse. Catherine declared, "Well, this is where I'm staying put while you young folks traipse off to the Hebrides or wherever." I had a feeling that Diane had suggested as much to her.

That evening as Diane and I strolled around the old part of Edinburgh, an evening of slanting sun, I remember, glinting off the windows of the blackened granite tenements, she stopped and looked at me for a long moment with a soft girlish look and her impish smile.

"I telephoned Mick today and told him he'd have to leave the house in Deep River." She did a little skip along the pavement in her flat folk dance shoes.

"I told him I was in love with someone else." She giggled.

Back at Mrs. Muir's, as we were parting to go to our rooms, she suddenly said, "Willie, would you kiss me?"

I was so taken aback that I kissed her before I knew it. Just like that, and then she was gone to her room.

In the dark, Scottish-smelling room I lay awake for a long time trying to untangle the jumbled fishing line of my emotions.

The following morning, at the School of Scottish Studies, we met Hamish Henderson, who was to take us on the odyssey to the Outer Hebrides. We were going to record "waulking" songs, work songs sung by the island women when they're processing homespun cloth; "port o' beal," or mouth music; and most important of all, the great Gaelic singer Flora McNeill. I was told that Hamish Henderson was a poet and an academic. What I was to discover was that he was a *Scottish* poet/academic. In other words, mad as a hatter.

"Flora McNeill, she's a queen, Diane!" he kept saying over and over as he pranced around the classroom singing snatches of Gaelic songs and taking the odd swig from a bottle.

"She's a queen, Diane . . . *Bioc an deoc so 'r labh mo ruin . . . deoc slainte le fer an doon.*" He'd sing a few lines and then get so overcome with enthusiasm he'd break into another. "*Mhic earla na mbratach bana—he-o hin-o huo-o eile.*" One at a time wasn't enough for him; little snippets of song kept bubbling out of him uncontrollably.

We drove up along the tiny lochside road on the western shore of Loch Lomond, headed for the port of Oban in the Highlands where we were to catch the overnight steamer to Castlebay on the Isle of Barra.

Diane drove, I was in the passenger seat, and Hamish was in the back-seat, not quite alone, having a bottle of something that kept the songs and stories going all the way. Diane was laughing nervously as she tried to maneuver the precarious track along the waterside, while Hamish grew ever more raucous, jumping around the backseat and having him-self a great time. Every once in a while he'd lean over the front seat for emphasis, overwhelming us with whiskey fumes.

Somewhere along the way he discovered my collarbone, which he began to tap on with growing fascination. I had never been exposed to anything like that before, so I just sat there not knowing what to do as my skin crawled. But if it made me uneasy, it made Diane see red. Since the kiss at Mrs. Muir's guesthouse, she seemed to think she had propri-etary rights over me. The last place in the world she saw competition from was a respected Scottish poet, male.

"Hamish, if you don't sit back, I'm putting you out of the car!" A minute later, "Hamish, if you keep bothering Willie, I'll drop you on the roadside! I swear it!" He'd sit back and laugh, shouting, "Flora Mc-Neill, she's a queen, a queen. Wait till you see her on the pier of Castle-bay!" Five minutes later he'd be back at my collarbone.

By the time we arrived in Oban I knew I was somewhere between the devil and the deep blue sea. But the real crux came when we were boarding the steamer. Diane had booked three separate cabins, but the wee clerk said cheerfully, "Only two cabins left. Some two of you are go-ing to have to share." Peering over the top of his specs with a wicked twinkle in his eye, he added, "I'm sure you can work it out among yoursel's."

I weighed it up from the perspective of my Catholic upbringing. Here was a mad, drunken poet who wanted my collarbone and here was an older woman, American, twice divorced, obviously no morals, who seemed to want the rest of me! But there was no choice, really. My Catholic conscience told me that the corridor to Diane's cabin was the way straight to hell!

Hamish was gleeful. There were two bunks in the cabin we were to share, one upper, one lower.

"Och, Willie, we'll put the two mattresses on the floor so no one falls out of the top bunk."

"We will not!" I said with such shock and horror that he immediately laughed and graciously gave me my choice of bunks. I opted for the lower, in case a quick escape was called for. It was hard to know whether to take him seriously or not. Was he having a great laugh at the lovesick Yank and the young greenhorn Paddy? I'm sure he was, but I wasn't taking any chances. Not that there was anything to worry about, the whiskey had done its job. He was snoring in no time.

In the morning we were in Tobermory harbor. I was up on deck watching the salvage boats searching for the wreck of the Spanish galleon that had sunk there during the Armada. When Hamish came on deck, he was a changed man, a serious and subdued academic. He told me the history of the Spanish Armada and the integration of some of the survivors into the island culture. It was much the same as happened in Galway.

There was a long, rough sea between the Inner and Outer Hebrides. Diane and Hamish were markedly absent for a lot of the voyage, but I stayed up on deck, exhilarated, no hint of seasickness.

Rounding the headland and coming into Castlebay harbor is a most extraordinary sight. The peak of Ben o' Chioch towers over the village and the harbor of massive, cut boulders, but it is Kishmol's castle that dominates the eye. It rises straight up out of the water as if it's just the tip of a great underwater fortress. Only the song about it in the Gaelic can convey the vision of its emergence from the sea. In translation it says:

High upon the Ben o' Chioch on the day of days
Seaward I gaze
Watching Kishmol's galley sailing.
Ochee Ochoo, Fallu-o.

Homeward now she bravely battles, 'gainst the hurtling waves
No moor, no rope,
Anchor, cable or tackle has she
Ochee Ochoo, Fallu-o.

Here is red wine and feast for heroes
And harping too

Ochee Ochoo
Here's red wine and feast for heroes
Ochee Ochoo, Fallu-o.

As the steamer pulled into the pier, there was a small cluster of people either waiting for someone arriving or waiting to board. Among them a woman stood out, a striking presence. This had to be Flora McNeill. Hamish became very animated. "Flora!" he shouted. She waved a greeting. Diane said, "Isn't this wonderful, she's here to meet us. He must have got word to her."

But Flora McNeill was not there to meet us. She was there to take the steamer to Glasgow to get married.

We stood on the pier with our luggage and equipment and watched the boat depart, not to return for five days.

A taxi took us to a guesthouse, neat and clean and modern with electric lightbulbs in the rooms. And switches, but that was it. The landlady apologized: "Och, the electric light was supposed to be in last month but now they tell us it will be another six months before we're connected up. Never you mind, we're used to the candle and the oil lamp and we're no fussed about it. We've waited a few centuries," she laughed, "I'm sure we can survive another six months without it. Besides, a lot of folks are against it. They're afeard of burnin' the house down."

So here we were on Barra, our singer gone, our recording equipment useless, our poet conversing loudly with the islanders in an unintelligible language at the pub. And the only way off the island, the steamer, gone for five days.

"Not to worry, Diane, there are wonderful singers on the island. Port o' beal—the waulking songs, wonderful."

"What about electricity, Hamish?"

"Aha! I have solved that little problem, Diane. It appears there are film shows in the hall on Friday nights and they use the generator belonging to the doctor. That's how Alan Lomax got his recordings. Now I'll need a fiver for a taxi to make arrangements with the doctor and get the singers. They're on the other side of the island."

That was the last we saw of Hamish that day. For the next few days he would show up at the guesthouse before noon, none knew where he slept, and with elaborate excuses and promises, collect the also ever-inflating expense money, and take off into the unknown.

Diane was not perturbed. She was in love. And I was not perturbed because the full impact of my entrapment by this woman would not hit me till much later.

I loved Barra. I soon heard the sounds of Irish Gaelic within the strangeness of the island Gaelic. I felt the common bond of Celtic blood: the love of language, of music, of a good laugh and a hearty cry, and the heart worn on the sleeve like a badge. The weather was with us. The days were languorous. Sometimes we climbed the ben, sometimes we ran on the deserted beaches, cavorting like puppies. Sometimes we visited.

In a cottage on the winding road up the side of the hill, living alone, was Annie Johnson, who had been recorded by Alan Lomax and Robin Roberts a couple of years before. She reminded me so much of my mother. The welcome and the tea, the tea, always the tea, and the fussing.

She had an old windup gramophone with a big trumpet horn on it and a box of needles that looked like rusty barbed-wire spikes. Shyly but proudly she brought out the purple test-play disc that Lomax had sent her of her own singing. As she put it on the turntable and wound the machine up, I wanted to tell her that this was a modern microgroove record to be played using only a modern stylus, but what was the point? She had already plonked the great chisel needle in the groove. It played, barely, but it was fascinating to watch the purple strand of vinyl that curled away from the needle and onto the floor, carrying on it her last recorded performance.

The night the steamer that would take us back to the mainland returned, the film was on in the village hall. The film, I will never forget, was *Please Don't Eat the Daisies* with Doris Day. Hamish had finally come through and brought three women from the far end of the island to the doctor's house, where we had set up the equipment and been connected up to the generator by the local electrician.

The three women were straight out of *Macbeth*. They had, possibly, two and a half teeth among them, not one word of English, and a brand of Gaelic that even the Castlebay folk had trouble with. Hamish, however, conversed with them freely as he placed them around the microphone in the sitting room. So as not to have the whir of the tape recorder be picked up on the microphone, it, and I, were set up in the surgery.

When the three witches were ready, I switched on the machine to get a level. I put the headphones on. I listened for a few moments in disbelief, then called Diane from the sitting room.

"Listen to this."

She looked at me quizzically and put the headphones on. Her eyes widened. She shouted, as people wearing headphones tend to do, "My God, it's Doris Day!"

We checked out the sound in the sitting room. There was no extraneous sound to be heard in the hall, but on the headphones, there she was, Doris! We could also hear the wail and thud of the waulking songs, mind you, but try as we may, we could not get rid of Doris. Here were three hags from another century reenacting a timeless island tradition, waulking, the process of thickening the homespun cloth by dipping it in a bath of communal urine, placing the saturated cloth on a huge table surrounded by women, who pounded the, whatever, out of the cloth in front of them, then passing it on round and round the table time after time for maybe days, to the rhythmic chant of the ancient song form. And there, right with them on the tape, to this day, somewhere in Diane's recording archives: "Don't, don't, don't eat the daisies":

> *Hiri hurann-o*
> *Hiri hurann-o*
> Don't, don't, don't eat the daisies.

Between the Barra time and December, Diane and I did some hectic traveling. Catherine had been dispatched from Edinburgh home to New York. Back in Ireland I suddenly acquired a 16mm Bolex movie camera which we used to film the dances and traditions of the Dungeer Mummers in Wexford. We traveled to Wales and back with the troupe for the Mummers Festival in Fishguard. A week later we took the boat to Fishguard again and on by train to London to see Josh White, my favorite singer, at the Festival Hall. We went to Cecil Sharp House (a shrine for Diane), the Tower of London, St. Paul's Cathedral, all the tourist things, then back to Ireland, recording singers and fiddlers and accordion players. Driving, driving all the time, and talking. Oh my God, the talking! And the questioning.

Diane had been years in psychoanalysis, and people in psychoanalysis have a mind capacity akin to a finely tuned athlete's muscles. Questioning, doubting, analyzing, teasing out, chewing on, quantum-leaping, U-turning, mood-changing, more doubting, more questioning. The unfortunate simple person on the receiving end of this mental marathon is left panting, exhausted, and brain-dead, like trying to keep up on a child's tricycle with a Tour de France cyclist on a souped-up Raleigh.

Not that our forays didn't have their moments of humor. Diane had an endless capacity for putting her foot in it. Once, having filled up the rental car with petrol [gas], we were only a few miles down the road when Diane had to pee. We pulled into the next petrol station (in Ireland they are *not* called gas stations), and in a desperate rush Diane jumped out of the car and asked the bemused and blushing young attendant, "I'm-all-full-up-with-gas-can-I-use-your-ladies'-room?"

Another night in Wexford, when we were filming late, we got back to the hotel and tumbled exhausted into our separate rooms. Separate but next door. Before I could get to sleep I heard, way down the corridor, the sound of drunken footsteps. I heard a squeaky door handle turn. Then the steps came to the next door. Door handle again. Whoever was up and about was trying each door along the corridor and coming our direction. I switched on the light to make sure my door was bolted. It was. I barely breathed as the sounds came closer. The steps stopped outside my door, I was in number 16, and, like something from a suspense film, I watched with horror as the handle slowly turned and I heard the push against the locked door. The handle went back slowly. Then the footsteps went on to number 17, Diane's room. In the two seconds that I was thinking "Oh God! I bet she didn't lock her room" (she never did), I heard the door handle creak and the door open. I heard the brief silence, then the scream.

What a dilemma! I was dressed only in a short shirt: Fruit of the

Loom still hadn't arrived in Ireland. I had to tackle whatever monster was in there without revealing my nakedness. I put a hand in through the slightly open door of Diane's room, not knowing what might grab it, and found a light switch. There on the bed was Diane screaming and flailing with a very large half-naked man on top of her. He turned wild eyes at me and growled, "Get out!" Standing in the darkness of the hallway, holding my shirt over my privates as best I could, I shouted, "You come out! I'll fight you out here!" He gave me a glazed look, then looked at Diane in feigned confusion and in a posh English accent said, "I'm terribly sorry. I thought I was in my wife's room." He lifted himself shakily off Diane and made his way out into the corridor.

"I'm terribly sorry, old boy. I went for a piddle and these damned hotels, they put the lights out to save electricity and I couldn't find my room. This is *so* embarrassing. I was quite sure the lady was my wife."

He put his arm around my shoulder in a fatherly fashion and I, being so relieved that I didn't have to fight him, put my arm around his shoulder.

"Tell you what, old boy," he said as I steered him away from Diane's room, "why don't you and I go down to the night porter and have ourselves a little drinky-poo just to show there's no hard feelings? What?"

I assured him there were no hard feelings and declined. But what a sight we must have been going arm in arm down the corridor like old pals, he in his briefs (they had them in England) and me with my white bottom peeping out from under my skimpy shirttail.

10

"She's a grand girl and all that— whoever she is, but I'm glad she's gone back. My God, she'd wear you out," my mother said. She was right. Diane left for America in early December a bit weepy but without any great scene. I felt utterly drained but, now that the whirlwind was over, I couldn't help wondering, who *was* this wealthy woman really? But then, in those days, we thought *all* Americans were wealthy. So, satisfied with that answer, for now at least, I fell into an exhausted sleep.

My mother was quite frail and constantly ailing at that time. What woman wouldn't be after bearing eleven children, losing two of them, and going through the hardships she went through? But she was still the queen bee and my sisters were constantly coming and going to the William Street hive.

Her main problem was her back, and the "heat," as she called it. Sometimes all that would help the back pain was a sensation worse than the one she had.

"Willie boy, would you get the nettles? Take these gloves so you won't burn yourself." And I'd have to go down to the park at the bottom of New Street and pull a bunch of nettles to sting her back. It was awful. Her back would break out in big blisters, but somehow it gave her ease.

Her energy was gone, too, and often she'd say to me at night, "I don't have the strength to go up to bed, boy. Would you give me a push up the stairs?" She'd pull herself up the first two steps, then I'd get my head under her bottom and, like an elephant pushing a small log, hoist her up the flight of stairs. Some mornings when she'd get up, the "heat" would be very bad.

"It's a terrible sensation, boy. When I first wake up I'm fine, then the heat starts, first in my tongue, then bit by bit it spreads all over my body."

In one of her letters she wrote: "We are all well, thank God, only that I have the heat, the back, and the rash back again after paying 6 pounds for the treatment I got from Manchester. Such ointments, bottles of stuff, I have it on my scalp now and I'm really going bald. Otherwise I'm strong and able to do everything in the house, so the story could be worse."

Then she'd offer it all up "for the poor souls in Purgatory."

We'd moved the couch (she called it "the lounge") into the kitchen for her so she wouldn't have to get up when an insurance client came into the "room" cum office. There she'd sit after she got the fire going, she had a great knack with lighting the fire, and out would come the snuffbox. She was addicted to snuff. She'd take a pinch between her thumb and finger and put it to her nose as if to snuff it up. But no. She'd hold that pose for the longest time, almost like a time of contemplation, and then, *snuff, snuff,* a big pinch into each nostril. I used to do pencil drawings of her in that pose over and over. She had great patience. The snuff never made her sneeze. I suppose the membranes were long since tanned and numbed. Her sense of smell I know was gone for a long time, which was a pity since she had a passion for flowers.

In spite of all her physical frailty she managed to get everything done that needed doing and always with a sense of humor: "keeping the best side out like the Piltown girls," she'd say. That December she got the plum pudding made and bagged and hung on the nail earlier than usual. Oh, what a smell that had! I'd often stand on a chair and put my nose against the pudding-stained cloth, inhaling that quintessential aroma of the festive season. That was the year, fortunately after she got the Christmas cakes made and had most of the preparations done, that I accidentally cracked two of her ribs just giving her a hug. I didn't know my strength, or rather her frailty. I hugged her and tried to lift her onto the counter at Lory Kiely's bakery shop when I heard the crack. I felt so guilty. She was bandaged up and confined to bed over most of Christmas. But even from her bed she ran everything cheerfully, with the girls doing their best, coming and going, dividing their time between their own families and the queen's hive.

Rehearsals for the panto *Snow White* were in full swing. Since the success of *The Playboy,* Christy Butler and Father Harty seemed to think that I could do anything related to the stage, so I got the job of painting the scenery and making the posters. I threw myself into the work with the enthusiasm of being back on familiar ground. Christy and his coproducer, Jerry Moran, went regularly to London to see shows and get ideas. The latest idea was black lighting. They devised a real, working waterfall onstage that would glow when the lights went out. My job was to design Snow White's cottage and the surrounding woods and paint them with fluorescent paints that would also glow under the ultraviolet light. Great fun. To get the trees just right I cycled out to Millvale where some very ancient, gnarled beeches grew, and these became my models. The poster depicted a Disney Dopey, easy to draw and paint over and over on slabs of cardboard.

By now Angela, who was always involved with the pantos, and I were hitting it off and going out on dates together. I loved the way, when she kissed me, she kept her head down so I had to put my hand under her chin to raise her mouth to mine. She had changed, in time, from not needing or heeding me to being in love with me. But it was too late. Even though I was still in love with her, the time was not now right to make commitments since I was all fired up with dreams of going to America to follow my destiny. It had never even occurred to me to question the inner voice that told me I must leave my hometown, go off into the big world, and make something unusual of my life. I had no idea how this was going to happen, but then, what do little things like reality mean to a dreamer?

The choir was in Christmas rehearsals, and the usual traditions were being observed of piecing together Felice's nativity scene for the church and making forays into the country in search of red berry holly. Bobby was running the insurance business, supposedly (he hated it even more than I did). My father was still totally confused by the new filing system I had introduced.

In the midst of all this, the first American phone call came. It came late at night, actually about 4 A.M. The nearest phone was at the chemist shop at the bottom of William Street, Paddy Meade's. I woke up from a deep sleep to a banging on the front door. I opened the window and looked down on the street to see a bleary and not too happy Paddy Meade in a dressing gown. "There's an urgent phone call for you from America. Some woman. She says it's an emergency. She's holding on, so come as quick as you can."

I threw on some clothes and ran down to the chemist shop not knowing what to expect. Was Paddy or Tom killed, or what? It was Diane, of course, in a state of distress.

"Willie, it's Diane. I had to call you. I'm very upset. I feel I can't go on. I have to know if you love me or not. If you don't love me, I don't think I can go on living. Our time together has changed my whole life. I've told Mick. Do you love me? Can you learn to love me?" On and on she went, teetering on hysteria. I was evasive. I tried to tell her I was on someone else's phone at four in the morning, freezing cold. She burst into hysterical tears and said, "Well, if that means more to you than my life . . ." *Slam!* The phone went dead.

Two nights later, another call. Paddy Meade was now quite angry, understandably.

"I can't keep doing this, you know," he told me. This time her threat was to fly back to Ireland, come to Carrick, and commit suicide in front of my house.

At that point I was getting truly frightened. How do you explain these phone calls to your father and mother? I asked Paddy Meade not to take any more calls in the night, that the person calling was a bit crazy and there were no emergencies. He got onto the switchboard operator in the post office and from then on the operator made the excuses, phone off the hook, line broken down, or whatever, and the frantic calls each night didn't get beyond Paddy Joe at the post office.

Just after Christmas, Diane arrived in Carrick unannounced, bearing gifts for everyone and full of the joys of spring. Not a hint of the dark side. It was as if the phone calls had never happened. "I'm looking for a cottage here," she announced happily. "And I'm going to the Aran Islands on a collecting trip at New Year's. Would you and Bobby like to come?"

Oh, she was cunning. She knew my passion for the writings of J. M. Synge and particularly his chronicle of the Aran Islands. She knew I wanted to make his *Riders to the Sea* and Liam O'Flaherty's *The Cow's Death* into short films. She also knew that by asking Bobby along it would take the harm, as they say, out of it. I had no defenses against a woman of such wiles.

On the first of January we took the steamer the *Dun Aengus*, Diane, Bobby, and I, from the quay in Galway to Inisheer, the smallest of the three Aran Islands. It turned out to be quite an adventure, in spite of the circumstances, or rather because of them.

Life on Inisheer had changed little, if at all, since Synge had described it in his essay "The Aran Islands" or since Robert Flaherty had made his film *Man of Aran*. It was a harsh life of survival with little or no time for frivolities like music. I don't recall us recording a single musician or singer during our weeklong stay there. Just getting ashore was a major feat.

There was no pier on the island at that time. The *Dun Aengus* had to lay off about a mile or so on the leeward side while the currachs, or canvas canoes, came out to off-load people and supplies. The necessities were loaded into the first currachs, foodstuffs and, more important, barrels of Guinness. Only when they were safely on their way were the passengers, like an afterthought, allowed to board the other currachs. We had to take off our shoes and sit exactly where we were told. Seated in the currach, with the craft undulating under you with every rise and fall, you began to realize the frailty of the thing. A mere skin of tarred canvas covering a skeleton of laths was keeping you from the icy black depths of the winter Atlantic. All that was needed was the high heel of a shoe to slip between the laths and through the canvas, and you were literally sunk.

The sea was seething that day and a mist of spray nearly hid the land from us. The islands are the first barrier that the great combers meet as they are driven eastward by the winter gales, uninterrupted, across three thousand miles of ocean. These mighty rollers grow to forty or more feet high and, at a half mile or so apart, attack, in timeless and unrelenting regiments, the cliffs of Aran. They seem to hurl themselves with malicious fury at these audacious obstructions, the spray-laden gales stripping every grain of soil or vegetation off the western side of the island, then eating, like living things, into the very rock itself. Only on the leeward side was it possible to get ashore in the currachs.

Even in the relative shelter of the lee side we were soaked to the skin before we got to the edge of the breakers. We had four mighty rowers, with faces that looked as if they'd been carved out of the rocks of Aran, handling our boat. I had the Bolex camera and was intent on getting another *Man of Aran* on film, but there was no way I could keep the lenses dry, so I abandoned myself completely to the adventure of getting ashore. The rowers pulled, silently, on the long, shapeless oars until we got to the outer surf. There they stopped rowing and watched the oncoming seas. The thunder of big surf was deafening. It seemed impossible that any craft could get through that turmoil and live. Looking around, we could see, dimly through the spray, shadowy figures wading waist-deep in the foam by the shore. Our rowers watched silently. Then, without any signal that I could detect, they heaved as one man and had us riding high on the landward wall of a cascading wave. We shot forward at incredible speed. What a roller-coaster, hair-raising, exhilarating, laughing, shouting ride! In, in we went with the speed of a runaway train at a crazy plunging angle, the figures in the surf rushing nearer, their arms outstretched, poised to make the last run with us up onto the beach. Suddenly hands were on the sides of the currach, running with us, lifting, heaving, pulling, and with a grunt and a shout there we were, high and dry on the sand and sea wrack, safe from the following, lesser waves, at least momentarily. I tried to use the camera and was curtly abused in Irish and hastily hauled out of the currach. I was a danger to the serious work at hand. There was no time for posing or pleasantries here. This, I discovered, was the pervasive mind-set of the people of Inisheer.

Later in the pub/guesthouse I studied the men who huddled over pints of the newly arrived black stuff. Everything about them, except the stout, spoke of self-reliance. All their clothes were homemade. Their caps, like their sweaters, were hand-knit from woolen thread straight from the spinning wheel. Their jackets and trousers were of homespun *bainin* or frieze cloth. At their waist, a multicolored woven belt, or *criss*, and on their feet, rawhide moccasins called *pampooties*. This footwear had to be kept perpetually moist, otherwise it became shriveled up and unwearable.

The weather cleared that night, and Diane asked me to go for a walk with her down the boreen to the beach. Bobby was having a pint with the men at the bar. Whatever romantic notions Diane may have had setting out on our stroll were quickly dispelled. First on our left we heard a rock being knocked over. Then the shuffle and scurry of pampootie-clad feet on our right. On our left again the silhouettes of running figures through the latticework of the high stone walls against the moonlit sky. The stifled giggles erupted into laughter. We were being followed on both sides of the boreen by young bucks hoping to see the long-legged Yank get a rub of the relic and provide them with food for new fantasies for another year.

"May God forgive them their innocent mirth," as Seamus Ennis, the old folklordy-lordy himself, used to say.

Back in the pub, Bobby had struck up a conversation with the assistant lighthouse keeper, who invited us to visit the lighthouse on the western side of the island the following day.

From just outside the patchwork of little man-made fields surrounding the village there was no road or track; the going was on bare, pitted rock. It was a moonscape all the way to the cliffs to the west and the lighthouse. Not a grain of anything movable could last here. As we got closer to the cliffs, we had to lean on the wind as great gobs of spume, like shaving cream, were flung past us at hectic speed.

The sight from atop the lighthouse was awesome in the true sense of that word. The ranks of house-high combers could now be seen in all their majesty. Where they hit the cliffs a seething brew was created, with spectacular jets of spray shooting up through them like fountains. The yellow froth created in this cauldron built up and up to the clifftop until, free of the rock, the wind whipped it away and flung it clear across the island.

Nothing was ever dry, not our clothes, our hair, the towels Diane brought (and the toilet paper). Everything was wet all the time. I came down with a cold and fever, and after a week we could take it no more. The surf was calmer as we were rowed out again to the *Dun Aengus* in silence. We had experienced something primal and elemental that silenced us. It didn't matter that we took back with us not a foot of film, not a reel of usable tape, not even a rendition of "Don't Eat the Daisies."

The Connemara landscape, which had looked to me so forbidding when last I'd seen it, now seemed soft and benign compared with Aran. So did the people. We went west along the coast of Galway Bay, called Cois Farraige, to spend a night of recording with the Conlon family of Spiddle: Festy, Finian, and the matriarch, Mamo. Mrs. Conlon. Here in Spiddle and on to the west, the seam of folklore, language, and tradition was deep and rich and healthy. Festy's slow airs on the tin whistle brought tears and goose bumps. Festy himself cried freely at the beauty of the music he was playing. Finian sang in the *sean nos,* the ancient style, a song called "An Caisideach Ban," about a young priest on pilgrimage who fell in love with a girl and was tortured by the mountain of his guilt "bigger than Croagh Patrick itself."

During the inevitable tea break Mrs. Conlon took me aback by asking earnestly, "Are you afraid of the fairies?"

I said, "Well, I think I heard the banshee one time, but no, I don't really believe in the fairies, Mrs. Conlon."

Festy broke in. "What's all this 'Mrs. Conlon' business? Can't you call her 'Mamo' like the rest of us?"

His mother ignored him. "Aren't you very lucky?" she said, her eyes focused on some other world. "When I think of all the things I could have done in my life if I wasn't afraid of the fairies."

Before the night was over I felt like the Conlons were family. Even years later, after his mother had died, I'd meet Festy at a *fleadh* or a music session or on the street in Cork where he worked for a while and he'd fill up with tears and give me a bear hug. Then, with his forehead against mine, he'd say, *"O sha Liam a mhacin, Mamo, Mamo."* He always thought of the night with his mother when he saw me.

I think now that Diane, with all her problems, had a very important talent: she was a catalyst. Never mind her singing or playing or collecting. That was just covering ground that others had traveled before, but she had an uncanny instinct for bringing people together whose combined energies and interests made a magical new element. She saw the potential in a situation, and she had the money to make it happen.

Meeting the Conlon family through her brought me to a love of the *sean nos* singing, to Joe Heany and Seamus Ennis, to Willie Clancy the piper, people who were to become friends and teachers. She brought the Clancys and Makems together, then started the record company, Tradition Records, which would be the launching pad for Paddy, Tom, Tommy Makem, and myself as The Clancy Brothers and Tommy Makem. She introduced us to Josh White, whose managers would guide us onto the world's stages.

Through Tradition Records, too, we would form longtime associations with people like David Hammond of Belfast, Ewan McColl and A. L. Lloyd, Richard "Uncle Dick" Chase, Odetta, John Jacob Niles, and Etta Baker. These contacts went on and out to include all kinds of people in the fields of folk music and the theater: Alan Lomax and

Robin Roberts and Jean Ritchie, John Henry Faulk, Frank O'Connor, Pete Seeger, and, just before he died, Woody Guthrie. Woody's disciples Ramblin' Jack Elliot and Bob Dylan became friends, too, and the producer of Woody's film biography *Bound for Glory* and longtime associate Harold Leventhal became our partner in the publishing company Tiparm Music, and for fifteen years produced our biyearly concerts at Carnegie Hall. The list could go on and on.

But a most interesting connection she made at that time in January 1956 was the one with the Behan family in Dublin, which is where we headed after our Connemara and Aran experiences.

Dublin city seemed not miles removed from Inisheer and Spiddle, but centuries. That the two worlds could exist on the same small island seemed beyond imagining.

Brendan was the Behan that Diane had heard of from her sources and the one whose trail we were on. He was not well known at the time except as a Dublin "character." But he was elusive. We never did find him in our tour of the Dublin pubs that were known to be his haunts. However, we found his mother and father, Kathleen and Stephen, and brother Dominic. I can't remember where the house was, but it was a small little place with a cozy kitchen warmed by a coal-burning range.

Kathleen made us welcome when Diane explained who she was and that she was looking for songs, and Stephen stood up briefly from reading his paper by the stove to look us up and down. He reminded me of a little bantam cock. He kind of fluttered. He had a small Hitler-type mustache, and by way of greeting he pulled himself up to his full height of five foot nothing and stuck out his chest, checking us out from toe to top to see if we passed muster. Eventually he said loudly, "Hello!" in a tone that implied, "That's fuckin' tellin' yous!"

Kathleen ordered Dominic, "Go down to the pub and get some drinks."

"I have no fuckin' money. What am I supposed to buy drink with?"

"Don't use that language in front of your father!"

"I've got some money right here," Diane piped up, producing some notes whose value she obviously had no idea of.

"That'll do. That'll do," said Dominic, taking whatever was in her hand.

"I'll go and help you," said Bobby.

Needless to say, we never saw tail nor hide of either of them again that night.

Unlike the country people, Kathleen needed no coaxing to get her singing. The woman was unstoppable. She sang rebel song after rebel song interspersed with tirades on the British and treatises on the rights of the workingman. She found some whiskey someplace, and, peering at us through her thick glasses with her one fogged eye, she held us spell-bound for hours.

"Connolly was the greatest man to ever come out of Ireland. An Irishman through and through. Didn't he die for Ireland? Didn't he lay down his life for the ordinary workin' man?" Then she'd burst into song: "I'll tell you a tale of a row in the town / When the green flag went up and the red rag came down."

"And me brother, Peader, God rest him. He was a great Irishman. Peader Kearney, Kearney was me maiden name before I became a Fur-long, me first husband, and when he died I married himself," nodding toward the figure at the fire studying the racing page. "Sure it was me brother Peader who wrote the national anthem, 'Amhran na bhFiann,' the 'Soldier's Song,' wasn't it, Stephen? And 'The Foggy Dew': 'And Britannia's huns / with their long-range guns sailed in from the Foggy Dew,' he wrote that. Didn't he, Stephen?"

Stephen grunted, shifted his arse on the chair, and gave the newspaper a good shake. As far as he was concerned we were dismissed.

Later that night, sitting in a car outside the Central Hotel in Dublin with the rain whipping the streets and the car windows streaming with condensation, Diane finally told me at length all about herself, as if it was a secret she'd been withholding. She was thirty-two. She had a daughter, Carol, by her second marriage, to the singer John Langstaff, whom she'd met at the English and Scottish Country Dance Society. Their marriage didn't last long. She was too immature to be a good wife. She knew nothing of running a house. "One day John said he'd like lamb chops for dinner. So I went and bought two lamb chops, which I put in a pot of water and boiled up. I didn't know what else to do with them. He was mad at me and I was in tears. Shortly after Carol was born John and I were divorced. That's when I started seeing Mick. I was all mixed up and there was a kind of security in having a psychiatry student around. Mick treated me very well. Poor Mick, I hope he's not too upset at my throwing him out of the house in Deep River."

Names would pour out of her without any expansion on who these people might be, as if I knew them all intimately. Mick and John, Carol, Jean Ritchie, Freda Winton, Harry Jackson, Robin Roberts, Cecil Sharp, Frank Lloyd Wright, her father Harry. It was as if whatever was in her mind should automatically be in mine. Similarly if she had an interest in something, she assumed I was interested, too. If she was in love, I must be in love. When two people are in love, there's a marvelous magnetic energy flow between them. When only one is in love, that energy flow desperately seeks a response from the other and tries to suck the energy from them. I found it all exhausting.

Suddenly she got very silent and distant. After a time she said, "I've got something to tell you. Very few people know it and I'd prefer if you kept it a secret between us. My name is not really Hamilton. My real name is Guggenheim."

She looked at me for the expression of shock. I had never heard the name before. She might as well have said she was one of the O'Shaughnessys from the mountains of Kerry. She explained: "You see, the Guggenheims were, are, quite wealthy, and since I was determined to set out in the world on my own, they all thought it better if I changed my name. They were afraid I'd be taken advantage of."

She never qualified the ominous "they." "You see, my father, Harry Guggenheim, was a neighbor and close friend of Charles Lindbergh. He financed all his flying experiments, including his trip across the Atlantic. They still refer to Harry Guggenheim as the father of American aviation. He flies everywhere for free. But when the Lindbergh baby was kidnapped, have you heard about that? Do you know the story? It was awful. He was snatched from his bedroom. A kidnapper climbed up a ladder and took him. They never saw him again. But when he was kidnapped, my mother was sure they would try to kidnap me. I was protected day and night. I couldn't go anywhere alone or with my friends. It was like being a prisoner. My mother got more and more paranoid about it. It drove her kind of crazy. She was locked up for the last few years of her life. In the house, of course, at Falaise, our estate on Long Island. It would have been unheard-of to have her in an institution. She was kept upstairs in one of the wings. She used to call down to me in a singsong voice, 'Ooh Diane.'

"You may have heard of my cousin Peggy, lives in Venice? We don't talk much about her. Peggy collects writers, Hemingway and Beckett, people like that. I like Florence. Florence is a beautiful city. Would you like to come there sometime with me? I've got to go over soon with my friend Harry Jackson. He's a cowboy. You'd love Harry. He's a wonderful painter. Cowboy scenes. Stampedes and all that. Recently he started doing model sculptures in wax as sketches for his paintings. But now his sculptures are better than his paintings, so we are going to Italy to cast them in bronze. I must bring him to Carrick on the way. He sings, too. Cowboy songs. Real ones. He was a real working cowboy."

Her monologue was like the flight of a butterfly. We were parked outside the Central Hotel, with the rain still lashing the deserted streets, till after midnight. A lone figure went up Dame Street, a hawker pushing his cart, hunched over with a canvas sack covering his head and shoulders. I'd seen him that day on O'Connell Bridge.

I said to Diane, "He probably hasn't collected two shillings today. You'd wonder what kind of hovel he's going back to now to throw himself down in, soaked to the bone, nothing to eat and nothing to show for his day on the bridge. Imagine if we drove up to him now, put a twenty-pound note in his hand, and just drove off."

Diane looked at me, her eyes welling up with mischief. "Let's do it. Here, I've got one. We'll just pull up quickly beside him and you just hand it to him." She pulled out a big red twenty-pound note. I had never owned one and hardly ever seen one. We drove by and I stuffed it in the old man's wet hand and drove off. We laughed and talked for an hour of what a shock it must have been when he saw the miracle.

The joy of giving must have infected her because a few days later, back in Carrick, she announced to my parents, "With all the music we've collected and the film we made of the mummers, I've been talking to Paddy on the telephone about starting a record company in New York. I know that Willie's heart's desire is to study acting and film-making and I would really like to help out. He could come and work on editing the Irish tapes and do a film course at New York University. I'd like to pay for his passage to New York and for the NYU course, if that's all right with everyone. I've already made tentative arrangements for a berth on board the SS *Ivernia* sailing out of Cobh at the end of January."

I was fascinated and moved by her flashes of generosity. My parents looked a little stunned but there were no objections, and for me that was the main thing. And that's when it hit me, the excitement, that the realization of all my dreams was not only possible, but even imminent.

My mother used to tell of a woman in the town of Carrick who was given passage to San Francisco by relatives. From the very day she got her steamship ticket she never washed her face. When her neighbors would ask, "Agnes, wouldn't you wash your face, girl?"

"What?" she'd say indignantly. "Wash your face in Carrick? Carrick? Hah!"

I knew how she felt. I was impatient to be off now that the decision had been made. But I also began to look at my family and friends in a new light. Perhaps I'd never see them again. After all, the woman who wouldn't wash her face in Carrick arrived in San Francisco two days before the great earthquake of 1906. She was never heard of again. I made my visits around the town.

Uncle Tommy was commissioned to make a new suit for my trip. Poor Uncle Tommy, nothing ever seemed to work for him. He had been a good tailor, in the old style, sitting cross-legged on the big tailor's table, stitching by hand, often long into the night. But the craft had abandoned him. The suit would not come right. The shoulders, between the collar and the shoulder seam, buckled up no matter how he tried to recut and smooth them. My mother felt very bad for him and tried to make light of it, but he could not be comforted. He took to the drink. Then he took to his bed. The day before I left for America I went to the old room he slept in, top of the stairs, past the pig's head plinth, to say good-bye. The room smelled like death. He knew I came to forgive him for the suit.

"I'm sorry, boy, I'm sorry. I couldn't get it right."

I tried to pass it off. "Ah sure 'tis nothing. We'll have a laugh about it when I come home. I'm only going for six months. It's not like an American wake, you know."

"I won't be here when you get back, boy, I know that. I want to say good-bye to you now." I tried to shush him. He stopped me. "No, Willie boy, 'twas a botched job and I know it." I hugged him and left.

A few weeks later I got the letter in New York. I'd missed his funeral. I knew that the botched suit was the death of him.

11

Grayness and depression seeped from the rain-drenched, tear-drenched cobble-stones of the Cobh of Cork that January morning as I waited for the tender to take me out to the ship for America. What scenes of lamentation and distress this place had witnessed as countless thousands of emigrants were severed from beloved places, beloved families, over the generations stretching back to the famine and beyond. Even though my going had none of the finality of the American wake—I was only going for six months to learn about filmmaking, I kept telling myself—the anguish and loss I felt seemed as deep and desolate as could be borne by any soul.

The memory of the farewells of the evening before in Carrick kept playing back like a film loop over and over on my mind's inner screen. The lump in my throat ached. I fought, second by second, to hold back tears. Speech was difficult.

The farewells to the friends at the Musical Society were full of frivolities and hollow jokes and bits of silly advice. But it was all cover-up; underneath there was a genuine sadness. Christy Butler was particularly upset to see me go. Christy was a passionate family man. I think Angela was upset, too; at least I wanted to think so. She and I had become very close of late.

The farewells at home were particularly harrowing, with Aunt Alice and with Uncle Tommy on his deathbed. My sisters came to the house with hugs and tears. My father had been more withdrawn and distant lately and often talked of "handing in my gun." Perhaps the cancer had started already.

But it was my mother's heartbreak that was hardest to take. I would tell her over and over that it was only six months, but she'd say, "Oh, sure I know that, boy, but I know what America can do to people. It has some terrible hold. It robs ye of all yer faith and yer religion. I thought I'd shed all the tears I had to shed when you went off to Dublin. Losing the last, the baby, is the hardest thing of all for a mother. When you were in Dublin, I'd go upstairs to the garret to look for something or maybe clean up and I'd find something you left behind, that old pair of brown shoes or your old school jotters. It would all come over me again and I'd have to sit on the bed and have a good cry. Finally I had to gather up all your old clothes and the shoes and I put them in a bag and gave them to that nice tinker woman that comes around. And you know, she saw how upset I was, and told me about her own sons that went off to England, and the two of us sat down and had a good cry together like old friends. Every time she comes around now she asks me how you're getting on."

The steam was rising off us like cattle as we lined up in the rain to take our turn boarding the tenders coming and going to the SS *Ivernia* anchored out in the channel. I was wearing a long American overcoat, straight out of a Chicago gangster film, with huge winglike lapels that went from the padded shoulders straight down to the navel with no protection for the chest against the bitter January wind off Cork harbor. Everything I wore, except the botched suit of Uncle Tommy's, was a castoff belonging to one or another of my brothers. The overcoat was a trade with Bobby for the Raleigh racing bike. I had a white starched shirt that had belonged to Paddy and a very loud American tie that even Tom, with all his flamboyance, refused to wear. He called it his "appendicitis tie" because the big leaves growing out on either side of a stem down the middle looked like huge stitches holding together an incision.

Bobby had come down with me the night before to see me off. We'd stayed in a guesthouse. As we stood there now, feeling miserable, my arm throbbing from the vaccination, Bobby, always the joker, looked up and down at my castoffs, my brown cardboard suitcase, the battered guitar case, the big envelope with my chest x ray under my oxter, and said, "Jesus, that's a great overcoat. I think you swindled me on that deal. I'll never use that old bike and there you are goin' off with me lovely coat."

As the tender pulled away from the quayside, I saluted a farewell to him, but I couldn't help thinking from the look on his drawn face that he'd rather be the one setting off on a new adventure than facing back to Carrick, the house on William Street, and the insurance office.

On board the SS Ivernia, I was shown to cabin A30, which I was to share with three other lads. I was in the top bunk. I stowed my x ray, without which there was no hope of entry into the paradise known as the United States of America, and my suitcase, with its pathetic handful of belongings: a change of shirt, socks, clean handkerchiefs, shoe polish, toothbrush, and rosary beads. I also stashed my old Martin guitar in its flimsy case. The action on it was too high and it cut into my fingers, but I have been told by those in the know that if I had it now, it would fetch a fortune. Little did I know at the time that though it might not make me a fortune, that old Martin would befriend me on the road to a lifelong, adventure-filled career.

As the engines grumbled into life and the anchor was weighed, everyone came up on deck to get a last look at the holy ground of Ireland.

The friends and family we left at home become frozen as we last saw them, as in a snapshot. But it's the sense of place that haunts us most, the images of places we played in as children, quick flashes of places we loved, that stand out in high relief: sitting in a dark wood at evening looking out under the fringe of pine branches on the Suir valley in its winter light, holding an old blunderbuss and waiting for the pigeons to come in to roost, pretending you're there to shoot them; diving into the cold, crystalline water of the mill pond in Kilonerry early on a summer's morning; sitting around the fire in the woodman's hut high up on Carraigadoon late at night telling ghost stories, dreading the inevitable time when you'll have to pee on the fire and face the darkness of the woods all the way back to Driscoll's farmhouse in Ballinurra, and safety. All the accumulated memories of youth are already being swamped by the rush of new experiences. And mingled among the flashes of memory and waves of emotion is the excitement in the pit of your stomach, of starting out into the unknown, of swimming out into the middle of the lake where you'd dropped your stone in the beginning. Reaching down a toe, you find there's no bottom and you feel, not frightened, but liberated, liberated from the safety of firm ground, to float free out on the great adventure of Life.

Five young Irish lads were at our designated table in the dining room and one bald Englishwoman, very posh indeed. She must have had the same disease as Wiggy Dugan, the Christian Brother, because she had no eyebrows or lashes and you could see the shiny, hairless skin up under the bad wig. She was not a woman that one would be likely to forget in a hurry.

Some people say that seasickness is all in the mind. I was inclined to agree with that, since on my crossings to Wales and my rough trips to Aran and Barra, I had never felt squeamish while people all around me were chucking their guts up. So it was with a certain sense of superiority that I took my place at the dinner table that first night as the ship made its way toward the open sea. I smiled to myself as, one by one, the lads turned green and made their departure while her ladyship, as we came to call her, regaled us with tales of "Injia" and other exotic corners of the empire she had graced with her presence.

We got to the dessert about the same time as we reached the open ocean and encountered, from a different perspective, the mighty swells we had recently seen from atop the lighthouse on Inisheer. At this point her ladyship and I were the only ones still in the dining room apart from the waiters, who were careering wildly toward the galleys with laden trays, trying not to slip on the patches of vomit. As she droned on with her story, something about elephants, the first wave of nausea hit me. I went out on deck but that was awash with people holding on for dear life to anything stable as the ship heaved mightily. "I have to get to the cabin. I must get to the cabin," I kept telling myself. My control held as I made my way down the two flights of stairs, clinging to the handrail. When I got to the corridor, which stretched the full length of the ship, and saw the other end of it, way off in the distance, rising up at an unimaginable angle as the ship labored up the side of a mountainous wave, crushing me to the deck, I lost it. Lost it completely and utterly. Psychological my arse!

Those few days were the only time in my life that I truly longed to die, to be at rest. I prayed that the ship would sink, and over and over I would imagine the blessed moment when it would settle on the ocean bed and all motion would cease.

I lived from minute to minute. The roll and the plunge, the bottom-out and the labored climb, the awful levitating moment of going over the top with the attendant scream of the propellers churning air: knowing there was no escaping this relentless motion for seven days of twenty-four hours each, I longed for death. Give me death, please, God! Eventually, on the third day, my cabinmates, who had bounced right back, the bastards, got worried and sent the nurse. She gave me some pills, which I managed to keep down long enough for them to dry up my mouth, my eyes, and my nose like blotting paper and make my brain all woozy. But they did the trick.

That night at dinner her ladyship was holding forth, looking as if she had never left her seat, or her composure, since I'd bolted on that first night. Later the lads took me to a dance and introduced me to some of the female talent they'd befriended. Zap! An instant hormonal cure.

Each mealtime her ladyship would entertain us with tales of her world travels, but if we tried to pry a little under the surface on matters such as the identity of her husband, she would go back to picking at her food daintily and smiling enigmatically.

By the time we reached Halifax, Nova Scotia, we were bonded, the lads and myself and the bald woman. When we steamed into New York harbor under Lady Liberty, we were swapping addresses and swearing that we would always keep in touch. Even her ladyship seemed truly emotional at our parting but evaded the address exchanges with, "Oh, I'm sure we'll meet again. The world is much smaller than it seems, you know."

Shipboard bonding, like shipboard romance, is brief and intense, and the moment the feet touch solid ground, the squib burns out. In our heart of hearts we all knew that we would be swallowed up by the vast New World with no real hope of our paths crossing again. But I would be proved wrong.

My first impression of New York City as seen from the ship's deck when we berthed at Pier 18 was of dirt and dowdiness. Hollywood's New York it was not. The buildings that lined the West Side Highway were ugly and down-at-the-heel with painted advertisements peeling off the flaking brick facades.

Ellis Island had been closed, but the replacement system for admitting immigrants can't have been an improvement. We were treated like beasts coming off a cattle boat and were herded for hours through pens, smiled down on all the while by a somewhat shy-looking Dwight D. Eisenhower. Eventually, having got through most of the red tape, I came to the last hurdle, the medical officer. He examined my chest x ray for a long and uneasy time. Then he pointed to a spot on the negative and said, "You're a lucky boy. Did you know you'd had TB as a child? You were sure lucky you beat it. Go ahead, next!" I thought back to the time when I first joined the St. Nicholas choir and the looks I used to get for the barking cough I had that echoed through the whole church. So that was what it was.

Diane met me, and after she'd hustled me into a car she announced gleefully, "I have a surprise for you." That night she threw a party at her apartment on West Tenth Street near Fifth Avenue. It was a surprise, all right. Brothers Paddy and Tom were there, of course, but I had expected that. But there, too, were Oscar Brand, Cynthia Gooding, Logan English, Paul Clayton, Robin Roberts—all people I'd heard Diane talk about. Over by the window on a large couch, with an amazing blonde wrapped around him, was Josh White, the man that Diane had taken me all the way from Tipperary to London to hear in concert. This was her big surprise.

What a party it was! What a megajolt of culture shock! Not a word could I understand, the volume of the conversation was so loud and the mannerisms so foreign and, to me, phony. The deafening clink of ice in all those strange drinks being consumed by totally involved people arguing passionately in small groups everywhere: phrases jumped out over the din like "I know!" or "Oh my Gawd, she did?"

I felt like a lost child, but Tom took me over.

"Have a drink. Relax. What ye havin'?"

"I don't drink."

"Ya don't drink! Ya sick? Have a smoke." His American accent appalled me.

"I don't smoke, either." I laughed.

"Jesus! Are you sure you're my brother? Do you like girls?"

"Of course I like girls."

"Thanks be to Christ. I was beginning to think you were a fuckin' queer!"

He and Paddy asked me about home and all that, but in this setting I realized, with new clarity, what total strangers we really were, what few points of contact there were in our utterly different experiences. I had known them only as big men home on leave from the RAF full of loud stories and the braggadocio and condescension that seemed to be common to all the people I'd known coming back to the small hometown from the big, vastly superior world. I had always been the child in the corner. In a way, through our long career together as the Clancy

Brothers, that never really changed. Things like that never do in families. It's the pecking order.

Diane pulled me away to meet Josh White.

"Josh, I'd like you to meet a great admirer of yours. This is Liam Clancy." (I'd been coaching her to call me Liam.) "He traveled all the way from Ireland to London to see your concert at the Festival Hall."

Josh raised his left eyebrow in that way he had and flashed the smile that devastated women all across America and beyond. He got the woman off his lap and focused his full attention on me.

"You came all the way to London? Man! You must love the blues or else you must be crazy. Do you sing, do you play?"

"A little bit," I said. "I brought a guitar."

He thought briefly.

"Go get it," he said suddenly.

I got the Martin, thinking he'd never be able to play it. The action was too high.

He took the guitar as only Josh could take a guitar, something I would later discover. He took it softly, he took it slowly, he took it reverently. He looked at it the way he'd look at a beautiful, fragile woman.

"A Martin. Old. Beautiful, man."

He touched it voluptuously. In the flash of an eye he untuned and retuned each string perfectly. He looked at me and laughed an evil, gutsy laugh. Then he looked deep into the blonde's eyes and started:

> "I gave my love a cherry
> That had no stone."

To my amazement the guitar spoke: it came to life in his hands and effortlessly, beautifully did his bidding.

He sang "John Henry" and "Free and Equal Blues." He sang "Molly Malone" as no one had ever heard it before, bending the tune, caressing the words, creating a dialogue with the Martin. He became the center of the party. He went into his raunchy repertoire, and the blonde played her role as the love object. She squirmed her bottom, pressed her breasts, tongued her lips, closed her eyes, and threw her head back in suggested orgasm. Then, as suddenly as he had started, he handed me back the guitar and said, "Now you can get me a Jack Daniel's, a large one."

A little while later the blonde eased past me on her way to the "little girls' room," as she called it. She paused and touched me on the cheek. She let her finger just feather down my face and under my chin and said, "You're so young. So innocent. So," she paused, "refreshing." She just breathed the word "refreshing" and let her breast slowly brush past me.

I was the only one at the party who didn't know who she was. I learned later she was the most high-profile call girl in New York, splashed all over the papers for weeks before. Something to do with a political scandal.

Oh yeah! I had arrived in New York!

After the welcoming party I went back to Paddy and Betty's apartment, where I was to stay. It was just a short walk west on the same street as Diane's place. Paddy and Betty's daughter, Leish, named after our sister Leish, of course, had been born just a few weeks before my arrival, and although I was made heartily welcome, I felt uneasy about intruding on a home with a mother and infant. However, I didn't have to worry. Diane had an agenda that got me out at cockcrow each morning and didn't allow for sleep at night. She was on one of her highs, and that first week was a dizzying blur of yellow cabs and subways and visits to family and friends. Tom and his wife, Laine, lived just a couple of blocks from Tenth Street on Perry Street. I quickly discovered that Greenwich Village was just that, a village, where friends met on the street and chatted, just like at home, where all was encompassable, all within walking distance.

But a good old-fashioned family welcome for the newcomer from Ireland, with the usual round of house parties and pub crawls and Irish dance halls, was not in the cards in my case. Paddy and Tom were both married, both working hard, and had long since given up the high jinks of the City Center Ballroom, the Jaeger House dances, and all the other

The Mountain of the Women.
If you look closely, you can see
why it got its name.
—*photo courtesy of Liam Clancy*

here I am at about fifteen years
of age. —*photo courtesy of Liam Clancy*

a self-portrait I took at the grave of my
namesake. —*photo courtesy of Liam Clancy*

generations break like waves on the shore

The people I never knew. Family photograph of the McGraths. My parents are fourth and fifth from the left in the back row.

—*photo courtesy of Liam Clancy*

Here I am in elementary school. I'm the little lad in the bottom left corner.

—*photo courtesy of Liam Clancy*

The last photo of the Clancy family all together. Front row, left to right: Liam, Bobby, Paddy, and Tom. Back row, left to right: Peg, Lili, Mammie, Daddy, Leish, Joan, Cait.

—*photo courtesy of Liam Clancy*

Frank Driscoll and I
on the set of *Playboy of
the Western World*, 1954.
—*photo courtesy of
Liam Clancy*

Frank O'Connor,
Murray Lerner, and I
discuss the possibility
of making a film based
on O'Connor's story
"Guests of the Nation."
—*photo courtesy of*
Sunday Independent

ouis Le Brocquy, whom I greatly admired, created original artwork for the first two LP covers for the Clancy Brothers and Tommy Makem. Here is the art from *The Rising of the Moon.*

—artwork reproduced with the permission of Louis Le Brocquy

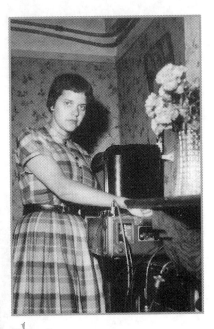

iane Hamilton (Guggenheim) during the recording of Mammie Clancy's song.

—photo courtesy of Joan Butler

Our citadel of singing—the White Horse Tavern in Greenwich Village.

—photo courtesy of Eban Clancy

Ꝺig deal, Dublin, 1965.

—both photos reprinted with the permission of Fionnbar Callanan

Limelight, 1964 . . . Left to right: Liam Clancy, Tommy Makem, a woman in a black hat, Paddy Clancy, Tom Clancy, Theodore Bikel (behind the Clancys), Peter La Farge, Billy Faire, and Odetta.

—photo taken by Daniel Lanois. Reprinted with permission of The Saturday Evening Post, *1954, (renewed) BFL&MS, Inc.*

Father and daughter, Anya.
—*photo courtesy of Liam Clancy*

Paddy and I at National
Stadium, Ireland.
—*photo reprinted with the permission
of Fionnbar Callanan*

S erenading the sharks in Sydney Bay, Australia, 1965.

—*photograph courtesy of Wendy Farnan-Dale and the family of the late Kevin Dale, Melbourne, Australia*

things that young Irish immigrants had been led to expect. Paddy was exhausted every time I saw him. He was working as a draftsman for an advertising firm in Queens and very often had to bring his work home with him, and the new baby wasn't giving him, or Betty, much rest. Tom was totally preoccupied with rehearsals for the upcoming production of *Saint Joan,* which Siobhan McKenna had brought to New York. So Diane showed me the city.

The New York she lived in was not the New York any immigrant was likely to see. We did the tourist things, of course, like the Empire State Building, the Central Park zoo, the drive up Fifth Avenue, and all that. On my insistence we climbed the Statue of Liberty, right up the spiral stairs to the tiara on the lady's head. Diane wouldn't chance it, but I ventured up the arm into the torch. But mainly Diane wanted me to meet her friends in the world of art and music. Robin Roberts was a particular friend. She had been a girlfriend of Paddy's once and had gone on collecting trips with the famed folklorist Alan Lomax. Together they had collected a massive three-volume, six-disc series of field recordings in Ireland, England, and Scotland for Columbia Records, which were considered to be of almost biblical importance in the realm of folk music. God knows Diane and I had heard their names often enough in our travels, from the Hebrides to the west of Ireland to South Armagh and London.

Harry Jackson was another friend I had to meet. He sang cowboy songs in his studio on the Lower East Side of Manhattan at the top of his voice as he showed us around. The place was full of paintings of horses and prairie scenes and elaborate clay models of stampedes and cowboy burials.

Diane introduced me to Murray Lerner, the film director. Murray and I would work a lot together later on. Oscar Brand lived upstairs from Murray in a West Twelfth Street apartment building. His folk music broadcasts on New York Public Radio started before I came to America and will probably run forever. From Diane's circle of friends in the English and Scottish Country Dance Society, I met two extraordinary singers, a tenor and his partner, a countertenor, named Hartly and Huntley or some such combination. They reminded me so much of MacLiammor and Edwards back in Dublin. We took tea at their

Gramercy Park apartment one afternoon and listened to a recording of their madrigals.

We took in plays and films, we ate Chinese food in Chinatown, Italian food in Little Italy, borscht at the Russian Tea Room, even ate at a kosher restaurant, where Diane persuaded me to order bacon and eggs with a glass of milk, out of devilment. Of course, I couldn't understand what got the waiter so incensed and agitated while Diane wet herself laughing. The Orthodox waiter was not amused. We couldn't get served until she explained that I was from Ireland and had never heard of kosher food. We ended up having lox and bagels, a novel experience for me. When Diane was in that mood, the practical jokes and stream of apocryphal stories never stopped.

We hit the museums, the Metropolitan, the Museum of Natural History, the Museum of Modern Art, and, by way of a throwaway line, she asked if I'd like to see the museum her Uncle Solomon was building on Fifth Avenue. It wasn't finished yet, she added apologetically, but it was nearing completion under the scrutiny of an architect friend. His name was Frank Lloyd Wright. People weren't allowed to see it yet, but she was sure she could get us in somehow. Needless to say we got the grand tour. It looked rather bleak to me without artwork but very impressive nonetheless. As we walked down the spiral ramp, she asked me what I thought. I said, "A great place for roller-skating."

In Port Washington, Long Island, at the home of Jean Ritchie and her photographer husband George Pickow, we encountered a young man they'd met in Belfast. His name was David Hammond. After the fun and songs we had that afternoon, Davy and I became fast friends and later collaborators in music and film (not to mention drunken slapstick in Belfast). After a short time in their company I understood a lot more about Diane. It was obvious that she was searching for an identity and that Jean Ritchie was her role model. Jean sang the old songs of close family deep-rooted in old tradition, and Diane wanted that. Jean played the mountain dulcimer; Diane wanted to learn that. Jean and George had gone on a collecting trip to Ireland. Diane now had to go. I don't think any of this was done in malice or conscious imitation, just a desperate need. Because of her background, Diane had no family life, no warmth of brothers or sisters, and I could see that she looked to Jean Ritchie and to my family to fill some of the vacuum she felt in her life. My sisters became her sisters. My mother became her Mammie Clancy. For me the difficult part was that she also wanted to become Mrs. Willie Clancy, and although we were now having a great time, I knew that that wasn't for me. Diane's mood swings frightened me and I knew that I was too inexperienced to handle them. The forces surrounding us were outside the comprehension of this young lad from small-town Ireland.

Jean Ritchie understood. I knew by the way she treated me, the way she looked at Diane and me, and even the way she scolded her husband for telling risqué stories that she knew would embarrass me. She was a country girl.

Jean was from Viper, Kentucky, one of a large musical family. Like the Carter family, the Ritchies had come to prominence when America started to search for its real musical heritage. The onslaught of popular television and radio programming was threatening to swallow up all that was valuable in America's rich cultural past. But then, in the fifties, little radio stations in the South started airing local talent, and soon it wasn't so local anymore. Regional traditions began to capture the national imagination. New York magazines sent writers and photographers out to what they called the boondocks to find out what was going on. George Pickow was sent to a "Viper" in the hills of Kentucky to photograph the singing Ritchie family. He and Jean fell in love, got married, and moved to Port Washington. They lived only a short distance from the great gates of Falaise, the Sands Point estate and castle belonging to Harry F. Guggenheim, Diane's father.

Brought over from the Normandy town of the same name, stone by numbered stone and reconstructed, complete with its great entrance hall, sunken living room cum art gallery, library, spiral stone stairs leading up to towers and outer wings, Falaise was on a huge estate on the Long Island waterfront. Iron railings protected the estate on the landward side, the sea and a great stretch of private beach sheltered the other. The estate had its own stables and racecourse.

Diane took me to meet her father. She had to make an appointment by phone. As we went through the big gates and up the winding avenue, I thought, "What have I gotten myself into?"

A butler ushered us into the entrance hall, where we waited until we were announced. How strange, to go to your own home, where you grew up, and have to wait in a foyer for permission to be let in.

It was a little while before Harry Guggenheim emerged to greet his daughter. He looked none too pleased but brought us through to the great living room. The introductions were brief and chilly. He asked Diane to step into the library with him. I could only surmise that the hushed voices that filtered back to the sunken gallery were voices of controlled remonstration and anger. In retrospect, can I blame him? His only daughter, his heir, shows up at his castle with a twenty-year-old Irish Catholic peasant and expects him to bless the union, her third?

There was nothing for me to do but wander among the works of art.

Much of the room space was taken up by larger-than-life oak sculptures, black and cracked. Brass plaques said they were medieval German pieces. The paintings intrigued me more. One in particular fascinated me, a luminous depiction of a Madonna and child. I had labored with brushstrokes and texture enough to know that the effect I was seeing in this small painting was impossible to achieve. Time and again I would stand back and marvel at its glow, then come close and touch the paint and feel the flow of the brushstroke and the astounding ease of the application of the paint combined with the complexity of the pigments the artist had used. After long contemplation, while the voices in the library ebbed and flowed, I sought a name plaque on the painting. Sure enough, there it was. Michelangelo.

Afterward, as we walked along the private beach, Diane told me how much she hated the place. She told me again how her mother had gone mad there and died, hidden and screaming, in one of the towers.

When I asked her what she and her father had talked about, she was evasive at first. Then she started giggling, divulging that he didn't approve of this relationship with a young Irish lad. But she had outmaneuvered him and got us invited down to his camping-out place in

South Carolina, Cainhoy Plantation. The pretext was that George Pickow needed me as an assistant cameraman for the documentary he was commissioned to make about the animals on the vast plantation. That was exciting news. I was going to make a start at fulfilling my dream of learning about filmmaking. However, that wasn't scheduled to happen until June, and in the intervening months, this was only February, I would be bombarded by a host of new experiences.

12

George Pickow worked as a photog-
rapher with a company called Three Lions
Studio, which made calendars and postcards and such. That winter he was doing a
series of calendar shots of New England
snow scenes and, on Diane's suggestion, of
course, invited me along as his assistant
(Diane came along as *my* assistant). I was
eager to learn anything I could about pho-
tography, including stills. It was a start.

Another photographer had done a series of postcards on the same subject.
George set out with a batch of these to
photograph the same spots. He explained,
"It's cheaper for Three Lions Studio to
send me up to ski country to get these

shots again than to buy the copyright from whoever. I'm not com-plaining."

"In other words," I said, "they're just being copycats." I was some-what scornful of that approach, being twenty, romantic, idealistic, arro-gant, penniless, and all the other noble attributes that youth is briefly allowed. Most of all, the company's approach to making calendars was practical, something utterly foreign to my nature.

The big highways of present-day New England had not yet been built, so we had a very leisurely and scenic trip up the Merritt Parkway, through Connecticut on rural roads, and on up through New Hamp-shire and Vermont. What amazed me was the extent of the forest wilderness starting just north of New York City. Just past the George Washington Bridge you could look across the majestic Hudson at the Palisades, high rock faces carved out by the river. At that time of year their vertical outcrops were gleaming in the sun with huge cascades of ice sculptures.

About a three-hour drive north of New York we made our first stop at Diane's house in Deep River on the Connecticut River. It was a con-verted old farmhouse straight out of a Robert Frost poem, on what had been a "faam," now reclaimed by the woods, its stone boundary walls meandering off to nowhere. The woods were covered in virgin snow, sparkling in the slanting evening light, yet there was a redolent scent of decayed leaves from under the silent woodscape and the smell of trees in winter sleep. The house itself was clad in weathered, gray shingles, and the modest lawn was surrounded by split-rail fencing. Inside, the house held the ghost of aromatic cedar and old pine beams, split and cracked with age, and the lingering scent of generations of log fires in the great stone fireplace that formed the core of the house from ground to roof. Everything in the house was handcrafted in the traditional Yankee style. Even the modernization that Diane had carried out was so tastefully done that the old and the new meshed seamlessly together. Her electric stove top in the modernized kitchen was of local green slate with holes cut out for the electric rings. The fridge and dishwasher were paneled in pine. The central heating unit was hidden underground in the root cel-lar, with the warm air filtering through vents of old brick.

If Falaise had been beautiful and artistic on a grand scale, the house in Deep River had the beauty of folk simplicity and understatement. That was a quality Diane brought to everything she touched, including the cottage outside Carrick, which she would soon buy and refurbish.

On the way up to ski country in North Conway in New Hampshire's White Mountains we stopped off in Dover in southern New Hampshire to visit Tommy Makem, who had come out there in December of 1955 and now lived with the Boyle family, his mother's brother and sisters: Uncle Barney, Aunt Annie, and Aunt Molly. Dover had been a cotton mill town until the mills moved south to cotton-growing country after the Great Depression. The processing of cotton was very similar to the processing of flax for the linen industry in parts of the north of Ireland and in County Cork in the south. Thousands of workers from Cork and Armagh went out there as cheap labor, mainly as "scutchers," although some of the girls took to being housemaids and nannies for the wealthy mill owners.

Tommy's Aunt Annie put on the tea for us, and Tommy and I got into a huddle to talk about our common ambition, acting in New York. He had a job at the time in a printing works, and his plan was to save enough money to buy time in New York to break into theatrical work. It seemed to me that it could take a long time on Dover wages. But fate took a hand in things. Shortly after our get-together in Dover, Tommy's left hand was crushed in a printing press, severing all the tendons to his fingers. His job was finished, and it looked as if his days of playing the pipes and pennywhistle were over, too.

George Pickow, Diane, and I forged up north through the snowy villages and towns of the White Mountains. The hamlets we passed through reminded me of the little decorative houses made of icing sugar on the Christmas cakes from Lory Kiely's bakery back in Carrick.

George and I would trudge through waist-high powder snow up hillsides, lugging tripods, camera cases, and lens bags to find just the right spot where the white New England spire would be the focal point of the composition among the snow-laden houses of the picturesque village, all suitably framed by sagging piney boughs. I learned how to load Hasselblad camera magazines and make some sense out of the upside-down images on the camera viewfinder. Not very creative work, but worth it for the wonderful New England inns we stayed in, with their big blazing fires and Old World charm.

When we returned to New York, Diane set in motion the plan she'd been hatching ever since we took the Irish recordings back to America. Her original idea was to have one of the established record labels release them. But in discussions with a professor of folklore at Columbia University, Kenny Goldstein, who had worked on building up catalogs for companies like Folkways, Electra, and Stinson, the concept of starting a new record company had taken shape. Paddy and Diane had talked about this before, but now we all got down to the nitty-gritty of making it happen. The more we talked, the more appeal it had. We had the material for one album ready to go. Paddy could run the company. The job he had was driving him crazy, anyway. Kenny Goldstein had access to a wide range of artists and unreleased material, while Diane and I would go off to the southern Appalachian Mountains to collect "old-timey" music. All that was needed now was a name, an office, a logo, and lots of money.

The name Tradition Records was quickly agreed on. An office was rented at 131 Christopher Street, a half block from Paddy's apartment, and the partners liked my idea of a maple leaf as a logo. It all seemed so easy, but then, with Guggenheim money, many things seem easy.

The Lark in the Morning was the name of our first release. On it was the best of the material we'd collected in Ireland. That was fine, but what we needed in order to be credible was a catalog. We wanted Tradition to be a record label that would specialize in folk music but also open up to poetry and the spoken word.

Siobhan McKenna had just starred in the brilliant New York version of Shaw's *Saint Joan* and was still in the city. Tom was in that production. I had known Siobhan from the Dublin production of *The Playboy of the Western World.* We were all in the right place at the right time, so when we approached her about recording *The Countess Cathleen* by W. B. Yeats for Tradition Records, she immediately agreed. Tom assembled the cast, which included John Neville, from the London Old Vic Company, to play the part of Aleel, the poet opposite Siobhan. We recorded in March 1956 on the stage of Town Hall in New York.

As far as I recall, it was Kenny Goldstein who suggested that we make an album of Irish rebel songs. Tommy had arrived in New York by then with his poor busted hand. A young surgeon in Dover had undertaken the reconstruction of it by using tendons from his feet and skin and flesh from his backside. But it was a long process that had to be done in stages, and Tommy figured he might as well spend his time recuperating in New York as in Dover.

At the new office of Tradition Records we researched and rehearsed by night. By day we had the use of the back room of Leon Seidel's restaurant, the Lion's Head, on Hudson Street, forerunner of the famous Lion's Head on Christopher Street. Just north on Hudson was the White Horse Tavern where Paddy and Tom used to drink. After rehearsals we would go there at night and invariably start a singsong.

There in the back room of the White Horse we took our first tentative steps at performing in front of a real, albeit drunk, audience. Out of that experience came the offer to sing at a benefit for Woody Guthrie at the Circle in the Square Theater. He was permanently hospitalized by then at Greystone Hospital in New Jersey, and that didn't come cheap. He needed all the financial help he could get. The concert was on a snowy night in March and all the folksingers of the Village were there. I remember Pete Seeger and Lee Hays because I was a great fan of the Weavers, and Harold Leventhal, their manager (soon to become a major influence in our singing careers). Alan Lomax, Cisco Houston, Woody's old pal, and a lot of the people from my arrival party were also in attendance. After the concert I met Woody Guthrie. Huntington's chorea had taken all his muscular control and it was hard to shake his hand. It was a sad way to meet a great soul for the first and last time.

It was shortly after that concert that I went to confession for the first time since leaving Ireland. Intimations of mortality, perhaps. I went to St. Patrick's Cathedral on Fifth Avenue and confessed to a big, beefy man whose accent and demeanor reminded me more of a banker than a priest. In my examination of conscience I rounded up the usual suspects, and told him the one about impure thoughts and touches. I still hadn't lost my virginity, believe it or not, and I intended, for now, to hold on to it.

"Masturbation," he growled. "It's called masturbation." I had never before heard the word.

Later in the church I said my three Our Fathers, Hail Marys, and Glory Bes. I went out into the day, not walking on air as I should be after confession, but feeling kind of stale, yes, that's it, stale, like the taste of old milk at Prendergast's dairy.

I went to a barber and had a haircut. I had to shed something. I haven't been to confession from that day to this, nor to a barber. That day, I decided it was time to cut my own hair and tend my own soul.

Our first recording of The Rising of the Moon was not exactly a polished work of art. Tommy's hand was still bandaged and mine might as well have been. My guitar style was commonly known as the boxing glove method. The album was a bunch of songs belted out in unison by four raw voices with occasional accompaniment from Paddy's harmonica, recorded around Kenny Goldstein's kitchen table in the Bronx, with Kenny's wife Rochelle holding her hand over the baby's mouth to keep her from wailing during a take. Amazingly, people thought it was wonderful, and we heard reactions like "powerful, passionate renditions" and "raw masculinity." To us it was just plain embarrassing, and as soon as Tommy could play again we withdrew the first effort from circulation, all two hundred copies, and with guitar and harp accompaniment by Jack Keenan and Jack Melady, released the revised edition, which was, sadly, not much of an improvement.

The first three albums to be released on Tradition were *The Lark in the Morning, The Rising of the Moon,* and *The Countess Cathleen,* all ready to go but for the artwork on the covers. For *Countess* there was no problem: we would feature a wonderful photograph of Siobhan McKenna costumed for the part. But for the others we were at a bit of a loss. I had been a great admirer of the work of Irish artist Louis Le Brocquy, so I wrote to him asking if he'd design two album covers. I fully expected a scornful no, but to my surprise I got a warm yes. For *The Lark in the*

Morning he did a gray-on-white rendition of the Newgrange spirals as a background to the title, and for *The Rising of the Moon* he sent us a square of green plywood with a quarter moon and a bloodstained piece of calico, roughly cut in the shape of a shirt, glued to it. They both made powerful album covers and both won graphics awards for best album designs of the year. We were off to a good start.

Tapes started coming in hot and heavy: Ed McCurdy, Odetta, Alan Lomax, John Jacob Niles, Robin Roberts, Glenn Yarborough, Davy Hammond, Seamus Ennis, Ewan McColl, A. L. Lloyd, Lightnin' Hopkins, along with flamenco, Italian, and Greek albums.

I desperately wanted to have one artist on the label, Mary O'Hara, a lovely young singer/harpist who I had fallen madly in love with (from a distance as usual) in Ireland. Paddy told me to write to her and ask if she'd be interested. I tried, but "Dear Miss O'Hara" was as far as I could get. The words just wouldn't come to me, and for weeks Paddy kept finding sheets of paper all over the apartment that had only Dear Miss O'Hara on them.

My father saying "Oh, the bloody love!" came to mind.

Diane's moods were a roller coaster. When the lads and I were working on the *Rising* album, she went into the lower depths. She was fine as long as we were involved in something together, but as soon as I drifted outside her orbit she'd start to panic. I began to dread the phone calls, a repeat of the small hours' calls to Carrick before Christmas. There was a question mark over each day. Will she be calm? Or will those telltale signs of trouble make their appearance?—the thumb sucking, the silences, the sighs, the teetering on the verge of control, the hints, sometimes open threats, of suicide.

Though I was staying at Paddy and Betty's apartment, I wasn't entitled to disrupt their lives. They had a small baby. I dreaded the evenings at Diane's apartment. The closer the time came to saying good night, the more agitated she'd get. She'd sit, thumb in mouth, sunk deep in the armchair. There were fearful, fearful things behind those eyes, and then she would focus her eyes on me, they would soften, and I would know with a chill that she was seeing in me her only bridge to sanity. But I didn't want to be, couldn't be, that bridge. I'd calm her down, reassure her, break it to her gently that I must go home: Paddy, Betty, the baby, must go home. She'd fight to keep me. Then weaken. Sometimes I'd get to the elevator before she'd panic. Sometimes I'd make it to the street. Halfway down the block I'd hear the window open up on the third floor and the scream, "I'll jump! I'm going to jump!" The windows along the block would open. Heads would appear. I'd have to run back up and start the whole process of calming her all over again. Other nights would be easier. If I could get down to the end of the block and across Sixth Avenue, I felt safe. My shoulders would drop. The burden would lighten. All I had to face then was 240 West Tenth, hoping that Paddy and Betty weren't having a tiff, hoping Leish was asleep. When I'd finally get to my mattress on the floor in the back room, it was a welcome escape, even with the cockroaches scampering across my body.

Mornings I'd be wrecked. Diane might call up full of fun. Come to breakfast, meet me at such and such. Devilment in her eyes, she'd be like a mischievous little girl. "Drink up your ice water. It's good for you." Then she'd crack up with laughter when I'd discover the plastic ice cube with the dead fly in the middle of it.

Sometimes she'd give me the money to take her out to breakfast. She wanted to be a poor helpless thing, to be given a treat. She desperately wanted to come from the same starting point as those around her. But how can you do that when you're one of the wealthy Guggenheims? Wealth won't go away any more than poverty. You can't act out the struggle that is real to the rest of us. There could be no reconciliation for her between the life of privilege she came from and the life of struggle she wanted so desperately to live.

My need for independence was turning to desperation. I'd made a number of friends in the Village who, without ever saying so, understood my predicament. Murray Lerner was one of them. Murray was the filmmaker who lived on Twelfth Street. He and Oscar Brand were involved in the making of a short independent film called *Night in a Pet Shop* about the adventures of a chimp who gets loose in Treflick's famous pet shop after closing time. Murray, who was directing, offered me the job of assistant cameraman and general grip. It was an ideal opportunity for me to gain experience and independence at the same time. The work involved being on location at the pet shop in the Wall Street area at six o'clock closing time and working through the night. That got me away from the scenes with Diane, which I had come to dread.

It was also a fascinating job. Treflick's was not an ordinary pet shop. They supplied animals, anything from a toucan to an elephant, to zoos, animal trainers for circuses, films, you name it. At night it was a five-story Noah's ark filled with a jungle-like cacophony. There were floors for domestic pets, exotic birds, reptiles, spiders, snakes, monkeys.

One night I had to go to the basement for bananas for the chimp, who was being temperamental. It was actually about three in the morning, pitch-dark, very scary amid all those jungle sounds. All I had for light was a torch with a weak battery. At the bottom of the basement stairs was a crate covered with sacking, which was where I thought they kept their supply of bananas. I threw back the cover and as I shone the torch into the crate I heard a low growl. Then I saw the shining eyes, the bared teeth, and before I could jump back it came at me with a sudden snarl, claws and teeth flashing. It was a black panther! I leaped backward shouting "Jesus Christ Almighty!" and losing the torch in the process. In total blackness I scrambled on all fours blindly up the stairs, not knowing when the beast would land on my back, sinking fangs and claws into my flesh. I've had frights and I've had frights, but that was a fright!

Next evening I showed up for work at the usual time and there, already moving lights about, was Diane.

"Hi!" she said cheerily. "I got a job!"

I pulled Murray Lerner aside—"What the hell's going on? I took this job to get away from her. How did she get involved?"

He put his hands out in a gesture of hopelessness. "What can I tell you?" he said. "She bought out the production company."

The filming trip to Cainhoy Plantation, Harry Guggenheim's ranch in South Carolina, was planned to coincide with the spring break from school so that Diane's daughter Carol would be free to join us. Carol lived mostly with her father, singer John Langstaff, in McLean, Virginia, where she also went to school. She was twelve at the time and a great pet of her grandfather Harry, or Skipper, as she called him. Her friend Binnie Aiello, from near Deep River, was coming along to keep Carol company. I half expected Carol to be messed up, considering the instability of her mother, but instead, the tall, lovely girl I met was very calm and self-possessed. She and I hit it off straightaway. She obviously knew her mother's temperament very well because when Diane would pull a foot-in-the-mouth or a silly practical joke, Carol would give me a knowing look and roll her eyes up to heaven.

Her friend Binnie was one of the Aiello family who would later take me in as a kind of orphan, even convert part of their attic into a bedroom for me.

Diane, Carol, Binnie, and I took the overnight train from Grand Central Station to Charleston, South Carolina. George Pickow had undertaken the long drive with a station wagon full of camera equipment.

We had dinner and played card games till about Washington. Then the porters came along and transformed the whole carriage into a *Some Like It Hot* sleeping car, like magic.

Crawling into the top bunk and lacing up the curtain behind me reminded me of the cozy dens we used to build in the garret at home with beds and blankets. But this was even better with the *clickety-click* of the rails and the louvered blinds you could peep through and watch the lights of the towns that we were passing in the night.

In Charleston we were picked up by a chauffeur and driven the forty miles south to the big gates of Cainhoy Plantation. It was so humid that sometimes you felt like you were breathing more water than air. The avenue from the main gates to the big house seemed to go on forever, all lined with ancient trees festooned in drooping Spanish moss.

When at last the trees opened out to reveal the vista of broad lawns and gardens surrounding the house, it was breathtaking. It looked just like Tara from *Gone With the Wind.*

Skipper/Harry (I never knew what to call him) greeted the girls with a warm welcome. I got the limp handshake. George had just arrived with his laden station wagon and already had his assigned room and was resting on his four-poster bed. We were given a brief tour. The mansion had been restored to burnished perfection. Black servants glided around silently. Out on the western terrace, smelling of humid sweet growth and glowing now with the afternoon light, a "houseboy" with white hair and white gloves served us iced tea. Harry showed us the old slave bell, very much like a big church bell with its wheel and rope, which had pealed out over the cotton fields to call in the slaves, before the Civil War and Emancipation ruined all that. He seemed proud of it.

When everyone else had gone to freshen up and dress before dinner, I was told to follow two black maids who would show me my quarters. As we left the main house and headed for the woods, my Irish blood began to overheat. A quarter of a mile away there was a cabin in the woods. This, I was told by the maids, was all mine and they were my staff if I needed any little thing. They folded down my bed, checked my towels, small kitchen, bathroom, sprayed everywhere for bugs, and left. There was no phone, no radio, no television. Diane had told me, "When my father is at Cainhoy, he thinks he's camping out." If he was camping out, what was I doing? Playing caveman?

Carol and Binnie came to fetch me to the big house for dinner. It was 7 P.M. and the sun was getting lower. The air was soft and warm and the dining room was full of golden light glinting off the crystal and silver settings on the polished mahogany table. Casablanca fans turned slowly high overhead. Everything moved slowly and silently. We stood behind our chairs talking in hushed tones until Harry arrived and sat. Our servants then seated us.

The meal was not spectacular, we were, after all, camping out, and the atmosphere was, to put it mildly, strained. Harry's stiff conversation was directed mostly at Diane and Carol and didn't stray much beyond school and such. It was a major calamity when Carol sent her piece of chicken flying off the plate, scattering peas all over the mahogany table and into Harry's lap. Carol and Binnie got an uncontrollable fit of the giggles, which in turn infected the rest of us, except Harry, damn near choking us in our attempts to stifle it. Harry excused himself and Carol scooted her plate across to me to cut up the chicken before Skipper came back. I just took it up in my fists and tore it apart to the controlled amusement of the servants standing behind us, one of whom slipped me a conspiratorial cloth to clean my hands.

Filming at the ranch was to start the following morning. The calves were being branded and the young bulls castrated. Breakfast was at seven. "Seven o'clock, sharp!" Harry warned as I made my exit from the brightly lit porch with its gleaming white columns into the darkness of the woods to find my lonely cabin.

At six o'clock the following morning I woke up to the clanging of the slave bell. As I headed for the house I thought it was the girls playing games. But no, it was Harry who had rung the bell. My Irish rebel blood came to a boil: he wasn't going to get away with that!

We spent the day filming the roping and branding—all the things we were used to seeing in the cowboy films at home. This time, though, it was very real with the stench of burning hair and skin as the white-hot branding irons burned through to flesh and the blood ran red as the knives snipped off the little calves' balls. One big difference from the movies: all the cowboys were black.

That night in bed the frightful imagery of the song "Strange Fruit" from an old Josh White album plagued my dreams:

> Southern trees bear a strange fruit,
> Blood on the leaves and blood at the root.
> Black bodies swinging in the Southern breeze,
> Strange fruit hanging from the poplar trees.
> Pastoral scenes of the gallant South,
> The bulging eyes and the twisted mouth.
> Scent of magnolia, clean and fresh—
> Then the sudden smell of burning flesh.

The images of the slave days and the lynchings that probably took place right here on this plantation came before my eyes. And I thought of the similar terrors and monstrous injustices inflicted on the blacks and the Irish at the hands of arrogant, greedy men of power and how ironic it was that lynching should be called after an Irishman named Lynch when one of the most moving ballads of emigration from Ireland should start:

> On the deck of Patrick Lynch's boat
> I sat in woeful plight.

Sighing all the weary day
And weeping all the night.

At a quarter to six the following morning I was up at the big house ringing the holy bejeesus out of the slave bell to get Harry Guggenheim out of his bed. But my effort was wasted. He was half-deaf and didn't hear a thing.

We filmed the wild deer and the possums, the gigantic butterflies and the tiny hummingbirds. With the help of an old character called Turkey Tucker, we set up a blind in a wilderness clearing and filmed the wild turkeys coming in at twilight to the call of his magic box.

He was an old-timey storyteller, too, and he told us, as we trudged through the woods, how his mule and he had blundered into a nest of deadly snakes one day, right there where we were walking. The mule stumbled and threw him clear. He ran to get help, but when they came back, the mule was dead and swollen up to twice its size. We didn't believe him, of course, but we watched every step.

George needed film, and Diane suggested that she and I take the station wagon into Charleston to pick up some. It had been a while since she and I had been alone together and she was getting edgy. We picked up the film and had some lunch. Charleston looked beautiful at that time of year and we decided to do some sight-seeing.

"There's a wonderful Civil War museum on the other side of this park. Would you like to go see it?"

"Why not? We're in no rush. George has plenty of things to keep him occupied."

We walked down one of the myriad paths that crisscrossed the park, stopping occasionally to inhale the wonderful scents of the public gardens. Suddenly I stopped and looked in amazement. Diane was a little startled.

"What's wrong?" she said.

There, on the path coming toward us, was her ladyship, the bald woman from the ship! I couldn't believe my eyes. Here we were, a thousand miles from New York, on the same path, in the same park, in the same city, at the same moment in time: the coincidence was unimaginable. As these thoughts flashed through my mind, a strange thing happened. The bald woman stopped. She looked at me in shock and horror. I put out my hands in greeting. She grabbed the three children that were with her and fled down a side path.

I was dumbfounded. I had to sit on a park bench to let the questions rankle round my head.

"Why?" I was asking myself. "Why would she do that? What reason? We got to be such good friends on the ship! She told us such great stories. I just don't understand."

"Didn't you notice she had three little children with her?" Diane said. "And she was traveling steerage on the ship? Not first-class? Don't you see? You found her out! It was all a lie about her being a somebody. She's just a *nanny*. I should know."

13

One of the new releases from Tradition Records was an album of whaling
songs by a young folksinger, Paul Clayton, from New Bedford, Massachusetts.
Paul was living and studying in Chapel
Hill, North Carolina, and had a lot of contacts with people who had the pure tradition. Again Diane was the catalyst for a
new venture.

Not long after the South Carolina escapade, Diane and I set out for Chapel
Hill to meet Paul Clayton for a collecting
trip to Appalachia. An intense love of old
traditional songs and folklore was what
bonded the three of us. It was a pity that
the sexual tensions between Diane and me

blurred some of the focus of our quest, but then, that was part of the chemistry.

In the hills and dark hollows of the western part of North Carolina there were treasures to be found. We knew these pearls of folklore were there from the work of collectors going back to the 1930s. At least Diane and Paul did; I was the novice, but no less excited. We had the best recording equipment of the time, an Ampex 600 recorder and Shure 55 mikes, and we knew that the time capsules of medieval culture held in the pockets and folds of the southern Appalachian Mountains were untouched, as yet, by the influences of radio and television.

Paul had a whole itinerary worked out for us when we picked him up. One of the things he'd arranged was a recording session of spirituals at a black Baptist church somewhere around Chapel Hill. That was a real culture shock to me. All those shy, timid women greeted us, and minutes later the singing started and they were seized by the "spirit" and all heaven broke loose. Within minutes of turning on the tape machine, tears were streaming down my face as I stood in the midst of a possessed people, their eyes closed, their bodies convulsed. I was surrounded by a wild abandon of voices and harmonies.

Then there was a college where Paul and Diane had arranged for me to give a lecture on Irish music and poetry. Before we left I had made a tape of my favorite songs and poems. When I started to play it, the listeners were obviously bored, especially when I had to reel the tape back and forth trying to find the right song, so I abandoned it and started to sing and recite and tell stories, and to my surprise the whole thing came to life. I got a bit of a glow from it.

The following day at an outdoor picnic at the college Paul was involved with, Diane asked me to sing "Buachaill on Eirne," or "The Boy from the Erne," for the picnickers sitting on the grass under a great oak tree. It was my favorite song at the time. They wanted more, so I ended up singing the handful of songs I knew. That set me thinking about taking the singing a little more seriously.

One of the great finds on that trip was the guitarist Etta Baker. Her style of guitar picking on tunes like "Railroad Bill" became legendary and influenced just about every young folk guitarist who ever came down the line afterward. I don't know if Paul or Diane had known of her before or if it was purely by accident that we were driving by her house that sweltering day in Morganton, North Carolina, as she was sitting on the porch just picking away on the guitar for her own amusement. To my memory it seems accidental because we pulled up when we heard the music and got a conversation going. We had no recording equipment with us, so we arranged to come back that evening when she had fed the children and put them to bed.

Of course, when we did come back and set up our gear, the kids were still up, full of curiosity and excitement. What fascinated me at the time was the way that such incredible music flowed from this young housewife while she kept complete control over her whole family just with her eyes, two totally different activities at the same time. When she glared at the kids, they daren't breathe. The tunes we recorded that evening in her kitchen can be heard on an album called *Instrumental Music of the Southern Appalachian Mountains* on Tradition Records.

Beech Mountain and environs, known locally as the Beech, was famous for its singers, storytellers, liars, dulcimer players, whittlers, and whimmydiddle makers. The man who knew them all, the man who became our guide, friend, and teacher, was Richard Chase, known affectionately to all as Uncle Dick.

Uncle Dick lived in Beech Creek when we met him, although he was born in Alabama. He was a one-man traveling show: a writer, entertainer, lecturer, dance teacher, whittler. He even played the harmonica, badly. But he had a way about him that everyone loved. Everywhere we went with Uncle Dick we were made welcome. He knew all the families who were the torchbearers of the old traditions: the Presnells, Harmons, Wards, Hickses. He'd learned songs and tales from the best, including the tall tales of "Lie-hue," John Calvin Younts, reputed to be the best liar of them all. Uncle Dick, in a characteristically underplayed way, also helped the poorest families in the area earn some cash by getting them to use the long winter months doing local crafts, making such things as quilts, whittled figurines, and, a big seller, gee-haw whimmydiddles. Whimmydiddles were made from two sticks and a little propeller that went one way if you told it to "gee," then stopped and reversed when you told it to "haw." He sold these out of the back of his station wagon on his summer travels to folk festivals, seminars, and square dances and to highway restaurants and shops like Howard Johnson. The income he brought back to the families was sometimes literally a lifesaver.

I thought I had seen poverty in Ireland in the 40s, but never had I seen anything like the poverty in rural North Carolina in the fifties—and that was only among the poor white folks. What the worst-off black communities must have suffered is hard to imagine.

Uncle Dick took us along to one of the families whose whittlings he'd been selling on his travels. He had some cash for them and a batch of whimmydiddles to pick up.

He warned us that this was really a backwoods outing we were on. Still, I wasn't prepared for what we encountered. We drove from bad roads to dirt roads to no roads. Then we set out on foot across some cleared land under wooded hills. Even the land looked hungry. The heat was soupy thick. The flies swarmed around us in a cloud looking for the meal that cattle would normally provide. Here I saw no cattle, or anything else, to sustain a family. On the verge of the trees leaned a crumbling wooden shack with the remains of a porch in front. A pack of assorted mangy dogs emerged from under this porch, but they looked too weak and listless to be threatening. They couldn't even bark. As we approached I heard a joyous whoop from the house. Uncle Dick had been spotted from the window. A roly-poly woman emerged followed by a clatter of kids, from teens down to a bare-bottomed crawler.

"Well, hiiiaiiahi!!" It was by far the longest, most musically modulated "hi" I ever heard in my whole life. It was also just about the only word I understood of the animated chat that ensued. There was one other word, "piiiieaihi," as in apple pie. I was looking blankly at this jolly woman, Sally Mae, when I got a kick from Diane. "She wants to know if you'd like some pie." I looked at the two pies she had on the table and my stomach turned. They had been sugar-coated, but the sugar had melted in the soggy heat and had turned into a flytrap. The piecrusts were black with a coating of dead and dying flies. But how could I refuse? She had baked these pies especially for Uncle Dick's visit and, judging by the hungry looks on the children's faces, it was a rare treat. "Yes, please. I'd love some pie," I said, at which point she took her thumb and with one deft, sidelong scoop, cleared the fly soup onto the rough floorboards.

I only understood snatches of the conversation, but a lot of it seemed to concern a brother Bill and a missing husband called Hank. There was an awful lot of gesticulating toward the woods behind the shack, and once or twice a rusty shotgun was produced and pointed out the window by way of demonstration.

When we left with much ado and "byeyeyeis," Uncle Dick filled us in on the basics of the conversation. Her husband had gone to Boone looking for work and stayed gone for six months, not working, from the reports she got, but drinking himself to death. Her brother Bill had moved in and was taking care of the family, but Hank finally came back, roaring drunk, with a jug of moonshine under his arm and wildly waving a shotgun, shouting that he was going to kill them all but first he was going to get Bill for trying to steal his holding and his house and turning his own family against him. She had hidden Bill under the house, which was up on stilts to keep out the floods and snakes, and sent the kids off into the woods while she held off Hank alone, herself and the shotgun. She and the family had a strategy worked out now for when Hank would make his drunken visits. What really struck me was how a woman with so many troubles could be so cheerful. You could hear her laughing in the next county.

It was Uncle Dick who led us to old Monroe Presnell, an impressive man. He had been tall in his youth, though age was pulling him toward the ground when we first recorded him that summer of 1956. He was from a time and place that the modern world had somehow skipped over. A lot of his speech was Elizabethan or even earlier. He sang the word "lover" as "lovyer," which, I believe, is from the Middle English of Chaucer's time. How strange to hear this man sing, "Fother, fother build me a boat / that on the ocean I might float," and tell us that he learned the song from an old-timer in Arkansas, where he worked as a young man. He pronounced it ArKANsas, not Arkansaw. Six short months before, Diane and I had recorded the same song in the dead of winter from two sisters in Kilmore Quay in Ireland, in County Wexford, who told us they never heard of the song anywhere else except in their family.

Lee Monroe Presnell lived on a ridge way up on Beech Mountain. It was a tortuous trip on the dirt roads every day for the week or more that we spent recording with him, but a beautiful trip, too, up through the small tobacco farms with their drying sheds overlooking the valley, fading into the blue haze so characteristic of the Blue Ridge and southern Appalachian Mountains. By the time we'd get way up to the Presnell place you could feel the lightness of the air, which was full of birdsong, making a complement to the old man's singing. Each day Diane would ask him, "What can we bring you? We have to give something back for all the time and lovely songs you've given us. You won't take money, so tell us what you would like."

"No, no," he'd protest. "Can't spend money on Beech Mountain. Nowhere to spend it. No-o, don't need nothin'," then he'd look around to see if anyone was in earshot and whisper conspiratorially, "Could you get me some Sen-Sen? Covers up the smell of tobacco!"

From then on we always smuggled him some Sen-Sen (little licorice bits) and a wad of black plug tobacco. Personally I think it was the smell of the occasional swig from the hidden jug that he really wanted to cover up.

"One time there was an old blacksmith named John." That was the way Uncle Dick started off a story one day as we drove the back roads of Watauga County. The story was called "Wicked John and the Devil," and it started to sound familiar to me when Wicked John had a visit from St. Peter, who gave him three wishes. When the devil appeared in the story, words came back to me from my school days, but they were Gaelic words: *Bhí fear ann fadó agus is e ainm a bhí ar na Seadhna.* Same story, "Seadhna and the Three Wishes," in Irish.

Many things began to sound familiar to me. One day we recorded an old, old man, over ninety, his daughter told us, playing a mountain tune on a homemade fretless banjo. He was blind and almost deaf and shook like a leaf until the banjo was put in his hands, at which point he became steady as a rock and the years fell away from him. He wanted to know who we were and where we came from. When he was told that I came from Ireland he perked up. "Ah'm Scotch-Irish!" he announced with a burst of pride.

I had never heard the expression before, but I soon found out the story. Back in the 1600s the native Irish were ejected from their land, forcibly, to make way for the troublesome Lowland Scots that the English wanted to be rid of. The exercise was called the Plantation of Ulster. It had been only partly successful, because the land could not support all the Lowlanders transplanted there. After the Battle of the Boyne in 1690 many of the planters, who now called themselves Scotch-Irish, moved on to the American colonies, especially to Jamestown, in Virginia. They weren't welcomed there and had to move on west to the wilderness and mountainous lands of Virginia and North Carolina. They kept their heroes and their cultural identity from the old country, though, their foremost icon being William of Orange, the same King Billy who had bivouacked his army outside the walls of my hometown, Carrick-on-Suir, after whom my street, William Street, was named, after whom my next-door neighbor, Ned Orange, was named. So enamored were they of the name of their hero that every second boy was called William, or Billy.

The "hill Billies" took their place in the American tapestry. With them came the songs, the dances, stories, the bright side of their culture, but with them, too, came the dark side. The Orange Order became the Ku Klux Klan, the fear and intolerance of Catholics mutated into hatred of black people, Jewish people, everyone, in fact, who wasn't white Anglo-Saxon Protestant. Their inability to adapt was both their strength and their weakness.

Apart from the curiosity of seeing signs in restaurants and toilets reading "Coloreds only" and "Whites only," I was naively unaware of the racial tensions in the American South. I would have a lot of growing up to do before I would come to political awareness. At that time I was still only twenty years of age and full of the in-between world of the Celtic twilight.

. . .

Back in Deep River I mentioned to Diane that the story of "Wicked John and the Devil" would make a nice short film. All I had to say was the word and next morning we were on our way to New York City to buy cameras, lights, tripods, sound equipment, the whole shebang. That was on a Friday. By Sunday we were back in Connecticut checking out an old forge in the hills above Lyme on the Connecticut River and auditioning young locals for the parts of "little devils." On Monday morning at 7 A.M. we were shooting the outdoor scenes with my brother Tom, who jumped into the fray at short notice, playing the leading role, while a local leather worker repaired the huge antique bellows of the old fieldstone blacksmith's forge. Meantime, a local butcher was delivering a cow's leg, which we needed for the big devil's cloven hoof. He left the location looking a little worried.

The film was never finished. The heaven and hell parts of the story, which would have required costly sets and major funding, never got done. But at least I got to make a film before returning to Ireland. I submitted what I had completed to the Children's Television Workshop, but the reply I got was that the devil looked too black. It wasn't acceptable in America anymore that the devil should look like "a Negro" (I quote!). Hell! Shoveling coal all day into them thar furnaces down below, how could you be white?

My honeymoon with America was nearly over. The time I'd set for going home had come and gone. But I had never experienced summer before, not like a New England summer. And I couldn't contemplate going back to the misery of Ireland, its weather and its hang-ups. I wallowed in the last of my childish innocence, cycling every day with Carol and another one of the Aiello family, Annette, to Cedar Lake to swim and cavort and do handsprings off the raft anchored a hundred yards from the beach, and to sail when the chance arose with some of the young lads who found something different in this Irish guy in their midst. Freedom! It was new, and heady, and not to be given up so soon.

There is a time in everyone's life when Life, in the big sense, is at its most intense. It has to be savored then, because that peak can never again be reached. Mine was the summer in Deep River before my twenty-first birthday, before the backlash of a tormented woman thrust me dismissively into the reality of adulthood.

From Ireland there was not a word. Apparently the family was convinced that their worst fears had come true, as they knew they would. I had been seduced and corrupted by America. I was supposed to come home in June, but June had come and gone, as had July and August. Judging by the deafening silence from across the Atlantic, I had obviously been written off.

As my twenty-first birthday approached, I was totally alone and feeling a glowing warmth of self-pity. Diane had taken off for Florence or Ireland or somewhere to show me how much I needed her and how little she needed me. I was helpless, stranded in the farmhouse alone, no money, no company but my own, my stomach being eaten by ulcers, day after day talking to myself, and even worse, night after fearful night in that house, which I was convinced was haunted. The sounds I heard there at night were not caused by anything I could explain, like old timbers settling or changes in temperature. One night, as I tried to brave it out and find sleep, the noises grew and grew in the attic. "It's only the house settling," I kept telling myself until, with a great crash, the attic window burst out onto the dark lawn. At that point I said, "Fuck this!" and hightailed it out to the Volkswagen bus that Diane had converted to a camper for a trip we'd made to the Asheville, North Carolina, festival. I found the window glass scattered all over the grass the next morning.

There were no two ways about it: Diane had me where she wanted me, and I had to do something drastic, and soon.

My twenty-first birthday should have been a happy time, but on September 2, there I was alone in the farmhouse in Deep River. Diane didn't want me in New York. I knew that: I might meet people. I was safe in Deep River. She gave me a job to keep me from feeling useless, painting the big extension to the back of the farmhouse. All morning I waited in growing agitation for the postman. Nothing! Not from home, not from anyone. By the afternoon I was in deep depression. All the old religious arguments were going over and over in my head: pitting Teilhard de Chardin against the Penny Catechism and my growing agnosticism, all the nonsense that now seems so inconsequential, having arrived at the state of being happier with the mysteries of life than with questions or answers.

Then about three-thirty young Donnie Clarke came by on his bike. Donnie was about fifteen and thought an older guy from a foreign land was kind of exotic.

"I told my mom it was your birthday. She wants to know if you'll come down for supper. She's baked you a cake. Five o'clock?"

"Great, I'd love to." I drove down in the VW bus to Donnie and his mom's place. They lived in a mobile home down Route 80. It was just the three of us.

"Oh, I just couldn't bear the thought of you there alone in that old farmhouse on your birthday. Especially your twenty-first, my goodness. When Donald told me, I just said that ain't right, now I'll bake a nice little cake and you go right over there and you get him. My goodness! A twenty-first birthday all alone!"

She rattled on and on, but to me it was such music. I'd been alone in the farmhouse for so long I was starting to go funny, going over and over the same old script in my head about religion and philosophy and sexuality and, above all, my present predicament and what to do about it. I was like a horse going round and round the paddock not knowing what else to do. The chitchat now was a great relief. She played some records and we had some Coke and then a real New England supper of baked beans and wieners with homemade corn bread followed by the cake with twenty-one candles.

What a great surprise and what a bitter irony: here I was in the warm friendliness of a mobile home on a Connecticut side road with a woman I'd never met before and a kid on a bike, a world away from family and friends, none, not one of whom, had given a tuppenny damn for my coming of age. I didn't know what religion these people were, but they had more humanity than all the holier-than-thou hypocrites did in Catholic-fucking-Ireland. Once more my conviction was growing stronger and stronger that the only one you can count on is yourself. Take the divil by the tail, as they say, and do your own thing.

Diane returned with Carol for Thanksgiving. Paddy and Betty and their daughter, Leish, came up from New York for the holiday. The weather was still good enough to go for the occasional swim in Cedar Lake with Carol and her pals, whom I'd grown so close to, especially the Aiellos. It was a great relief to have company again after the long period of solitude.

But my enjoyment was tempered by the helpless feeling that I wasn't in control of my own life. That realization had grown in the time I'd spent alone. Diane had done magnanimous things for me: she'd brought me to America, introduced me to people who would be lifelong friends. She had bankrolled Tradition Records and the film of "Wicked John," taken me on the adventure-filled collecting trips. She had given me her house to live in and had opened up a whole new world to me. It was all wonderful. Yet what good was all that if I didn't own myself? I was dependent on her for everything. What she wanted in return for all she'd given me was simple, my body and my soul. They weren't for sale.

I had tried very hard to understand her mood swings and the mental torment that she suffered, a torment I'd often suffered with her. If I'd had the ability to talk to her, to help her, and explain my feelings toward her like a mature man, events may not have unfolded as they did, but I was a callow youth and only time and experience can change that.

It was a hot Indian-summer night. There was no air-conditioning in the old part of the house. Paddy and Betty and the baby were sleeping in the new extension. I was in the small room at the top of the stairs next to Diane's room. Carol's room was down half a flight across the stairs. The old house was full of creaks. The air in the room was stifling and I lay in bed only in my underpants. The floorboard in Diane's room creaked and her door opened. Then my door opened but no light came in. A warm, naked body slid into the bed beside me. For a moment I lay there in confusion. Then I thought, "This is it, decision time. Her sanity or mine." Her body held no sexual pull for me. I wanted Angela. I wanted a young, loving but shy body to snuggle with and cling to in love and lust and affection. Not this. This was a kind of rape. I raised my leg and, with a choked cry, shoved her out of the bed onto the floor.

The gasp. The anguished cry of rejection. The finality. The absolute realization. He really doesn't want me. She scrambled naked out of the room.

I heard noises in her room, then a stumble down the steep old stairs. Water running in the kitchen sink, a glass being filled and filled again. Gasping sobs. A commotion of sounds. I lay there not breathing, interpreting sounds. Where are Paddy and Betty? Surely one of them had heard. Where's Carol? What's that sound? A glass dropped in the sink. The front door thrown open, a cry, a car door. An engine roared to life. Wheels tore gravel. A screeching of tires on road surface. Oh Jesus, the station wagon, going away at high speed. Which way? Toward Route 80.

I jumped up and threw on a pair of jeans. No time for shoes or shirt. I ran downstairs, no sign of Carol, Paddy, or Betty. In the sink a broken glass. On the slate countertop a pill bottle. Cotton. What does the label say? Dr. Weinberger, where? Old Saybrook, forty miles away. Date! Date! When were they prescribed? The bottle was empty. The name of the medicine meant nothing. Phone number for the doctor! What time is it? Four-thirty A.M. He's in bed. Try anyway.

Ring.

"Yes?" (How dare you call at this hour.)

"Dr. Weinberger?"

"Yes."

"I'm a guest at Mrs. Hamilton's house in Deep River. You prescribed some pills for her the day before yesterday. I think she's taken them all. Could they be dangerous?" Pause.

"If she did take them all, yes, they would be dangerous. Were they all gone? Where is she now? May I talk to her?"

"She just drove away at high speed. I don't know where. What could happen?"

"Well, they are quite powerful sleeping pills. She would pass out in thirty or forty minutes. If her stomach is not pumped out, she could die. Can you find her somehow?"

"There's another car. I'll try. Will I bring her to your office if I do?"

"I'm not equipped to pump out her stomach. She must go to the emergency room at the nearest hospital. Let's see, from Deep River, that would be Middletown. But you must try to find her immediately!"

I ran out, jumped in the VW, and took off toward Route 80. Four or five miles down the road a station wagon doing high speed passed me going the opposite direction. I wheeled around but it quickly lost me. The VW was no match for the powerful station wagon. I arrived back at the house and sighed with relief to see the station wagon parked, albeit at a crazy angle, near the split-rail fence. I looked in, no Diane, no keys. I ran into the house and saw no one. Upstairs sprawled across her bed was Diane in her nightdress, unconscious. She was a heavy woman, but I got her down the stairs and into the VW. I only knew the way to Middletown vaguely. It was all little country roads, now slippery from wet leaves.

There was no time for terror, no time for caution. All I could think of was to get to the emergency room at the hospital. At each bend Diane's body would either fall over on me or slam against the window. Once she sort of revived and said, "I have to pee." She couldn't open the door. I had to run around the car and haul her out and hold her while she peed. Back in the car she passed out again.

Finally I saw the lights of a big town reflected in the low cloud cover and prayed it was Middletown. It was. As I sped through the wet streets looking for the hospital, a flashing light and the siren of a squad car closed behind me.

"Out of the car. Why aren't you dressed? Is this woman drunk? Where's your license and registration?"

"Please, we don't have time. She's taken an overdose of sleeping pills. We have to get her to a hospital immediately."

"Follow us."

While she was being pumped out and put to bed, I was left sitting in a waiting room in just my jeans, flanked by the two cops.

"I have to get back to Deep River. Her daughter doesn't know. She's only twelve. My brother and sister-in-law are there but they don't know, either."

"You can take it easy, fella. You're not going anywhere for a while. If she recovers she can tell her story. If she dies, you may be charged. Okay, name?"

At six in the morning they finally gave me a blanket. At about nine Diane recovered consciousness. I called Paddy and woke him up. He'd slept through the whole commotion. He called Freda Winton, Diane's financial adviser. She called Harry Guggenheim.

The Aiellos picked up Carol before I got back to the house. Paddy and Betty came and took over at the hospital. I had packed my stuff by the time they got back in the afternoon. When they arrived, they said that Diane had been moved to a mental hospital.

For the next few nights I stayed in the Aiellos' house and went to visit Diane at the most luxurious hospital I had ever seen. When I first saw her, she said, "Oh, Willie, I'm so sorry. I gave you an awful fright. I'm alright now but they won't let me out. You won't believe this, but all the doctors and nurses here are crazy." She started laughing. "They're all crazy. You've got to get me out. Phone Freda. Tell her to tell my father they're all crazy."

I made the phone call. Two weeks later Diane was out of the hospital and on her way to Italy.

Meantime, I was in New York, a complete basket case. But free. Free at last.

14

I was desolate: penniless, jobless, and basically homeless.

The Aiello family of Killingworth, Connecticut, took me in. They built me a bedroom in their attic, and there I was, cozy and content, back in a garret again. Lou and Marge Aiello helped me through the aftershocks of the suicide attempt, and their kids Annette and Binnie, Walter and Chris, and little Elaine helped me come back to life.

Small-town and rural America were there in Killingworth. The Norman Rockwell America, clichéd but lovely, full of the smell of apples and pumpkin pie and cinnamon. When the corn was ripe, the firemen's picnic was held under a great spreading chestnut tree in the cornfield. I had never tasted fresh corn on the cob dipped in melted butter before. Oh, it was so good! And the slow-baked beans and the barbecued hot dogs and chicken and steaks, the mounds of potato salad and coleslaw and a big pot of spaghetti sauce as only Lou Aiello could make it. And later the kids dragged me off to the state fair in Old Lyme, or was it Hadlyme? East Lyme? They wanted me to go square dancing!

"I can't dance," I told them, but when we got there I discovered it was no problem at all. The Virginia reel was really what we called the Walls of Limerick back in Ireland, the haymaker's jig was the Siege of Ennis. With the "caller" telling everyone what to do, "Promenade, do-si-do your partner," I had their adaptations of the old Irish dances off in no time at all. Before the night was over I was teaching them the traditional *ceilidh* ornamentations to the dances that had been lost on the boat over. Throwing the Sheaf, Tug-o'-War, Trick-o'-the-Loop, Three-Card Trick, Find the Pea, Clydesdale showing, prize sheep, squealing pigs, monster vegetables, all were familiar to me from the Bar'ny Meeting in Piltown, my father's village. The only things new to me, and I loved them, were candied apples and popcorn.

The fun we had at the Aiello household went a long way to saving my sanity. Marge was a mother to me, loving without demanding. Lou had us laughing all the time. He was a sculptor, but to augment his income, he had a little factory behind the house where he made parts for manikins. Some of the big supply companies of store window dummies were Lou's customers, his bread and butter, or rather, spaghetti.

Even when I went back to New York (I just had to find work), it was comforting to know that a small garret and a big welcome awaited me in Killingworth.

The trip was now coming to an end. I was in love with it all: the land, the seasons, the amazing light, the people, the freedom. My mother was right. I had been seduced. The dark attic of my soul, with its dust-collecting baggage of other generations, had its windows flung open and a great fresh breath of sunlit air swept through it.

The snow-laden woods of New England, its villages pungent with the smell of woodsmoke; the frosty tingle of its crisp air; the smell of old hand-adzed beams in Diane's ancient farmhouse: these things were part of an America I had never envisioned.

South Carolina in the spring was seductive with scents of growing things, of magnolia and hibiscus, the air heavy with noontime heat and the swampy buzz of katydids and flying critters. The nights there belonged to frogs and bats and flying beetles and the countless mingled smells of a land at rest after a burgeoning day's work fermenting life.

In the mountains of Appalachia the warmth was of a different sort, the warmth of a simple, almost childlike people, a people who in the midst of poverty the like of which I had never seen could laugh and sing and share without stint the riches of humor, song, story, whittling, and drawled Elizabethan turn of phrase. After this southern odyssey, I return to a summery New England, a land of green forests and clear lakes, a land where a young immigrant like me kept a watchful eye on the woods for the possible sighting of an Indian hunter. It was all a revelation.

With the dark days coming, I headed for New York and borrowed the money from Paddy to fly back to Ireland, out of Idlewild Airport on an old Constellation airplane, back to Rinanna, stopping off at Gander, Newfoundland, to refuel before the big jump across the Atlantic to the little landing strip beside the Shannon. I was at last going home. Home for Christmas.

Yes, some of the Yank had rubbed off on me, as they had told me it would before I left. How I had been disgusted when Bobby came home to Ireland with an American twang. And here I was driving home from the airport thinking, "It all looks so small and so poor, so shabby and mean." Passing through Limerick city, I thought how red the faces of the people looked, particularly the children, and how ugly the shopfronts. And the women, so pinched-looking, so badly dressed. Why were they all hunched like that, men and women? Was it the cold or was it that they were a cowed, hopeless people, unlike Americans, who had appeared to me so confident, so loud and seemingly arrogant when I first arrived?

Bobby had picked me up at the airport. He was a much happier-looking fellow than the down-in-the-mouth one who had seen me off at Cobh back in January. He had obviously settled in and gotten himself a girlfriend, judging by the smile on his face. Also his Carrick accent was back in full bloom. After we had left the dowdiness of Limerick behind us, Bobby's good humor and wisecracks, his stories about all "the lads" and the shenanigans at the pantomime rehearsals, began to cheer me up, that together with the startling green of the countryside. It was one of those sharp, clear frosty days you often get in Ireland just before Christmas, not a hint of a cloud in the winter blue of the sky and the filigree of bare hawthorn trees along the hedgerows etched against the low December light.

After we passed through Tipperary town we got the first glimpse of the Galty Mountains, a sprinkling of snow on the topmost peaks. They looked so majestic in the low eastern sun. With the town of Clonmel behind us, the sight of Slievenamon's lovely breast, nipple-topped, rising on our left, overwhelmed me with a feeling of home.

We drove down along by the river Suir, where every sight and sound and smell through the open window of the VW became familiar, the contour of the hills and woods of Carrickbeg, the boreen down to the fishing spot where Sker Driscoll and I used to leave our bikes on summer evenings when the trout rise was on. Mickey Murray's cottage on the left, then Miloko factory on our right. After that the old beech and elm trees at Dr. Murphy's place, and then past the council housing estate ("Keep away from that place, boy," my mother's line), past Claureen Well on our right, up the hill past the Ormond Hall (oh, the all-night dances and *The Song of Bernadette,* how lovely she was!). Then turn left onto Lough Street and (my heart starts pounding now) turn right onto Town Wall past the Garryrue and the Level, past Gilman the cobbler's (snapapple on Halloween night, his deaf-mute daughter making strange sounds), and then we're blessing ourselves passing St. Nicholas' Church (the smell of incense, the choir loft, the crib, the hymns, the drone of Latin). Here we are on William Street. Paulie's shop, the Verringtons, Agnes and Ellie, the two Driscolls, Nell the pessimist and Ned the barber, Miss O'Connor's, Freddy Reck, the motorbike man, Nurse Shanahan's, Felice's window all Christmas lights,

O'Keeffe's, the Irishes, and in among them, our house, and the front door opening and my father clearing his throat and my mother biting her lip and holding back the tears. "Oh *sha,* Willie boy, you're home!"

After the cup of tea and the telling of some of my adventures, I plodded up the two flights of stairs past the landing where the May altar was, May the month and May my sister's altar, past the lattice-wired window where the stray kitten had squeezed through to become our pet, up to my own little room in the garret. It all felt so right. Stacks of my school copybooks still lay in the corner and in the recess of the floor-level window. And the smell! The smell of home drove a straight arrow to the core of my life's memory.

After I climbed in under the blanket, I lay back and looked at the patch of blue sky through the skylight as I reflected on all that had happened in the whole American experience, which, even now, began to take on a dreamlike haze of unreality. Either it was a dream or it had happened to someone else. For now, I wanted to forget it all and pick up the life I'd sailed away from that day back in January.

Just as I dozed off, the first shattering clang of the great bell of St. Nicholas' Church struck. I leaped two feet off the bed. My God, I'd forgotten how close that bell was. How loud it was. How could I have lived under that all my life? How could I have slept through it? As the eighteen strokes of the noon Angelus rankled my brain, I realized that I no longer remembered the prayers that went with it. I had escaped to my room just in time because, down in the kitchen now, they would be on their knees, my father and Bobby and probably Aunt Alice, my mother leading out the Angelus prayers with her most grievous fervor and I not remembering the responses, and that would let the cat out of the bag about the questionable religious life I had been living in America, just as she feared.

Before the last gong tolled, I was deep in sleep, having made a mental note that, from now on, I should be either in my bed or out of the house at Angelus time.

I woke to the smell of rashers [bacon] frying, wafting its way from the kitchen up the bends of the stairs to the garret. And there I was, induced back, by a smell, into a world I thought I'd left behind.

Daddy Clancy was like a young fellow. His hair looked blacker. Bobby told me he was using burnt cork to darken it. For another thing, he had Bobby working in the insurance business with him, which made him very happy. Now it really was "R. J. Clancy and Son"; maybe not "Sons" as he wanted, but better than nothing.

I had brought home the LPs of *The Rising of the Moon* and *The Lark in the Morning,* which had just been issued. Daddy Clancy felt the same way about recordings as Americans felt about television: if you were on them, you were famous; if you weren't, you were nobody. It thrilled him that his own sons were on an LP singing the rebel songs that had so impassioned his youth. It thrilled him because the only other people he had ever heard on recordings were his heroes like John McCormack and the great Italian tenor Beniamino Gigli and such. In turn that made me very happy because he had asked me once if I wanted to "act the goat" all my life. Now I was up there with his heroes, with the people who were immortalized on wax discs. Forever.

Since the first time that I had felt the squeeze of his hand, on our walk up Town Wall when I was a small child, I knew of my father's love and concern for me, but now I also knew that he was proud of me. And that was important.

Over and over as I ate breakfast, I heard "Roddy McCorley" and "Tipperary So Far Away" playing on the new electric gramophone. My brother-in-law Christy Butler, who now owned his own electrical business, had given it to my mother and father as a pre-Christmas present.

Maybe the actor in Daddy Clancy was reassessing his concept of the "and Sons" role as the embodiment of what he himself really wanted to be in his childhood dreams, dreams that could not be spoken of in his time, dreams of being onstage, singing, or of being on a real recording.

In my youthful fancy I had thought my own visions were purely my own, but now I realized that I was just an inheritor like everyone else. We ourselves bring so little to the scheme of things, except our own unique imprint, minute as it may be.

. . .

Mammie Clancy was worried about what America might have done to my religious faith. She watched me even though she tried to hide it. As always, she kept the best side out, and over Christmas she fulfilled her unquestioned role as "chief bottlewasher" for all occasions.

She had grown frail even in the short time I'd been away. The long years of childbearing had taken everything but her spirit, which was intact and strong. But her body was racked with pain. "Oh, the back, the back," she would say. Some days the noise in her head was so bad that she found all sounds unbearable. Worst of all was the heat. Some days she was consumed by it, but other days were bearable to the point that she could cheerily function without a mention of it.

She went to eight o'clock mass every morning, and afterward she'd light the fire and clean up. By the time Bobby and I surfaced, her back would have given out, and for most of the day the "lounge" in the kitchen would be her headquarters from which she directed the day's operations.

The day after I came home she piped up from the chaise lounge, "Do you know what? I just realized, Willie boy, that it's time for the red berry holly. The plum pudding is hanging up there over my head for the last three weeks and there's not a sprig of holly on it yet." Things like that never changed from year to year. It all felt alluringly safe. One could easily feel that the ritual would flow on forever.

Bobby and I made the rounds of our sisters' houses. Peg, Joan, Leish, and Cait all lived in Carrick. The eldest, Lili, lived in Waterford city sixteen miles away. They all were happily married and rearing their children. Strange the difference between the boys and girls in the family. The four boys felt the call of adventure and far-off places, while the girls were content to stay close to the nest amid the much quieter adventure of home and family and tradition.

My sister Lili married Jimmy O'Brien, who owned a bakery in Waterford, and Leish married Lory Kiely, the baker from Carrickbeg. One thing for sure, we would never go hungry.

Christmas Eve was strictly a fast day. There would be communion at midnight mass, and nothing could be eaten or drunk (except water) until after communion. Confessions were heard in the church all day, but Bobby, always a step ahead of these things, had dodged off somewhere. Since my experience with confession back in St. Patrick's Cathedral in New York the previous March, I was sticking to my vow to never again go to confession and never again to a barber. I had decided back then to tend my own hair and my own soul, and no weight of religious convention was going to change that. On the other hand, I wasn't going to upset my mother if I could help it, so I found just the right way out for now: I'd do as I always did, and sing in the choir. It was safe in the choir loft at the back of the church because you had to sing the Christmas hymns while the lines and lines of people waited for communion. And you got to look down and see all the people in the church, and my heart beat faster at the thought of seeing Angela again.

When I did see her, as always walking head down, hands clasped in front of her, coming down through the throng from communion, a surprising flood of emotion came over me, including all the hurt and all the jealousy I'd felt that long-ago summer's day when we were younger, swimming in the mill pond, when she had disappeared with the other fellow and the girls had come running to tell me, "Shhh! Angela and Nipper are kissin', up there lying among the ferns." I went numb with anguish at the time, and now, back again in the choir, I was overwhelmed at the sight of her and with the emotion of homecoming and midnight mass and the smell of incense, the sound of the Latin, and the rise and swell of the old familiar hymns.

Maybe it was because we were only steps away from the church, but, more likely, because Mammie Clancy was the epicenter of so many people's lives, the house was always full of people after mass, not just at Christmas but any Sunday of the year. Our neighbors across the street, the old maids Agnes and Ellie Verrington, used to laugh about it. One Sunday after mass our little cat was stranded out in the street, terrified, and Agnes had tried to let it in. The house was so full she couldn't open the door wide enough even to put the cat in.

But tonight they were all there, my sisters and their husbands, Aunt Alice and Uncle Peter, and all the cousins, the McGraths and the Drohans and the Lanigans. The ham was cut and the sherry was opened (whiskey for the men, lemonade for me), the fire was stoked, and soon the songs and stories began.

It was a Christmas of plenty. But the highlight as usual was the fun of the "wran day," St. Stephen's Day, December 26. No one knows where the ritual of killing the wren, the smallest and most innocent of birds, with its attendant wild pageant, started. Most probably in pre-Christian Celtic culture, but it had been given a Christian slant by telling how the wren had led the soldiers to Jesus as he hid in the garden of Gethsemane. The fun and celebrations carry on to this day without, I'm glad to say, the killing of the wren, although that was still done when I was a child. I remember one year when I was very small Bobby and his gang scouring the hedgerows of the "nun's fields" until they killed the poor little thing. The ceremony then was to tie the body of the wren (colloquially pronounced *ran)* in the middle of a holly bush all festooned with ribbons and colored paper, deck yourselves out in straw costumes (or women's clothes), disguise your faces with boot polish or makeup, and parade the wran from house to house singing, playing, and dancing and collecting money or imbibing in free drink. That year I remember coming down in the morning and finding the floor of the kitchen all covered with feathers. The cat had eaten the wren during the night.

We continued the fun the year I came home from America, but now we took the holly bush around in a car, not from house to house, but from one little country pub to another, singing the wran song in each one:

> The wran, the wran, the king of all birds
> St. Stephen's Day was caught in the furze
> Although he was little his honor was great
> Jump up me lads and give us a treat.

> As I was goin' to Killenaule
> I met a wran upon the wall
> Up with me wattle and knocked him down
> And brought him into Carrick Town.

"Dreoilin, dreoilin, where's your nest?"
"'Tis in the bush that I love best,
'Tis in the tree, the holly tree
Where all the boys do follow me."

Up with the kettle and down with the pan
And give us a penny to bury the wran.

We never missed the wran day. Years later, living in New York, the McCourt brothers and ourselves (and whatever bemused Greenwich Villagers we could gather up) would deck ourselves out. I remember Malachy McCourt in a ground-length black fur coat, going from pub to Irish pub up along Third and Second Avenues singing "The Wran, the Wran" to curious drinkers, who asked, "Is this Halloween? Am I that drunk?" and collecting money for UNICEF, the United Nations Children's Fund. We even showed up at Conor Cruise O'Brien's house, in a mews [alley] off Fifth Avenue, one Stephen's night, but there was no response to our knocking or serenading. Politicians are like that.

The meanest months of the year, January and February, were a torture to me. I felt useless again and I was penniless. My future looked as bleak as the endless days of rain and darkness that hung about the lanes and streets of Carrick. Only the glow of love for Angela and the nights of camaraderie at the pantomime kept me from trying to escape back to America, a thought that became ever more attractive.

My mind and my soul were in torment: I was in a spiritual vacuum. All the simple, unquestioning beliefs I'd lived with all my life were coming unstrung. Until they were resolved in my head I couldn't pretend. What I realize now in my sixties that I could not know in my twenties was that there *is* no resolution. The big world was making me ask questions I had never asked, or thought of asking, in the cozy little town of Catholic, bell-tolled Carrick that I'd left just last January, the Carrick that had been a haven of rightness in the nonquestioning, warm huddle of family.

It would be comforting to bask in that forever, but the press of curiosity, the engine that pushes life on, is unrelenting in its thrust.

In New York, Tradition Records was up and running, and *The Rising of the Moon* album was selling well. Paddy wrote to me suggesting we make another album, this time of drinking songs. He'd send me the money to fly over. I could do the recording and then work at Tradition's office editing the new albums for release while I was looking for acting jobs, the thing he knew my heart was set on. The letter was music to my ears and I booked a flight out to America for March 24. In the meantime I immersed myself in books, short stories, and plays.

When I read a character in the plays of Yeats or O'Neill or Shakespeare, I found myself living the part. No doubt it means something different to every actor, but to me it meant escape, as in a drug, of losing myself in a dreamworld where no one could reach me. On the stage, shielded by the character, as I had discovered when I played *The Playboy,* I could travel "every land my imagination knew," in the words of the poet Patrick Kavanagh.

In the midst of all these reveries, all the hours of questioning, questioning, of the shedding of the skin of former lives and beliefs, came the lonely turmoil of my mother's disintegration. In later years I would come to discover what hormonal changes could do to a woman's mind as well as body, but at twenty-one I knew nothing of all that.

There was a howling gale all that February. In the middle of the month the Redemptorist missionaries came to St. Nicholas' Church preaching about hell and damnation and the filth of sex. The town was thrown into a religious frenzy. I knew I had to get out of this place.

Something terrible had come over my mother. It frightened me.

One night when she came back from the church after one of the missionaries' fire-and-brimstone sermons, she pulled my head close to hers. She was trying to suppress some intense emotion. Her lip was quivering. Not since the night when she had told me of May's death had I seen that kind of look in her eyes, and it struck horror into me.

"You won't ever lose your faith, Willie boy, sure you won't? What curse is on America? A curse! That it lures ye all away and robs ye of the faith." An uncontrollable cry broke through her closed lips.

"I brought four sons into the world, and when Paddy was young I used to think, maybe he'll be a priest with the help of God. Imagine! Paddy a priest!

"Oh God, I'll never forget the first night Tom came in with the stench of drink off him. I was struck dumb. And him no age. All I could see was the leering old drunken men in the pub at home when I was a child and the black rim of stale porter crusted around their mouths, and the dirty talk of them.

"The nights I spent, couldn't sleep a wink until Paddy and Tom would come in. Every time I'd think of Tom with the glass of stout up to his mouth something awful would rise up inside me. That's how I'm left with the heat today, boy, the nights waiting for them fellas. And then when they were all gone off and I knew the kind of lives they were living, I used to say to meself, sure I have Willie left, anyway. He won't turn out like the rest of them. I thought you might even turn out to be a priest. You were me last hope, Willie boy. I tried to rear ye up for God and to be good Catholics. That's all I wanted. And God knows I've prayed. I'm worn out from praying. And there you are now, as bad as the rest of them. *Sha!* Willie boy! What did I do wrong? Where did I fail ye as a mother?"

The next day I tried to pretend, to myself and to my father and mother, that everything was normal. My father was all too familiar with the tension in the house and took the easy way out. In the afternoon he took one of his capsules, his "gobs" as he called them (I had to get them on the q.t. from the back door of the chemist shop for him), and sent himself into a state of oblivion for a few hours.

A little while later I heard my mother, also taking to her bed, talking to herself: "It is a kind of sickness, boy." She climbed the stairs slowly. "A strange sickness."

· · ·

In the small room in the half-dark, scales of gray light lay on the tossed papers on the big mahogany table. The fire was working up to a blaze at last. I had put paraffin oil on the dead ashes earlier, and a few flames flapped now like little flags. Outside I heard the dull thud of children's running feet on the concrete and heard the twilight sound of their voices as they ran up to Paulie Stuart's sweetshop. The senses heighten in a time of crisis.

Above all, the great bell of St. Nicholas' Church went on relentlessly clanging, clanging. It had started when my mother had closed the stairs door: "It is a kind of sickness, boy."

I felt bad, as bad as I ever felt in my life. I sat upright on the upholstered chair before the fire and felt the eighteen clangs of the evening's Angelus bell burn such an imprint on my soul that I will never be able to forget the torment of those minutes. Even then I knew that this inevitable law of nature was one of the bitterest I would ever have to obey: the law of change, change that tears apart the bond of mother and son.

My flight to New York was booked for Sunday evening. Bobby was driving me to Shannon. Kevin Driscoll was coming to keep Bobby company on the return journey. On Sunday morning no word passed between my mother and me as I washed and got ready. She had the breakfast all ready, eggs boiled and all. The tension was unbearable. Then she went upstairs. Bobby and I went for a silent drive out to the peaceful mill pond of Kilonerry just to gaze into the water and reflect. When we came back, my mother had left the house. That was the last I saw of her before leaving, and I couldn't help thinking that maybe it was the last time I would ever see her.

We went to my sister Peg's house. She burst into tears when I went in the door and she held her forehead against mine for a long time. I said good-bye to her and good-bye to Joan. My sisters were always together at such times. We all cried.

"Mammie is asleep at my house," Joan said. " 'Twill be easier if you just go."

I went.

15

On *March 24, 1957, I arrived back* at Paddy and Betty's apartment at 240 West Tenth Street in Greenwich Village and began my adult life. I was destitute as usual but brimful of ambitions and romantic notions. However, I couldn't keep sponging off Paddy, so he arranged for me to set up a tab at the White Horse Tavern, where he and Tom had been regulars for the past couple of years and where we'd had many a singing session after rehearsals for *The Rising of the Moon* album. Old Ernie the German was the gruff but big-hearted owner. Hamburgers and beer became my staple diet, frothy beer, the first alcoholic drink I'd ever had since taking the pledge at my confirmation to abstain from the stuff for life. Here I was at the White Horse Tavern, where Dylan Thomas had taken his last drink a short time before. I was having my very first drink at the same bar counter.

Tom was acting on Broadway at the time, in Orson Welles's production of *Othello,* and after the play at night he'd head for the White Horse. We'd get together in the back room and the singing would start. But in the meantime I had to find a way to make a living.

One day at the Tradition Records' office I was puttering around editing tape when the phone rang. Paddy talked to someone for a few minutes and I heard him say, "I'm sure he'd love to play Aleel. Why don't you ask him yourself? He's standing right here." What a shock. "Here, take it. It's the director of the Poets Theater in Cambridge. Michael somebody or other—take it!"

I had always wanted to play the part of Aleel in *The Countess Cathleen.* During the recording we'd made of the play I was a bit dismayed by John Neville's reading of the part. He didn't seem at all comfortable with it himself. He was a very well trained Old Vic actor, but he'd never been lost in the Celtic mists of Yeats's poetry as I had. Those mists were in the marrow of my bones. And I knew the play by heart.

"Hello?"

"Hello. My name is Michael Linenthal. I just spoke to your brother Tom." His voice was soft, Harvard, cultivated, with a definite theatrical inflection.

"Tom played here at Poets, as you know, in Molly Howe's adaptation of *Finnegans Wake.* He was so marvelous. We all wanted him so badly for the part of Aleel, the poet in *Countess Cathleen,* which is in production at the moment. I'm afraid the Aleel we had was so abysmally bad that Molly said get rid of him, you have to get Tom Clancy! But now Tom tells me he's in the Orson Welles production of *Othello* on Broadway which is *marvelous* for him. But we're so excited now that you've arrived in America. Tom has been telling us all about you, what a wonderful actor you are, so young and yet two years with the Abbey Theatre. My Gawd, we're all so excited!"

I looked at Paddy in dismay. What the hell had Tom been telling them? Tom was never one to let the truth interfere with the business at hand, but how would I tread my way through this minefield? What history had he concocted for me that might trip me up at any time?

"When would you need me?"

"Dear boy, on the last train! We're desperate! But you've missed that one, so let's see . . . you could be on the two-ten and be in South Station in time for me to take you to the symphony. I'm sure you love classical music, Tom told me! Well, I have tickets for tonight."

"How will I know you?"

"You can't miss me, dear boy. I'll be the only man on the station platform brave enough to wear a long fur coat. Oh, and I'm somewhat balding and my right eye is a bit funny. There's a room at my house for you, dear boy, not to worry."

I worried.

There was no mistaking Michael when the train jolted to a stop at the South Station platform. Poor Michael, as I would later come to think of him, stood out from the crowd, all right, a bald, walleyed bear with a great, shining, ground-length fur coat. To him I must have looked the picture of the young country greenhorn, because he walked straight up to me, gave me a limp hand, and in that soft, arched, cultivated voice of his, slightly tinged with some inner sadness, said, "You must be dear Liam. I'm so glad. I feel sure now all will be well. Do you like the symphony? I have tickets for us, as I told you, dear boy. We shall snack on the way."

I wondered again what Tom could have told him; did Michael think I was a cultured city aesthete? The Abbey Theatre and all that. How would I bluff my way through this one?

I don't remember much about the music, just the vastness and formality of the hall and all the dressed-up people who clapped and clapped and then clapped some more each time the orchestra finished a piece, and I remember the embarrassment and cringing discomfort of my feeling of foreignness in their company. Little did I realize then that one day the Clancy Brothers and Tommy Makem would be the ones on that stage singing to packed, wild houses and fanatical young men hoisting crates of beer up onstage—their antics finally getting us barred from appearing in Symphony Hall for years.

Michael took me to his parents' home in Cambridge after the concert. He was an only child. His parents greeted me in a very polite and somber way—with a certain apprehension, now that I look back on it.

Over tea Michael droned on and on about the play, his sad strange eyes roaming the walls and ceiling, talking of the "problems" and the "Poets" and Molly, Molly, Molly, as if I should know this woman Molly, who grew to immense proportions in my imagination as I listened to Michael for the next two hours before I finally got to bed.

I slept fitfully, with dreams of all the turmoil at home weaving and twisting in my head.

Next morning we had a tense breakfast served by a middle-aged woman with a thick Galway accent. I didn't much relish the thought of living in another troubled house, but it looked like that would be my lot for the time being. I wrote home to let them know that I had a job and to try and smooth things over. A little while later I got a letter back that put my mind somewhat at ease.

> *William St.*
> *Ck on Suir*
> *April 17th '57*

Dear Willie

During the course of conversation with Bobbie he told me I made a statement before you went away, that meant that if you and he went to Mass ye could do whatever ye liked after. Well in the name of God, I ask you, did ye think I didn't care if ye were sinners for the rest of the time— when I say "do what you like after" I meant that you'd enjoy yourselves as I always wanted all of you to do, boys and girls. I know I have a great many faults, but that's not one of them, that I wanted ye to be hypocrites. I thought if you went to Mass it would help in the fight against the weak-ening of your Faith. We all must fight for it some time or other. Think of the fight our forefathers made for it.

Well any way Willie I'm sorry for the very bad opinion you have of me, but nothing can be done about it.

I hope you are not lonesome away from Paddy and Betty, Tom and Laine and your friends. I hate to think of you being lonely or unhappy. I love you boy and I wanted very much to make your visit home very happy but I failed forgive me, Willie I can't write any more God bless.

An hour later and I feel better after a good cry, but its just plain lonesomeness, will you write and don't mention religion. I don't want to hear or say any more about it again.

Diane left for N.Y. on Sunday. She brought us so many presents from Italy I asked her if she left anything there after her. She liked the new kitchen. May God bless her she's a darling. Good life, love and more love.

Mammie

The morning after I arrived in Cambridge, Michael took me to the Poets Theater. I don't know what I expected, but this wasn't it. It was a tiny space up a flight of steep stairs in an old warehouse at 29 Palmer Street, Cambridge. There was a small stage and seating for about forty-five people, the seats at a slight rake. It was a goodly size place for poets, I suppose, in Harvard's vast academic complex. Yes, a tiny place—but what a cast of characters inhabited its little world.

Michael took me down the stairs and across an alleyway to a kind of antique or bric-a-brac shop, dark and musty and chaotic. A glimmer of fire glowed back in the depths of the clutter and Michael called out, as if to the darkness, "Morris, come and meet our Aleel."

I heard a quavery laugh and a faltering step and then from behind an ancient couch emerged a little bald, potbellied man, straight out of *A Christmas Carol,* dressed in Dickensian clothes with a fob watch chain across his greasy waistcoat, his cheeks round and rosy, his small eyes laughing out of a jolly face. Chuckling, he came toddling toward us out of the inner dark. He was Morris Pancoast, pushing eighty years, and every time I saw him, and I would see quite a lot of him over the next two years, he was laughing. Morris's shop was also his living room, with a fireplace at the far end and a big collapsed couch in front of it, oft used by courting couples. His toilet was also the only toilet available to the theatergoers as well as to the cast. Various mirrors of all sizes, shapes and periods were our makeup mirrors, and the entire shop was our dressing (and undressing) room, to Morris's great delight, at least when it came to the girls. I came to love him dearly, as did everyone who ever knew him.

The following day we got our scripts, and the cast started reading their parts together at a local restaurant, Chez Dreyfus, which was managed by a man who loved plays but whose name I can't recall, who loved the "poets" and loved Molly Howe. I had not yet met Molly; she was in New York visiting her sister-in-law Helen Howe. In back of the dining room Chez Dreyfus had a function hall which wasn't in use during the day, and there we paced out our small stage space and, with script in hand, started to tentatively block out the action of the play with Michael directing. I hardly needed a script since I knew most of the play by heart, and as we went through rehearsals the beauty of the poetry flowed over me again. I've never been able to understand the relative indifference of scholars to Yeats's plays as opposed to his poetry.

> —there is a kind of joy
> In casting hope away, in losing joy,
> In ceasing all resistance, in at last
> Opening one's arms to the eternal flames,
> In casting all sails out upon the wind;
> —full of the gaiety of the lost—

Much of Yeats's dramatic vision of what he called "tragic joy" is in the plays, as are some of his most vivid images:

> The years like great black oxen tread the world,
> And God the herdsman goads them on behind,
> And I am broken by their passing feet.

The Countess Cathleen is a very moving, passionate play about a noblewoman who sells her soul to save a starving people during a time of famine. Not a rehearsal or a performance went by but my cheeks were wet with tears and goose bumps out on my arms by the end of it. Living day after day in this frame of mind, and considering the emotional roller coaster I'd been on, between the trauma with Diane and the gut-wrenching parting with my mother, it's easy to see that I was ready to fall madly in love.

A few days after rehearsals started, Molly Howe returned from New York, and a small party was arranged at the big, rambling house on Highland Street, a street lined with massive old trees. When Michael and I got there, Molly was holding forth from a big armchair by the fire in the spacious, book-lined living room. She was in full flight, telling ghost stories, and Michael and I hung back in the doorway so as not to interrupt. I watched this woman about whom I'd heard so much.

She had a presence. There was an aura of glee about her. Her eyes were full of life and devilment. Her face was a tangle of laugh lines that told of a lifetime of seeing delight and humor in the world around her. Her voice had a soft but compelling Anglo-Irish music to it. She had written a play for the Gate Theatre in Dublin when it was under the management of Hilton Edwards and Micheal MacLiammoir, the most outrageously camp theatrical couple in all of Britain, and Ireland, and it seemed to me that some of MacLiammoir's dramatic style had rubbed off on Molly. Or perhaps it was the other way around.

We caught her eye and she leaped from her chair with amazing energy for a woman her size and greeted us effusively.

"Ah, you must be Liam. My Gawd! You're the image of Tom. You could be twins except you're much younger and taller than he is. I hear you're wonderful as Aleel. I've had great reports from Michael and Peter Carnihan. Oh, I'm so relieved. That chap we had cast in the part, dear Lord, not an idea did he have of the part. Yeats would turn in his grave, not an ounce of poetry in the poor fellow's body. That's why I thought of Tom. Oh, Tom was so wonderful as Shem, the last production we did, you know, *The Voices of Shem.* Joyce is so wonderful when he's read aloud by the right people. I always felt that *Finnegans* was intended to be read aloud. It all begins to make sense when you hear it."

Then she did one of her ninety-degree turns. "Have you met my daughters? This is Susan, the eldest. You must have heard of Sukey from Tom and Paddy, Provincetown Playhouse, summer theater, the O'Neill plays, all that. And this is the youngest, Helen, and Fanny the middle one, where's Fanny? Fan! Oh, Fan!" she shouted. Fanny, a seventeen-year-old, blond, shy, lovely mouse, came bouncing down the stairs with an armful of schoolbooks and said, "Hi." That's all. "Hi." And I was in love.

Molly Howe had come over from Dublin as Mary Manning with a touring group from the Abbey Theatre back in the thirties and stayed on in Boston to marry Mark DeWolfe Howe, a law professor at Harvard. Two more opposite personalities would be hard to find. Molly, childlike in her enthusiasms, ebullient, laughing, outrageous; Mark, serious and retiring. I can't recall ever seeing him smile. But it worked. They had a great house, always full of life. If Mark objected to the carryings-on, he never showed it. In my brief conversations with him all I gathered was that Oliver Wendell Holmes loomed large in his life.

Molly also had a lifelong friendship and correspondence with Samuel Beckett. His desolate view of life, at least as expressed in his work, is so at odds with Molly's insatiable optimism that their relationship is even harder to fathom than that between her and Mark.

On the following Thursday, I started the serious work on the part of Aleel, without the script. I immediately felt at home with the cast and the stage crew. They were as insecure as I was in a new venture, I realized. Very soon I saw that they all relaxed when it became apparent that I was bringing a sense of Irish authenticity to the production. I was very flattered when the stage manager, Peter Carnihan, advised me to become a full-time actor.

Michael Linenthal was astute in his directing of the play, but also in his observations of the interaction between the players and the crew. He saw the chemistry between Fanny Howe and myself. Fanny was the assistant stage manager, so we saw a lot of each other.

"She's a very sweet girl and she's in love with you, child. When you saw the other girl home the other night, I saw tears in her eyes."

I met her the following day and, for some reason, we walked silently together through the graveyard near Harvard Square.

She was seventeen and there was an empathy between us that needed no words.

Throughout rehearsals I stayed at the Linenthals' house, and in my many long talks with Michael I discovered that he was a very different person from the seemingly self-confident eccentric on the railway platform in the fur coat on that night I arrived in Boston.

One night he was talking about being in love and about Fanny and me when out of the blue he said, "I like a pretty boy as well as the rest." I thought it sounded funny. Later he said, with that wistful look he had, "Remember I told you about being in love? It was a boy in England. It was the only time I was ever in love, and I shall always love him. Does that shock you?" In a way it did, but I said, "No. But I just don't understand."

"Well," he said in a more frivolous tone, "some like chocolate and some like vanilla."

Love, I believed, was more important than sex to him. He had principles but he'd been a victim. He was very wise, I thought, and understanding. He talked to me a long time about my folks at home, how I must have felt arriving in Cambridge, and what a culture shock it must have been.

"No matter how understanding people are, you need somebody who speaks your language, who grew out of the same sort of background. Even if their ideas are different, at least they've deviated from the same norm."

Michael had a great understanding, but expressing himself sometimes didn't come easy. He confided in me completely. I suddenly felt very ashamed of my lack of concern and understanding of what he was going through. He said he felt very tense since his parents had come home.

"I have no money. I am dependent on them and they in turn are overconcerned about me. I want to be independent, financially and emotionally, so as to write and make something of myself, but the struggle to get that independence without hurting my parents takes all my energy and I can't do anything else. It's become my life's work. I can't smile. I find it physically impossible. And I can't look at people. Did you notice this eye goes way off when I'm tense? You're the kind of person that people want to give jobs to. Don't you find things opening up for you? For me, they don't. I'm special. At this stage I will only do certain things."

"Well, you always seem so self-sufficient and I always look kind of helpless," I told him.

"That's not quite it," he said. "There are some people that it's just nice to have around. They're light and cheerful. I'm either of two things: very serious, or a buffoon. And when I'm a buffoon, it's to cover up my seriousness."

Poor Michael. He was so right about himself. The pity is that he didn't realize how talented he was as an artist. He created beautiful pieces in metal and enamel filigree. If he had cut loose from his parents and moved to Greenwich Village, he would have blossomed. But as it happened he lived in the wrong place at the wrong time.

One Sunday morning, or rather afternoon, he showed up in the kitchen with two black eyes and his face a mess. He was too weak and distraught to even attempt to tell me what had happened. Fortunately his parents were away again. It emerged later that he had gone to the Boston docks area on Saturday night and some sailors had beaten him up and left him in the street.

Molly thought it would be better all round if I moved. The Howes fixed up a place in their attic for me. Once more I was living in the garret.

16

One day while I was having a free coffee in the restaurant part of Chez Dreyfus, the phone rang at the front desk, and after a pause, the receptionist looked down at me and asked, "Are you Liam Clancy? There's a call coming in for you from Italy."

When I picked up the phone, I heard, barely recognizable, Diane's voice. She was shouting over a bad international connection, trying to be heard.

"Willie? Sorry, Liam? I keep forgetting. Diane here. I'm calling from Florence. Can you hear me? Can you meet me for lunch on Thursday? I'm so confused. I need to talk to you. I met a wonderful singer, Mario is his name, Mario Polidori, he's just a wonderful singer. He has beautiful songs, Neapolitan songs. I like him very much but I don't know what to do. I think I am still in love with you. I just have to know. I'm so confused. I think I love Mario as well. Could you meet me on Thursday? What's a good place? That place I tracked you down? Chez Dreyfus? I'll be there. Don't worry about trying to meet me off the train or anything. I'll take a taxi to the restaurant. One-thirty Thursday. Good-bye."

I suppose I should have been flattered, but I was just confused by the squandering of money that I could have used for food.

And she did meet me on Thursday. She took a train from Florence to Rome, flew to New York, took a five-hour train ride to Boston, taxi to Cambridge, to have lunch! To find out if she was still in love with me.

She met me at Chez Dreyfus and her first words were, "I can't stay long." She talked for an hour, nonstop. Somewhere in the monologue I realized that I was really just a substitute for her psychotherapist.

"Willie, Liam. I'm so confused. I went to Florence with Harry, Harry Jackson. He's casting one of his sculptures there in bronze. Beautiful sculpture of a cowboy's burial, *Streets of Loredo,* all that." Her eyes were sad and distant. "I met Mario. I told you on the phone. You'd love him. He sings wonderful Neapolitan songs, plays beautiful guitar." Her eyes came to life.

"He's wonderful. I think I'm in love with him. But I still love you. It's so hard. I love you in a different way. Can you understand that? But I know you don't want me, so that's that. Liam, you have so much charm, you must learn to control that. You're going to break so many hearts and probably your own. I probably shouldn't tell you this: I took Mario to Ireland. Are you shocked? I took him to Carrick. Did your mother tell you? I asked her not to. He met Mammie and Daddy Clancy in William Street. When I went in, your mother burst out crying. But she's better now. We cooked an Italian meal for her. Your father and she drank a whole bottle of chianti between them." She laughed. "Can you believe it? We had a great talk. She talked about you all the time, how sorry she was for all that happened between you. She's so guilty. She thinks she's driven you away forever. 'He's probably better than myself,' she says. 'I know he's not hypocritical and I admire him for it.' Bobby and Mario really hit it off. Mario asked him to come back to Italy with us. They're there right now. Paul Clayton, too, the three of them are probably having a great old time. I think they went to Rome on a skite, as you'd say. They're like little boys."

Suddenly she looked at her watch. We were only halfway through lunch, but I could see that our psychiatric session was over. She was very happy. She was in love with Mario. It was all resolved. Her conscience was at ease. In her head she was already back in Italy. Now she had to quickly get her body there. She couldn't eat any more lunch. She had to catch a train. Stay and finish my lunch. She'd pay.

She left me with a parting shot that set me back on my heels. "I've been thinking about this and there's something I'd like to do for you if you'll let me. I know you love film. You have great integrity and wisdom beyond your years. I know you love the French film directors. Would you accept a gift from me? I'd like to pay for a year in Paris for you. Nothing fancy, I can't afford it; but an apartment, living allowance, a scooter to get around on. And whatever it takes to have you study with whatever director you choose."

It was a sincere offer, a true patronage, and I thanked her for it although I was totally taken aback by it. But it was an offer I just couldn't accept. Not that I felt ungrateful. Diane had been more than generous, not just to me, but to many people I knew, including some of my family. However, I knew that I could never feel a true sense of accomplishment in anything I did unless it was off my own bat. If my fortunes were going to rise it would have to be on the buoyancy of my own vision.

Diane took a taxi to South Station, a train to New York, a plane to Rome, and a train to Florence. Now she could meet Mario as a lover with a load lifted from her mind. Not too long afterward, back in New York and in Deep River, Diane, Mario, and I could and would become the best of friends. A load lifted from me, too.

The play opened and Fanny and I were together all the time now. Love blotted out everything else. I was happy. I loved acting even though it was hard, hard for an amateur to find some consistency of performance. One night would be great, the next night it could all fall apart. Little things caused huge distractions, like the shoes of the people in the front row sticking in under the curtain onto the little stage. You're trying to get inside the skin of a strolling player of the Middle Ages and all these modern shoes are looking up at you moments before the curtain creaks haltingly across.

Opening night coincided with Morris's birthday, and Fanny and I were going to his party. We were at that stage in a romance where jealousy over previous loves creeps in. As we were leaving the theater after the play, two fellows came over and started to talk to Fanny, Harvard chaps in a convertible. Posh. My inborn inferiority complex came bounding out. One of the chappies was trying to put his arm around Fan; they were trying to force her into a car. When I came over, one said, "Ho! To the rescue!" I said, "What's wrong?" and put my arm around Fanny. She in turn put her arm around me. The fellows jumped into their fancy car and drove off. Back at the party she was trembling like a leaf.

There were three cakes for Morris on his eightieth birthday. Fanny and I gave him a radio. When he came tottering in while we all sang "Happy Birthday," he didn't know quite what to do. He either had to cry or bluff his way through. He bluffed, in a charming, childish fashion.

Fanny and I left early and sat on the porch at her house. I hugged her very tightly. My love for her hurt.

"I feel like fathering you tonight," I said.

"I'm glad." We sat for a long time in silence.

"About that fellow tonight. Tell me about it."

"There's nothing to tell. I met him last summer when we worked in summer theater. Suddenly tonight he turned up drunk. He asked me to go to the Casablanca nightclub with him. He asked me back to his place. He tried to pull at me. He was drunk and he was driving. He might get killed."

I said, "I don't know. I just feel there's something, a barrier, between us. But we're being silly. Let's push it aside." So we did.

The following night, after a tense snack at the Linenthals', with Mrs. Linenthal hanging over us, we walked along by the river. It was one of those perfect evenings. The dusk began to thicken and there was a strange coloring in the sky, which was overcast with leaden clouds. A foreboding sort of red fell on everything. The air was hot. We sat down by the river Charles and watched the fish rising and threshing about just under the bank. A building on the other side of the river lighted up brilliantly, adding a further strange effect to the light. I took a drag on an imaginary cigarette and started to act like a tough guy with it. I sat apart from Fanny and she looked over and laughed.

For a moment I felt I was in Dublin. It was the coloring you see so often there, with the lights reflected on the Liffey from the far bank. I thought of Angela. I crawled over and sat beside Fanny, and a lovely feeling of peace fell upon my soul. The heat, the light, the sky, the warmth of love, life felt beautiful. I lay back and Fan lay back with her head on my arm and we made pictures in the clouds. I kissed her. She said, "It's wicked and stupid and naughty in public." I said, "I know, but the forces of nature are piled up against us and what can we do?"

"That's true."

The run of the play was coming to an end. But the Poets Theater wasn't just about the low-key productions at the little theater. There was old Harvard money available to help poets and playwrights get their work out to the public in larger theaters such as Sanders. There I heard e. e. cummings read his poetry and I ushered at a Marcel Marceau performance in order to see it for free. But during the run of *The Countess Cathleen* there was a production in the works of a play by Robert Penn Warren called *Brother to Dragons,* a kind of southern version of the Cain and Abel story to be staged at the cavernous Sanders Theater. I was asked to read the part of Isham for the author and he was obviously impressed by my southern accent (compliments of Uncle Dick Chase), because I got the part. Offers of acting jobs were starting to come in.

I felt lonesome finishing *The Countess Cathleen.* We recorded the play at a radio/television station in Cambridge. My last performance was the best because I loved every line; at the end the tears flowed down my cheeks. After the show, Basil Langton, the Shakespearean director, phoned me and asked if I was available to play Ferdinand in *The Tempest* in Virginia. I said yes.

Basil Langton, an actor and director, had spoken to me after the opening of *The Countess Cathleen,* sizing me up as an actor. At the time he asked a very interesting question: "Do you have the courage of failure?"

"What do you mean?" I asked him.

"Just that," he said. "Do you have the courage to get out onstage and face the fact that you may be a flop, that you may fall flat on your face, and still go on?"

I thought about that for a while.

"If I didn't, then I couldn't really be here."

He made up his mind. I got the job.

Robert Penn Warren came up to see his play, and after chopping and changing the script, we didn't know whether we were coming or going. After the rehearsal, Fanny and I went to a little coffee shop where folksingers got together. It was dimly lit, low-ceilinged, with almost all the yellow paint peeled off the walls and tables that had sketches on them made by customers. It was my first exposure to the new phenomenon called the sixties scene, the advent of what was to become the era of freedom, the era of so-called free love, an era when the individual, at least in America, first stood up and started challenging established authorities and hierarchies.

Fan and I walked home a new way. We felt happy. We danced along the street singing "Killyburn Brae," walking to the verse, "There was an old man lived in Killyburn Brae," then skipping to the nonsense line, "Right fol-right fol tiddy fol day."

The night was hot. We went into the Howes' kitchen and had strawberries and cream. Then I read the end of Synge's *Deirdre of the Sorrows* to her.

Molly came in and said Penn Warren thought I was very good, that I was a natural for the part on Broadway. Then she went off to bed. Fanny and I sat on the porch. The air was hot and there was a big yellow moon. I lay with my head on her lap. Fanny bent her head over my face to kiss me and her yellow hair fell like a curtain between me and the moon. It glistened in the diffused light and I thought of the Yeats line

> The shadowy blossoms of my hair
> Will hide us from the bitter storm.

That glow stayed with me all the following day on the long train ride to New York and yet another leap in the dark. Years later, Molly Howe described the little romance between Fanny and me to a friend of mine: "Sleeping in each other's arms on the front porch of the house on Highland Street, they were like 'babes in the wood.' " That was so true. Our physical love never went beyond sweet hugs and chaste kisses. It was all that our love demanded.

17

It was June 1957 and you could fry eggs on the shimmering car roofs in New York City. I had just returned from Virginia where I played in *The Tempest* with Basil Langton. Richmond was stifling, but it was a clean heat. In New York there was filth falling from the sky and everything was covered in a layer of grime. The noise came with the heat. Windows were open day and night. Nights brought car horns and anger and family squabbles into apartments all round. Smells of the Village, too, mostly Italian sausage, spicy and mouthwatering but too expensive for me, and even the smell made my ulcer scream. Mornings were the worst, when the garbage trucks set up their racket along Tenth Street with the shouts of the garbagemen and the banging of the garbage cans and that brain-piercing whine when the compactor went into high gear.

The Village doesn't have many happy memories for me at that time. The lovely madness hadn't started yet. The scene that was to be "the sixties" hadn't gotten into gear. The cogs hadn't meshed. But it had its moments. One evening the great Odetta phoned and invited me to a Bob Gibson concert at a church hall on Bleecker Street (she had just signed a recording contract with Tradition Records). I was shy about it, but what a thrill it was. It was also good to get away from the apartment for a space.

After the concert she and I went down the street to Izzy Young's Folklore Center, where the banjos and guitars were goin' at it. Paul Clayton was there singing whaling songs with his friend Jo El. It turned into a party, as it always did at Izzy's place. Odetta sang "The Lass from the Low Country," and Paul and I did some more sea shanties. I walked Odetta home and we had a long talk. She sang me some songs in that powerful voice of hers (even though she tried to sing sotto voce) that shook the walls of the hotel room as if they were the walls of Jericho. What a great woman!

Next evening Paddy and I had dinner with the singer Mary O'Hara, who had stolen every young man's heart back in Ireland when she performed. She was married now to a young New York writer, Richard Selig. They were so much in love it was a little embarrassing. They called each other "boney" (they were both on the skinny side) and pet names like that. I still remember the meal I had: snails and frogs' legs, a first for me. We swapped songs back at Paddy's apartment. I blushed to the gills when Paddy told Mary, to her great delight, of how I'd tried to write and ask her to record for Tradition Records when we first started the label. He told her about all the sheets of writing paper strewn around the apartment that had Dear Miss O'Hara on them and nothing more. Later we listened to a beautiful tape of Irish love songs she'd made for Decca Records. One of the songs she sang was "Ballinderry," which I had taught her over the phone.

'Twas pretty to be in Ballinderry
Pretty to be in Aghalee

'Twas prettier to be in bonny Ram's Island
Sittin' forever beneath the trees.
Ochone, Ochone
Ochone, Ochone.

She agreed to record an album for Tradition later on when she was free of her contract with Decca. I don't know if she or Richard knew at the time that he had terminal cancer.

She did make that album after his death. It must have been harrowing for her. She sang with beauty and control at those sessions, but between takes she'd go off alone for long periods.

When Diane came back from Italy with Mario, he and I hit it off. It didn't matter that we couldn't speak each other's language, we laughed a lot. Diane sent us off together and I took him around. He had the Italian obsession with big, fast cars. He specially loved Diane's big station wagon in which he tore up Fifth Avenue at high speed and then around Central Park as if it were a rally track. We bought strawberries at an Italian market and wolfed them down together while he rattled on in Italian to the gigantic proprietor. At night we went to the White Horse and sang and sang.

Bobby wrote from Ireland. Everything had eased up at home and all the tension had gone. Tom arrived back from his Irish trip with Laine heavily pregnant. Daddy Clancy had treated him like a little boy, he said. He thought Da's brain was gone but Ma was as sharp as a whistle.

Paddy, Betty, and the baby, and Diane, Mario, and I set off to Deep River to escape the heat. The atmosphere was much more relaxed now that Diane was happy and fulfilled. We all got along very well. Mario was picking up English at a rapid rate and having a lot of fun in the process. Often we'd fall around laughing, especially Carol and the Aiello girls, Binnie and Annette. Their father Lou, being Italian-American, got a great kick, of course, out of Mario's pronunciations.

On hot nights we'd go swimming in Cedar Lake by moonlight.

Mario would bring his guitar along and with the water warmer than the air and beautifully clear, the girls and I would swim out to the raft while Mario stayed on the little beach and sang Neapolitan songs to us. That was wondrous, swimming in the dark water, the moon, the heat, the Italian voice and guitar music floating over the lake.

Apart from cars, Mario loved guns, so we did a lot of shooting. We never killed anything, of course, but we worried the hell out of a lot of tin cans. Diane and Mario were full of puppy-love fun and I remember a lot of practical joking. I turned over in my new bed (a couch in the extension I'd painted) one night and found the end of a garden hose under the cushion. Straight off I knew their plan, to get up in the middle of the night and turn it on. I thought I'd turn the tables on them, and when they were sound asleep in their double bed in the next room, I crept in and put the hose under their blanket. They never woke up to turn the water on and neither did I, so the trick backfired all round.

The girls slept in a cabin near the house. Mario took to serenading them under their window or frightening them with firecrackers. Diane must have gotten a bit miffed, because one Sunday evening she announced, "Mario! Get your things together. We're going to New York. Right now!"

Little episodes like that made me realize the upside of still being a virgin. But how long can the "Luck of the Irish" hold out?

The summer went by back and forth between Deep River and Killingworth and New York, sometimes driving, sometimes by train. I always loved the evening train into the city, when it was a fairyland of lights in the twilight. It was so calm and innocent at this distance, the Empire State Building flinging its searchlight beams across the whole city, embracing it to its farthest limits. And way over, across the river, the twisted lights of the Palisades Amusement Park. Who'd ever guess the awful mess at its heart?

"Exterminator Maayn!" How I hated this guy! Why couldn't he come at a civilized hour, like late afternoon, when hangovers had eased? But no, the exterminator man was a sadistic New York institution who always showed up at the crack of dawn, when the head was pounding from the session in the White Horse the previous night. Not only that, but he had to have access to your apartment no matter how embarrassing the circumstances may be, and fill the place with the stench of chemicals that did God-knows-what to your lungs.

The cockroaches got so bad in the apartment buildings on Tenth Street that the landlord decided to fumigate all the properties he owned along the block. Paddy decided it was time for us to take a trip to Vermont, to the farmhouse in the hills owned by Betty's mother. It was a welcome escape to the woods and the wild. When we came back to the city a week later, the exterminators were still taking out the cockroach bodies by the bucketful.

I spent my days mostly doing bits and pieces at the Tradition Records office, working on the Irish tapes and fetching coffee and sandwiches at lunchtime. Hot pastrami sandwiches, *the* taste of New York to me, made by the short-order cook at the greasy spoon down the street, whose movements were pure ballet to watch. At night we'd go to the White Horse and sing with the regulars: Greg Zilbourg of the big walrus mustache, the mechanically inclined son of an eminent psychiatrist; our two tone-deaf lawyers, Joe Muraskin and Hilda Pollack; our three filmmakers, Murray Lerner, Ernie Nukanen, and Dick Bagley; plus the girls known as the "four virgins." Our close friend, Richard Farina, the poet/singer/revolutionary, was a regular, and we had our own personal psychiatrist, Dr. Mick Hill, Diane's former lover.

Bernice, my diminutive drinking pal at the White Horse, joined me at the public swimming pool on Hudson Street sometimes on hot days, or we'd go up to Central Park to watch rehearsals for "Shakespeare in the Park" in the evenings. One night, after a singing session at the pub, big Greg Zilbourg got a savage beer hunger at about one o'clock in the morning and decided that we should all go to Hong Fat's in Chinatown. Bernice, Mary Ann, Greg, and I took a cab. We were feeling frisky after a night of beer and Chinese food and Greg and I tossed Bernice between us on the way home. Later, Bernice and I ended up in the sack together and my virginity came to a clumsy and rather messy end, at last.

My career as a filmmaker was not to be. "Wicked John" would stay half finished in the can. Paddy went to Venezuela on a diamond-hunting expedition funded by a Wall Street guy. It was illegal to take diamonds out of Venezuela, so it was set up under the guise of a documentary film shoot about a pygmy tribe in some remote part of the Amazon. Ernie Nukanen was to be the main cameraman, with Paddy and me as his assistants. I was given the heave-ho for budget reasons, which was just as well. For one thing they were damn lucky to get back from the jungle alive, and for another I got a call to go back to the Poets Theater to play the lead in three Yeats plays.

When Paddy got back from Venezuela, he brought some truly incredible film footage with him. The tribe, he pronounced it Mykeery-tarry, were not only pygmies but also cannibals. Fortunately for the expedition members they had no taste for white meat. They ate only their enemies, and, rather gruesomely, their own dead. The tallest ones were barely up to Paddy's waist and they had huge protruding bellies. Paddy also brought back some of their bows and arrows, which were marvels of craftsmanship. In addition he brought a blowpipe and poison darts, which caused a huge fight when I blew one of the darts, gently I thought, at a windowpane. It didn't break the window and kill anyone on the street, but the dart itself did peel apart like a banana skin. The bore of the blowpipe was as straight as a rifle bore; strange that the technology these little people had should be so highly perfected and yet they hadn't discovered the wheel. But who needs a wheel in the jungle?

For a long time after he returned, Paddy was in a foul mood and the shouting matches in the office became unbearable. I was very glad when the time came to head for Cambridge, old friends, and Mr. Yeats.

I arrived in Cambridge in late October to start work on the three Yeats plays. In *On Baile's Strand* I played the part of the Fool, in *Words upon the Windowpane*, Corbet, and the Stroller in *King of the Great Clock Tower*. I got a bed once again in Molly Howe's attic. Fanny was away at college, but when she'd come home for a visit we'd chat like old friends. The romance was gone. The friendship lasts to this day. Loves come and go. Angela was never far from my thoughts. First love has staying power because it hits you at a time when your life is at the peak of its intensity. We move on, like it or not.

There was a new cast, apart from Michael Linenthal, new friends to be made, including Tina, the lighting girl.

Trying out for the part of Cuchullain's son in *On Baile's Strand* was a young man named Doug Anderson. He was eighteen years old, striking-looking with blond hair sticking out. He followed me around all evening and then suddenly disappeared. Next day he was back at the Poets and he got the part. He told me he was getting married at Thanksgiving because his girlfriend was pregnant. He was a wild, very emotional, nervous youth with down on his jaw. Outspoken and good-natured, he and Tina and I became good buddies. We hung out a lot together, mostly at Morris Pancoast's curio shop. Since none of us had any money that was one of the few places we could go for free. Besides, there was always a fire burning in the old grate. I recall bringing Morris to a play one night, *Antigone* it was, on a mover's dolly. I can't remember where the hell we got the dolly but Morris's legs were bad and he wanted to come to the play with us. He laughed all the way. At eighty he was still game for anything.

The following day Tina was still in the theater after rehearsals, so I asked her to have dinner with Doug and me since my tiny stipend had come through. We had a Chinese meal and then went to a movie, *The Third Man.* Later we had French toast (what luxury!) at the Waldorf Cafeteria surrounded by plastic flowers lit by a tungsten sun, and then walked Tina back to her dorm at Radcliffe. I kissed her goodnight. As we walked back to Harvard Square, Doug said, "She's a good girl. There's a girl could really love you. Sure, people take her out but nobody falls in love with her. It makes me feel sad." The following night the three of us went to Cronin's pub.

I got a day job at Widener Library in Harvard. The getting up early was hard (always had been), and eight hours a day was a very long time to be stuck in the stacks of books on sociology and economics, but the money augmented the pittance that the Poets Theater could afford to pay me.

As I was leaving work the first evening, a woman stopped me and said, "You're Liam Clancy, aren't you? I saw you in *Countess Cathleen* and *Brother to Dragons.*" That felt really good to be recognized as an actor.

. . .

I recall about that time a particularly wonderful evening of Dylan Thomas stories told by the Welsh actor Emlyn Williams at the Sanders Theater. It was a very moving, funny, and stimulating production. The opening and closing were particularly inventive. Williams came onstage with a sheaf of penny jotters, saying that Dylan Thomas wrote everything in longhand. He put the jotters on a high stool and proceeded to play all the parts of the characters within the covers of the slim volumes.

He ended the show with the poem "And Death Shall Have No Dominion," and as he slowly walked offstage, the lights dimmed until only a pin spot remained on the penny jotters, while from behind the scrim we heard the closing lines:

> Heads of the characters hammer through daisies;
> Break in the sun till the sun breaks down,
> And death shall have no dominion.

Life was good. I had a job in Widener Library, money, a girl, Tina and I were becoming very close, and each night I felt I gave a good performance. At the library I was transferred to the Slavic section of the stacks, so when things were slack I'd immerse myself in Stanislavsky, Tolstoy, and Dostoevsky. Happy days.

Not all the time, of course. At times I'd get depressed, nervous, and jumpy, almost frightened, after spending some time in intense thought. I learned to cast it off by sitting and playing the guitar for a while. One night before the show when I was feeling particularly down I tried the guitar cure. When I went onstage, something clicked. For the first time I came close to being consumed in my own feelings and reaching something resembling what I wanted to reach. For the first time I got the sense of control over my character, a command, a relaxation, and a true sense of timing. I could stand a little off and see what I was doing and have a quick enough reflex action to make myself do what I wanted. I came close to being the puppet and the puppeteer simultaneously, just what I'd always been striving for.

In addition to the guitar, I took to playing the tin whistle. With the dark days of November upon us, Doug, Tina, and I and, frequently now, Doug's friend Eben Given, who was to become such a close friend that I called my son after him, would gravitate to Morris Pancoast's tattery-arsed old shop each night after the plays. Morris loved the company. It was cozy there in front of the blazing fire, sitting on the broken-down couch while Morris dozed in his old armchair. We'd tell stories and play tunes, the firelight and the light of antique oil lamps casting shadows on the moldering collection of oddments which would never be sold. I'd tell tales of Cuchullain and Fionn McCool and the Fianna. Tales from Irish mythology. I'd describe climbing Slievenamon and the Comer-aghs, or recording music on the Aran Islands and the Hebrides. We'd have long young men's talks, full of the romance of things we'd love to do and places we'd love to go. Eben and Doug longed for a place where life is simple. Eben particularly was drawn to Ireland and Wales. His father, also Eben Given and also an artist, was a friend of Eugene O'Neill's on Cape Cod. We talked about children and fools, wisdom and knowl-edge, books and films. They were enthusiastic about the idea of an Irish film industry. I told them I thought it could be done, that Molly Howe had written a film script of Frank O'Connor's story "Guests of the Na-tion" for Dennis Johnston of Dublin's Gate Theatre, and they had really filmed it. We spoke of being terrorized by the mechanical feats of men and of the detail and human effort gone into even one motorcar, "those colored whores" as Eben called them. Cars *were* gaudy in the fifties, and huge! With their outrageous size and crazy-looking fins, they amazed me when I first saw them from the deck of the SS *Ivernia* at the quay-side in Halifax, Nova Scotia, when we briefly docked there on that first trip to America in 1956.

Perhaps the readings from "A Child's Christmas in Wales" at the Emlyn Williams production sparked it off, but I had a vivid, vivid dream of Christmas at home about that time. For days it kept coming back to me.

I saw the Christmas dinner things on the sideboard, among the cut glass bowl of peaches with the two plastic salad spoons, one broken. I saw the remains of trifle or jelly and the empty Orange Crush bottles from Paulie's. I saw the cut plum pudding and the rich cake with the almond icing that Jimmy and Lili had brought up in the blue van. It all became so clear: the lounge, the sideboard, Mammie and Daddy Clancy, Jimmy and Lili coming in and talking about what Peg did and what Joan did and how much fruit she put in the cake and the weight of the turkey and the "Oh listen, girl, wait till I tell ye what happened to me" and the "oh-ahs" and putting coal on the fire and the snuffbox on the mantelpiece. The feelings, too, of midnight mass: the clean, light feelings, the holiness, the closeness to God: I was so near Him. All I could say was, "O God, O God"; no more would come or need come because of the happiness and excitement and holiness. I could see Christy come and slip me five bob as the pals and I were checking how much money we had by the light of Felice's shop window, which was full of toys. And I would see Angela at mass and long to talk to her or just look at her. Colm Driscoll's clear tenor voice would be heard outside and the thud of feet on the concrete would sound dully through the floor and I would know that over there is the river Suir flowing dark through the arches of the old bridge and beyond the river to Peg's house with bright Christmas lights and a fire and Radio Eireann playing on the wireless. And beyond that, over the hill, was Ballyknock, where we used to shoot the rabbits. In the Comeragh Mountains, high in the deep glacial gouges, the black surfaces of Coumseangan Lake and Crotty's Lake are being shaken by lonely gusts of night winds, and the bleating of sheep and lambs is coming from the rocks and echoing back from the great cliffs. And Joan's house, bright and plentiful with food and Joan and Alice laughing, that's over there beside the "Burkie" House, as we called the old Burke asylum. Ballinurra and the woods and the woodman's hut are beyond. I could see again the night we walked back from there thinking about the fairies, and going to Leish's house under the hill. And over there is Slievenamon in the darkness, bare Slievenamon with the cairn on top and the cross with ice clinging to it.

For days I'd relive the images and then I'd remember I was in America. Millions of people around me who will never know what I know. And in a few hours now I will get up before an audience and people will see me be the Fool and be hungry and beat the Blind Man, but never will they know what's in the mind behind the white makeup and the raised eyebrows. And later I'll kiss a girl outside a college dormitory, lined up on the sidewalk with all the others getting a little love from a college girl. But even she can never know what's behind the lips that kiss her, what images are there, what longings, what memories, and what hopes.

Tina and I had been together a great deal before she went home for Christmas. At first she was very cold and unaffectionate with me, but that changed slowly. I realized from the beginning that nothing good could come from this, that as with the other girls I'd known, it would end in heartbreak. But I went on regardless and we were getting more and more used to each other, and more and more to need each other. Then when the play finished, we found ourselves on the first free night standing in the rain before the closed doors of Poets, both of us home-less, and Morris's closed. We laughed to keep from crying. We ended up at Dougle's apartment that night telling ghost stories. We went there several times after that, when Doug was away with his girlfriend, to be alone and just have tea, play the guitar, and kiss and cuddle.

The night before she left she became very emotional and told me how she hated Radcliffe. The dorm was driving her crazy (two girls had already gone to mental institutions from there). She spent all her time doing what would please her parents, pretending she liked it. She was worried about her own nature, the vividness of her imagination that she always had to fight against because of the strange paths it wanted to take. For several nights she had woken up to find herself out of bed and wandering around. The night before, she had found herself in the dark corridor. The reason was always the same. In her sleep she heard a knock on the door. When she opened it, someone was there, usually her aunt who had died the previous spring, telling her to come somewhere. She didn't know where, but she felt she must go.

This story worried me, so that night I stayed at Doug's apartment with her. She was completely exhausted and fell fast asleep. While Doug and I were talking she suddenly got up and went fumbling for the door, saying that someone was knocking. I forced her to sit down.

"Tina, Tina, there's no one there, there's no knock."

"But I heard it," she said. "I must open the door. Someone knocked. They want me to go with them."

We made coffee for her and forced her to walk around a bit. She became more rational.

"Where is it you want to go? Is it just to get away from here?"

"From Radcliffe and all it stands for, my parents, studying history."

"So you want to be free, to follow your own mind."

"Yes." She thought for a moment. "But I've already started, haven't I?"

"Yes, you're free, Tina," I said. "You're going to talk to your parents tomorrow. You don't have to go back to the dorm tonight. You've already answered the door and you're free."

She slept peacefully the rest of the night.

On Christmas Eve, Tina told me on the phone, "I'm not coming back anymore." She had told all to her parents and was going to New York to look for a job.

"Well, then, I'll see you in New York," I said. "I have a job offer to work on a film there after Christmas."

"You will?" she yelled with joy. She pleaded with me to tear up the letter she'd written me when I received it. I got it on Christmas Eve. Her comment on our innocent affair was, "Little one, this has only been another turn of the wheel for you but it has been so much more for me." She was now setting out alone for New York to face God knows what, very much afraid and without a thing in the world except her courage.

I was full of Christmas cheer as I took a trolley from Cambridge to Boston to wait for the train to Brattleboro. It was snowing heavily. I was excited about spending a Vermont Christmas with Paddy and Betty and little Leish, but I was also excited at the thought of meeting Tina in New York after Christmas. To my surprise I began to realize how very close we'd become in the last short time. I'd deeply miss this mysterious girl, with her straight black hair falling down below her waist and her long perfect legs, if I were never to see her again.

I decided to splurge with the last of my cash, so I put the train fare to Vermont in my left pocket plus four dollars emergency money and went to the Salisbury Steak House where I blew the rest on a big minced steak covered in their famous thick brown sauce. There was no reason to think there might be an emergency. I'd sent a card to Paddy and Betty in New York telling them I was taking them up on their offer to come to Vermont for Christmas at Betty's house in the woods near Townshend. It would be a great place to spend Christmas.

As I boarded the train for Brattleboro, the nearest train station to Townshend, I could visualize Paddy and the old VW Beetle waiting, snow-covered, at Brattleboro station. From there it was only nineteen miles to the old covered bridge at Townshend and then up the mile or so of dirt road into the wooded upland, and there at the crest of the hill was the house in the clearing. God, we'd had such good times there! Summer and winter. Now there would be a big blazing fire and the yellow glow of oil lamps and lots of glorious food.

Leaving the lights of Boston behind, the great warhorse of an engine plowed its way into the snowy dark woods of Massachusetts and Vermont using its great iron nose to push the deepening snow from the track. I wanted to forget for a while all that had happened in the last couple of weeks, so I lapsed into a reverie of the adventures of the summer when Paddy and I had gone deer stalking in the hills above the house. The house itself was a fairly typical turn-of-the-century New England house, but with a touch of money and class. It had no electricity or running water or flush toilet, but it had fireplaces and one big woodstove for heating and cooking. The oven in the woodstove could easily hold a large turkey, and the cast-iron top was designed to keep things warm or boil the devil out of them depending on where you put your pots. There was no shortage of wood to burn, and a clear, sweet stream flowed just a little way back in the woods.

The old house had its drawbacks. Being unoccupied for such long stretches, it had been home to the wild creatures of the woods for quite a while. The ornate furniture, fancy in its day, had been further carved up by some animal with chisel-sharp teeth. Under the back door a nest of copperhead snakes had taken up residence and you had to be sure to wipe the sleep from your eyes in the morning before you stepped out for a wash in the stream and a bucket of water for the breakfast.

The train pushed on through the dark, the glow from the windows lighting up the snow-laden branches as we sped past.

I started talking with a girl in the seat across from me who was heading home for Christmas. Our excitement, getting closer to Brattleboro and feeling the glow of the season, got us chatting like old friends. She told me all about college and her boyfriend and I told her all about the plays we were doing and my girlfriend leaving college because of the pressures.

"Yeah, it's really tough at times. That's why it's so nice to get a break like this. Gee, I can't wait to get home and see my folks an' all. My dad's picking me up but we still got a two-hour drive to our house. I sure hope the roads are not too bad."

"My brother is picking me up. We've only got nineteen miles to go, but I'm more worried about his old VW than I am about the roads. Still, the snow has been getting heavier the further west we go."

At Brattleboro station I went through the crowd of family reunions, looking for Paddy. There was no sign of him. I went outside. The roads were bad (the snow was really piling up at this stage), and I hoped he wasn't stuck in a snowdrift.

The station cleared quickly, except for my friend, who was sitting on her suitcase looking as forlorn as I was beginning to feel. An hour later it looked gloomy for both of us. She made a phone call, then came back smiling. "I called home. My dad left ages ago. He should be here soon. The roads must be really bad." Then she had a thought.

"Look, if your brother doesn't show by the time he comes, I'm sure my dad will drive you to Townshend. It's not on the way but it's not that far off. And it is Christmas. It would be awful to be stuck here for the night. Do you think your brother will show at this late stage?"

"No," I had to admit. "I've been thinking. I only sent the card a couple of days ago. I forgot about the Christmas logjam in the mail. I feel so stupid. I only now remember that he said he was coming up early to Vermont to get all the shopping done for Christmas. My card is sitting in his mailbox right now in New York and he has no idea I'm here."

"Don't worry. I'll sweet-talk my father. We'll get you home." I felt better. Peace on earth, goodwill to men.

Her father arrived at about 1 A.M. She winked at me and spoke earnestly to him as he got her luggage. He looked none too happy. His trip had obviously been grueling. There was smoke coming out his ears. He listened to her for a few minutes in disbelief as I saw her gesticulate.

He shot me a poisonous glance and I heard him say, "For Christ's sake, what do you think I am, a fuckin' taxi driver? Get in the car." She gave me a hopeless backward glance, held out her gloved hands in a gesture of despair, and left.

I was devastated. That a man could do that! On Christmas Eve. Goodwill to men? Bah, humbug.

But hurt and disappointment couldn't solve my problem of the moment. I was alone in the station. It was 1 A.M. The night porter had to lock up. "Can't stay here, son." No room at the inn.

"Is there a rooming house or someplace I could stay? I only have four dollars to my name."

"Well," he looked at me over his spectacles as he bundled up, "there is a place up the hill there that has rooms, if you can wake 'em up at this hour. Vermonters go to bed early, 'specially in wintertime."

At least my suitcase was light as I trudged up the hill slipping and sliding. It was still the brown cardboard suitcase I'd brought from Ireland.

The lady was up, all right, and yes, she had a room. Four dollars, up front. It was my emergency money and now I had the emergency. I gave a sigh of relief at the news that I'd have a warm room and a bed to sleep in tonight. I'd have to wait till tomorrow to see what Santy would bring. I stripped and went to the light switch at the door. I looked at the bed and took a mental compass setting of where it was, switched off the light, and ran for it.

Lying in the dark, shivering between the starched sheets, I thought of home and how my life had changed in such a short time. So many new experiences had come hurtling at me that it seemed like long ago. I drifted off with the pain of Christmas memories in Carrick burning me somewhere in my chest deeper than the acid in my gut.

The sheet was warming up now, but I shouldn't have thought of the Christmas food: one side of my stomach was trying to digest the other, and the ulcer pain was gnawing at me. Paddy would have some antacids tomorrow. Meantime think of home and say some prayers for all of them. Maybe in the morning I'd find a little Catholic church, but it wouldn't be the same. I couldn't pull the two parts of me together. This was Bing Crosby's "White Christmas," come to think of it, the only white Christmas I'd ever seen in my twenty-two years.

What Santy brought was a complimentary cup of coffee and a doughnut, and that was that. I set out on foot for Townshend, thinking I'd surely hitch a ride. Outside of town the road between the snowbanks narrowed to one lane. There wasn't a vehicle of any kind on the road. I trudged a mile or so, which took the best part of an hour. There was no feeling in my feet or hands. I could have sworn my nose and ears had fallen off. Things weren't looking good.

Then a car slowly and silently came up behind me.

"Need a lift? Ain't goin' far but the car's warm." It was a farmer. He had a small calf in the backseat. He took me another mile or so. The heat was glorious and the smell of the calf, his wide-eyed wonder, and his wet nose brought me back to Mrs. Prendergast's milking shed in Carrick. How I wished I was there now.

"This is as far as I go."

"Thank you. Merry Christmas."

"Ah-yeah," he replied, and turned off.

Now I was really stuck, out in the heart of the country and freezing to death. All I could think of was that bastard last night! I kicked a lump of ice and discovered I did have a toe. He doesn't deserve the lovely daughter he has. He doesn't deserve to be called a Christian. I rambled on like that in my head, using my anger to keep me warm.

Another car glided out of the whiteness and stopped. "Where are you headed for, son?"

"Townshend."

"Not goin' that far but I can take you a bit." He was an old-timer with skin like leather and a real Veh-mant accent.

"Thanks. I thought I was going to freeze out there."

"How'd you get yourself in such a predicament on Christmas Day?" I told him about the mix-up with my brother and how I had no option now but to get to Townshend however I could, even if I had to walk. He fell silent.

Two miles up the road he said, "Wish I could take you but here's where I live and the good wife has got the goose ready. Made me go into Brattleboro with some stuff for her sister. She gets awful mad if I don't eat when it's ready. 'Fraid I might stop in to my neighbor's for a little Christmas cheer and forget to come home. Can't blame her. It's happened. Wish I could help you." He shook his head. "Really wish I could."

"Thanks for the ride. It got me a little bit closer, anyway. Happy Christmas."

Alone on the road, the cold and despair really hit me. I could picture the goose and the cranberry sauce and the candles and the big blazing fire and his wife and children around him, if he had any. No way now would I get to Paddy and Betty's for dinner. I began to doubt if I'd get there at all. Try as I may, I couldn't hold back the tears. I was awash with self-pity. It felt good.

One foot in front of another, one foot in front of another, that's all I could do. "God is good and the divil is not that bad," as my mother used to say.

Fifteen minutes later I heard a car horn behind me. It was the same man who had just dropped me off.

"Get in," he said. "I just couldn't eat thinking of you on the road. What would they think back in Ireland if you went and told them a Vermonter had left you to freeze to death on a lonely road on Christmas Day? Wife said to me, 'Go on, I'll keep it warm,' Townshend, eh? Only fifteen miles. I'll be home in no time."

Through the white wonderland we drove. My cheekbones pained me from the cold and also from the smile that wouldn't leave my face. Up along the river everything began to look familiar, even with its white coat. We went across the old covered bridge at Townshend and up the dirt road, now deep in virgin snow. And there were the lights in the window of Betty's old house and the woodsmoke curling, pungent, from the chimneys, telling of good things cooking.

"Safe and sound," the old man said. "And judging by the smell from that good woodstove, I'd say just in time for Christmas dinner."

As Paddy and Betty came out with looks of amazement on their faces, and little Leish peered through the window and waved, I grasped the old Vermonter's hand.

"God bless you," I said. "May you never die. Last night I lost my faith in humanity for a while. Today you gave it back to me. Happy Christmas."

18

I moved in with Tina in January 1958. She had a job as a librarian and had rented an apartment on Seventy-fifth Street near Central Park West. I started work right away with our friend Murray Lerner on a short film called *The Return.* It was about the long process of rehabilitation that victims of serious accidents have to go through. Making the film was a harrowing experience and really opened my eyes to a kind of human suffering that few of us ever get to see. The film documented what the young man had to go through, physically and mentally, in his return to some sort of normal life. I played the part of a young lad in the bloom of youth who is paralyzed from the waist down in a car crash. Singer, actress, and friend Robin Roberts played the part of the nurse while Greg Zilbourg, whom we thought of as our mechanic from the White Horse, played the doctor. It transpired that Greg's father was an eminent psychiatrist, so Greg fitted the part perfectly when he was cleaned up.

Filming involved spending six days a week living in a rehabilitation hospital near Suffern, New York, on the Hudson River. Cast and crew would meet each morning at six o'clock at a coffee shop on Seventh Avenue and drive up the Palisades Parkway, a beautiful drive through glistening snowy woodland, to the hospital. There I was fitted with special shoes and leg braces, my own hospital clothes, my own wheelchair. To get inside the part, I would arrive at the hospital about eight o'clock in the morning, harness myself to my hospital garb in a private room, and then join the routine of the other patients for the rest of the day.

The role model I was given to befriend and learn the ropes from was a lad of my own age named Don. He had been paralyzed, not in a car crash, but in a shooting incident. We took to each other right away. He taught me to rear back and balance on the two big wheels of my wheelchair, how to whirl around in this position for playing basketball, which muscles could be moved and which couldn't. He talked at length to me about how he'd been shot and how it felt to wake up in the hospital and realize that your body, from the waist down, was like a ghost, a thing that could be seen but was without feeling. But mostly he talked about his determination to walk again.

At the end of the first day's shooting I did a very stupid thing. Murray, the director, stopped Don and me in the middle of a wheelchair race down the corridor and said to me, "Okay, Liam, we're all packed up and ready to go. See you outside as soon as you're changed. See you tomorrow, Don." Without thinking, even though I'd been concentrating on my muscles being dead from the waist down, I stood up stiffly and walked away from Don, saying, "Tomorrow morning, eight o'clock."

The next day he was very distant, and it wasn't till near the end of the day he softened up and said to me, "You know the way you just got up and walked away from the wheelchair yesterday evening? Well, I had a dream last night that I did the very same thing. And you know what? I know that dream is going to come true, by God!"

What he didn't know was what his doctor had told me: "Don doesn't know it but he'll never walk again. There's a small piece of spinal cord tissue left. If we cut it, there's no hope. If we don't cut it, he'll be spastic. He'll never stand up in braces, his legs will shake so much. His bones will become porous and brittle. His condition would be much worse. We've decided to cut."

From then on, when our shooting day was finished, I'd say my goodbyes and wheel myself to the crew room before getting out of the wheelchair and leaving by a back door.

On the last day's shooting at the end of our five weeks in that hospital I felt chastened. I felt angry. I felt lucky and I felt hopelessly sad. I took a deep breath of clean winter air off Bear Mountain and the Hudson River before getting in the car for New York, and I thanked God or Life or Chance, or whatever it is that deals us a hand in this brief existence of ours, for the life I'd been given and vowed to play it out as best I could with intensity and passion.

Watching the film *East of Eden,* I had been fascinated by Julie Harris's offbeat character portrayal of the torn-between-two-brothers role. Like most young actors at the time, I was pulled into the vortex of the "method" school of acting. I desperately wanted to be a part of the Actors Studio, run by Lee Strasberg and his associates. It was producing such talent as Marlon Brando and Paul Newman, Julie Harris and Lee Remick.

I had a crush on a young actress at the time, Kathleen Widdoes. I felt for her all the passion that I could never feel, naturally, for my sister Peg in the love scenes of *The Playboy of the Western World.* I asked her to do the "big" love scene with me from that play as an audition for the Actors Studio. We were brilliant. I had a crush on her. She felt it. I was too shy to make advances. So was she. The scene as we played it, as we lived it, and forgot ourselves before that august body, was exactly right.

We were both accepted on the spot. It was only when I got back to the apartment on Seventy-fifth Street, walking on air, that I caught myself. These actors from rich families, these Yale graduates, can indulge themselves in the luxury of the Actors Studio. I can't. That's when I told myself I couldn't have the Actors Studio or Kathleen Widdoes. I had Tina to think of and I had to work for a living. Be it singing, acting, standing on your head, whatever it takes, I had to make a living! I was also beginning to realize that I could never be a one-woman man.

That same day I got a call from the agency Milberg Productions to play a small part in a TV film, *Little Moon of Alban,* with Julie Harris and Christopher Plummer. It was a small part paying union scale, but what the hell? I was working.

George Schaefer was the director, a lovely man without any theatrical affectations. On the third of March, a raw day of bright sun, the kind of day that shows up the dirt of New York, I took a subway to Brooklyn for the first reading of the script at NBC's Brooklyn studios, in what looked like an old warehouse, bare and cold, hardly a place to make magic. The cast, which included a young, up-and-coming actor named George Peppard playing an IRA man, sat around a large table, reading scripts. Although my part was minute, mostly playing harmonica under a Dublin street lamp to set the mood, I was glued to the script. What really amazed and impressed me was that the two leads, Julie Harris and Christopher Plummer, never had to glance at their scripts. Not only were they both word-perfect on that first reading, they possessed such conviction that I sat there at that table and listened enthralled, as if I were at a live performance, which of course I was.

The other thing that impressed me about the true professionals was that they were so nice. No condescension, none of the prima donna posturing so common in amateur dramatic societies.

The TV show, a *Hallmark Hall of Fame* special, was a huge success and won an Emmy for best television drama of the year. *Little Moon,* as we came to call it, was a moving piece written by James Costigan, a man I never heard of before or since, in the mold of Sean O'Casey, then so popular in New York theater circles.

The title came from J. M. Synge's play *Deirdre of the Sorrows:* "Little moon, little moon of Alban, it's lonesome you'll be this night, and the long nights after, and you pacing the woods beyond Glen Laoi, looking every place for Deirdre and Naoise, the two lovers who slept so sweetly together." That was one of Deirdre's lines.

Julie Harris's character thought of herself as Deirdre and thought of her young lover, who was, of course, George Peppard, as Naoise. When he is shot by the British in a raid on her house, she becomes a nursing sister, and the conflict evolves when she first cares for, then falls in love with, the British officer (Christopher Plummer) who had conducted the raid.

During rehearsals and production the troupe of actors became a close and happy company, especially under the direction of George Schaefer. When we got to the real rehearsal on set, Schaefer used a very novel method of direction. He conducted the whole action of the play from a wheelchair. There was nothing wrong with his legs, he just wanted to be as mobile as the camera. With his humor and his earnestness he made us all feel important. He could make the cast do anything he wanted, the sure sign of a good director.

That production was to be the first of three versions of *Little Moon of Alban,* two on television and a Broadway stage production, which would be a part of my life for the next couple of years.

Meantime, I was living with Tina at 43 West Seventy-fifth Street, under the suspicious eye of a landlady of the old puritanical school. America was caught up in the hypocritical frenzy of puritanism still. Cohabitation was illegal in most states. Police raided apartments of couples suspected of having "lewd relationships."

Tina's job had to support both of us after my stint on television was finished. I had a lot of time on my hands in that apartment with nothing to do all day but wait for the agency to phone, and think. There's a time of questioning in most people's lives, a time of pushing and pulling, of trying to come *at* yourself, your individual philosophy. That was such a time for me.

Out of the blue Diane came back and we went to Cape Cod together to see Carol. We had a nice time sailing and swimming and we had hours of interesting discussions about things occult, the curse and boon of money, democracy and proportional representation, the good of conflict. We talked of religions, education, and just about everything else as well. She told me all about Carrick, where she now lived much of the time, and said she wanted to put up the money for a film of "Riders to the Sea" in about three years. Money gives such freedom if one's sanity can be kept intact.

But it was a good time. I needed that break.

Life became a juggling act between acting and singing, auditioning and recording, working on new songs and trying them out at the White Horse. Things would gallop along at a hectic pace for a while and then lapse into a trough of idleness and penury. At one point when Tina and I were both out of work we had to sell all our books to buy food. What broke my heart was that we had to sell beautiful books of great sentimental as well as monetary value, by weight! Tina's ballet books had to go. My collection of books on acting, mythology, and poetry, including a variorum first edition of the poems of Yeats which Diane had spent a fortune on, were all sold by the pound. I started working nights, either in plays or, more frequently now, singing in the Village in the emerging folk club scene.

Television was in its infancy at that time. There was no such thing as videotape, so all the shows were live. That created a lot of work for stage actors who were there on the spot in New York. Some of it was great, but a lot of the time live TV was a bitch. Tom played Robinson Crusoe in a one-man show that was shot live on an island out in New York harbor. It was on a Sunday afternoon and we all gathered around a television set to watch it. The first shot looked fine as he came up the beach, but halfway up his portable radio mike fell off and trailed along the ground behind him. He was so busy acting that he didn't even notice. For the rest of the half hour we saw this madman tearing around an island declaiming to the wind, with nothing to be heard but the grating sound of a microphone being dragged over stones and sand and dune grass and finally going completely kaput as he waded into the water.

Paddy, Tom, Tommy Makem, and I were becoming a formidable foursome by this time. All four of us did a *Camera Three* special for St. Patrick's Day called "Irish Songs of Rebellion." That one wasn't bad. But we had a whopper with a version of *Treasure Island*. It was big-budget stuff, too, starring Hugh Griffith as Long John Silver and Boris Karloff playing Billy Bones. We were playing four pirates as well as providing the sea shanties for the background music. We shared a dressing room with Boris Karloff, the *real* Frankenstein monster, and a true gentleman. I asked him one day if he ever regretted being stuck with the stereotyped role of the monster. Would he not have liked to move on to Shakespeare, like Olivier? He just gave me a quizzical look with those dark, hooded eyes.

But Hugh Griffith was the one who caused all the trouble. He was in terrible pain, of course, because his leg was tied up double and he had to walk on this wooden stump, but he just couldn't (or wouldn't) learn his lines. That becomes an issue when you're going out live to millions of people. Danny Petrie, the director, solved that problem. Each time he heard a silence accompanied by a look of desperation on Long John Silver's face, he'd cut the sound going out on air, open the intercom mike in the control room, and shout the line to Griffith.

It all worked out until, coming to the end of the play, all of us pirates, fifteen of us, are gathered around a hole in the sand where we've found the buried treasure. Up comes Captain Smollett and fires a shot, a single shot, and fifteen pirates fall dead into the hole. Danny had forgotten to tell us which one of us took that first magic bullet.

I also did some *Camera Three* shows as a solo performer, one on my favorite poet, Yeats. This is when I first got to meet Frank O'Connor, a writer I had revered since the day back in Carrick when I'd opened Paddy's trunk of books. O'Connor had been manager of the Abbey Theatre under Yeats and few men, if any, knew the poet as he did. A revival of the dramatized version of O'Connor's powerful story "Guests of the Nation" was running in the Theater Marquee at the time and I was playing one of the leading roles in it. Paddy, Tom, Tommy Makem, and I had done it in the Village in 1956 as a one-performance-only matinee. That production had won an Obie, the *Village Voice*'s award for off-Broadway theater. But O'Connor hadn't as yet been to see *Guests*. He seemed so austere at the time that it didn't seem possible that we would become very close shortly afterward. Not only would we work together on the Cuchullain cycle of Yeats plays, but he would prove incredibly generous with the insights he imparted to me, a young whippersnapper, into the world of Yeats, as poet and man. He became almost like a surrogate father to me.

Another program I did about the same time was on the poet John Keats. I was given a script on Thursday with over a hundred cues in it which had to be memorized by nine o'clock Sunday morning and performed word-perfect for millions of people. The pay was 150 dollars. I took it. One of the poems alone, "Ode to a Nightingale," lasted over five minutes on air. There were no zoom lenses at the time, which meant that the camera, in order to begin with a long shot and end in a close-up, had to start at the far side of the studio and slowly close in, like a stalker, to within a few inches of my face. And all the while I tried to remember the long-lost words I'd learned in the monastery school in Carrick years ago. One of the other poems on the program was "The Terror of Death." It was nothing compared to the terror I suffered that Sunday morning.

But 150 dollars pays rent and food bills. There was even a little left to pay off some of my White Horse tab. And that's poetry, too.

Guests of the Nation ran for two enjoyable months. The play always moved me. Frank O'Connor finally did show up, along with his agent, Bill Maxwell. He seemed quite excited by the production and we had a get-together at the White Horse afterward. Grania O'Malley came with us. Grania played the old woman of the house in *Guests,* and what a character she was. Abrasive and gentle by turns, she'd been in the theater business all her life and took no bull from anyone. She told us how she'd send bitchy telegrams to rivals on their opening nights, ones who she knew had gotten the part via the casting couch, that read, "I hope you get a warm hand on your opening, my dear."

We all got drunk that night, and I know of no better way of bonding.

Guests was a short play, so we had a "curtain-raiser" called *Aria da Capo* by Edna St. Vincent Millay. Plays, like songs, show their worth very quickly to an actor involved in a run of any length. There are songs that I have been singing for decades, through thousands of performances, that still move me, that continue to show new facets and layers. I wasn't in the acting game long enough to ever have been involved in a really long-running production (nor would I want to be), but from my experience in the two-month run of *Guests of the Nation* and *Aria da Capo* I learned the difference between a flashy piece like *Aria* and a story of great humanity like *Guests:* the one became boring after a few nights, while the other grew in stature with each performance. On closing night I was as moved at the powerful climax of *Guests of the Nation* as I had been on opening night.

Aria wasn't a total loss, though. We had fun. Through it I got to know Roscoe Lee Brown of the mellifluous voice. Roscoe would later work with us on the Yeats plays, playing the Red Man in *The Green Helmet*. He got a kick out of that. "Maybe if we had a séance we could get Yeats to change it to the Black Man in *The Red Helmet*."

I think it was through O'Connor that I met John Henry Faulk. John Henry was the most gripping storyteller I have ever met. He was a regular visitor to the Theater Marquee. O'Connor was the writer but John Henry was the teller. I'm convinced he would have been up there with Mark Twain and Will Rogers if not for that blot on U.S. history named Senator Joseph McCarthy. John Henry had been blacklisted. Now that I think of it, maybe that was why his stories of bigotry and compassion, of the blind hatreds and small tendernesses of a little Texas community, were so vividly and poignantly told in his private theater, his apartment, on the West Side, which so often became our haven at night after the last curtain call.

Theater, I was discovering, is a two-way street. You set out to bring a bit of drama, or romance, or enlightenment into people's lives, but you get back as much as or more than you give.

Shortly after the plays closed, Grania O'Malley's estranged husband died and was cremated in accordance with his wishes. Grania invited a bunch of us up to her apartment for a disposing-of-her-husband's-ashes party. She'd married this actor years before but soon discovered he was gay. In his will he had asked if Grania would spread his ashes on the Hudson River along his favorite walk, where he used to take his doggy at midnight before turning in with his latest.

It was a great party. I remember a big bottle of Paddy whiskey on the mantelpiece beside the urn. The Paddy whiskey label has a map of Ireland on it.

"When we get down as far as the Shannon," Grania announced, "we'll head for the Hudson."

We drained the bottle as far as the Shannon, then the Suir and down to the Blackwater. When we arrived back up at Belfast Lough on the second bottle, I said to Grania, "The tide's going out. Hadn't we better do the deed?"

By now midnight was long gone. The party was in full roar. Tom was belting out, "Was you ever on the Congo River? Blow, boys, blow." Grania winked at me and, taking the urn, beckoned me to go with her.

Dumping the ashes into the toilet, she said, "I hate to ruin a good party." She flushed the toilet and we watched in silence as the husband began to spin and then disappear down the hole. "The miserable bastard. He'll be in the Hudson in about five minutes!"

Tommy Makem had moved to New York permanently in March 1958 to find work as an actor. Paddy was running Tradition Records, which was flying at this point. Tom was in *Ulysses in Nighttown,* a dramatized segment from Joyce's novel. Almost immediately after Tommy arrived we started working on another album, this time a collection of drinking songs. We rehearsed by day at Tradition's office on Christopher Street and belted out the songs by night at the White Horse Tavern. When they were ripe, we collected some friends to help with the choruses and set off for the Rooftop Theater where *Nighttown* was playing. There, on their "dark" night, David Hancock, the engineer who made his own microphones, set up his recording equipment and within a couple of hours we had a new album, *Come Fill Your Glass with Us.* This album was to be the turning point. We had never really thought of ourselves as a group before, but now the concept was starting to sink in.

During the rehearsals and recording of *Come Fill Your Glass with Us,* I recall trying to formulate a style of singing. On the song "Finnegan's Wake," for instance, I knew that the little, thin voice coming out of my mouth was not the ballsy voice I was hearing in my head. Those nights on the *Ulysses* stage, having seen the larger-than-life performances of Zero Mostel as Leopold Bloom and Carroll O'Connor as "stately plump Buck Mulligan," I was aware of the lack of drama in our telling of the songs. Like taking on an acting role, I started to push at the boundaries of singing, trying to make the result conform to the inner voice. Brother Tom, of course, was a dynamic role model. A critic once said of Tom: "Tom Clancy is the only performer I know who starts at the top and tries to work his way *up."*

About the same time we were recording the drinking songs album, Helena Carroll and Dermot McNamara were running a theater company called the Irish Players. They were mounting a production of a play by Helena's father, Paul Vincent Carroll, called *Shadow and Substance*. Tommy and I were cast as the two football-mad curates. That threw us together a lot, and on our "dark" nights we would check out the scene in Greenwich Village.

Friends of ours, Izzy Young and Tom Prendergast, had opened a folk club called the Fifth Peg, which had a free-for-all hootenanny every Monday night. Tommy Makem and I would get up and sing, trading solos initially, but as we got more songs together from the recording gigs, we also became more of a duo. When the play closed, Prendergast and Izzy offered us a singing gig at 125 dollars a week each. It was a staggering amount, considering that an off-Broadway actor made only forty dollars. Needless to say, we jumped at it.

Tom was playing on Broadway at the time, and on his nights off he and Paddy would join us. This was the way, bit by bit, the group took shape, even though in our heads we were actors first and foremost. It would be a while yet before we'd face the fact that the money was in the singing business.

In December 1958, I got one step closer to that realization when I got a part in José Quintero's production of *The Quare Fella* by Brendan Behan. Every actor in New York wanted to work with Quintero, the hottest director in the city on or off Broadway. He had created a new vision in his staging of the plays of Eugene O'Neill. I had seen the world premiere of *The Iceman Cometh* at the Circle in the Square and been spellbound by it. Its length alone, two hours, then an hour dinner break, followed by the concluding two hours, made you live the action almost in real time. Later, on Broadway, I had seen *Long Day's Journey into Night*, in which Quintero had cast the husband-and-wife team Fredric and Elsbeth March, and again Jason Robards, who had been so brilliant in *The Iceman Cometh*. Now here I was in rehearsal, under Quintero's direction, playing Scolara in *The Quare Fella*.

Money was a real problem for me at the time. I was living on burgers and beers at the White Horse with the tab growing daily. I wasn't in the Actors' Equity Association so I couldn't have an Equity contract with the Circle in the Square when we started rehearsals. All the other actors were in the union and all on the same wage, forty bucks a week.

But Equity members were on a sliding scale, so if the box-office receipts were up, their wages went up. At the end of the first week there was jubilation among the cast. Not only were the reviews brilliant but everyone got a ten-dollar bonus—everyone except the one non-Equity actor, me.

I stormed up to the office of Ted Mann, the producer.

"Do you think this is fair?" I demanded. "I've given as much as anyone to this production. More! Where would you have gotten the Gaelic songs? Ten lousy bucks! Everyone in the cast got it except me. How do you think that makes me feel? Can you sit there and tell me that's fair?"

"Fair has nothing to do with it. They've got contracts, you don't. I can't pay you the extra and that's that!"

"Okay," I said. "They've got contracts so they have to stick with this cheap fuckin' production company. But I have no contract with you. If I walk, there's not a fuckin' thing you can do about it."

"You can't do that to us. We've got a show in two hours."

"Then pay me what the rest of the company is getting."

"I can't do that. You don't have an Equity contract."

"Then, in the immortal words of Brendan Behan, fuck you Mr. Mann and all belonging to you. Get yourself another Scolara!"

I walked out.

New York was knocking the shy Carrick lad out of me.

People wanted to help me get work. Dick Bagley, one of the three filmmakers who hung out at the White Horse (he had an obsession with Dylan Thomas), went to bat for me. One night he swore he would help me with my acting career. He knew every agent in New York. He had great faith in me, in my ability: this was the drink talking. "Tomorrow morning meet me here at ten and I'll take you to the best agents in this city."

I was there, and so was Dick! It must have been torture for him with the hangover he was bound to have. A man of his word, though, he paid for the cabs, he took me to the agencies, he sang my praises.

It paid off. A few weeks later I met Dermot McNamara of the Irish Players on the street.

"How did you pull it off?" says he.

"Pull what off?" I said.

"Don't give me that *oul' shite,* Liam," says he. "We were all up for that part. We all feckin' read for it. You, ya fecker, never even read for it and you got it. How did you pull it off? Who's pullin' the strings?"

"Dermot, I swear to God I don't know what you're talking about. What part am I supposed to have landed?"

"Jesus, you're telling the truth, aren't you? Johnny Boyle. The part of Johnny Boyle in *Juno and the Paycock,* the TV version with Matthau—Walter Matthau and Hume Cronyn. Pauline Flanagan is playing Juno. Malachy McCourt told me not ten minutes ago. He'd heard you'd got it."

I rushed back to the apartment. Without even auditioning, without as much as a phone call, it was not possible. I called the William Morris agency. "Oh, yes, Mr. Clancy, we've been trying to call you. Rehearsals start next Tuesday. Columbus Circle rehearsal studio. That's at Fifty-ninth Street. Ten A.M."

Good old Bagley. I couldn't even thank him. Marshall Allen, of the long cigarette holder, had given him the key to his Spanish retreat so that he could write the screenplay for the definitive film on Dylan Thomas. He was already in Wales doing research.

Juno and the Paycock is one of Sean O'Casey's great tragicomedies. The production in which I played the one-armed IRA man who is pushed over the edge by guilt was *not* the ultimate *Juno.* Walter Matthau and Hume Cronyn, excellent actors though they may have been, were about as far from Dublin slum dwellers as is possible to imagine. Their attempt at "Oirish" accents was good for a laugh and that's about it. Matthau was exactly the same when we went to lunch as he was in the part—and every part he's ever played—a lovely, big, ambling, jowly bear, cranky and totally up front. Hume Cronyn was—Hume Cronyn. Pauline Flanagan played Juno with a clear ring of truth.

The whole production would have been eminently forgettable except for an incident that befell me at the dress rehearsal, just before the live transmission. I'd been off gallivanting. Tina had given up trying to corral the young stallion in me. The stable door of sexual repression had been flung open and the animal had bolted. For three days before the dress rehearsal for *Juno* I had been strung out—days rehearsing, nights involved with a woman who sucked every last drop of energy from me, body and soul.

When, on the fourth day of our romantic escapade, and still without sleep, I had to make the early rehearsal, she gave me two green triangular tablets.

"Just swallow them back," she told me. "They'll make you act like you never acted before."

She was right. I took them just before getting into costume, which involved having my right arm bandaged very tightly to my body, leaving the sleeve of my jacket empty. It was only when I was in this straitjacket that the "uppers" kicked in. I went into total panic. I started gasping and trying to tear off my bindings like a mad mummy who has just discovered he's being buried alive. Rehearsals had to be stopped. A doctor had to be called. He had to tranquilize me before we could get on with the show. The director was delighted. My part called for exactly the kind of behavior I was exhibiting. The green pills had done the director's job for him.

Meantime, Bagley came back from Spain. I met him in the White Horse.

"How's your screenplay?" I asked him over a stein of ale.

"Never wrote a fuckin' word."

"What happened?"

"Marshall-fuckin'-Allen. That's what happened. I get to his place hungry. I've bought myself some eggs—that's the only fuckin' word I know in Spanish, *huevos*. I'm lookin' for some pepper or something to put on the fuckin' eggs. All he's got is a whole fuckin' shelf of these fuckin' herbs. I think, why not? I shake these fuckin' herbs all over my scrambled-fuckin'-*huevos*. Ten minutes later I'm floatin'. Cloud-fuckin'-cuckooland. It's fuckin' marijuana. I live on scrambled *huevos* for three weeks. Never write a fuckin' word."

19

The arrival in New York of Eben Given, the artist I'd become friends with in Cambridge, and his friend Danny Richter, who was studying mime, opened up a whole new episode of life in New York. They crashed out with Tina and me, among others, while they hunted for an apartment, a thing that proved to be very difficult. Maybe it had something to do with the bohemian garb and that sixties air about them that was ahead of its time. They called on my acting ability, plus some borrowed "respectable" clothes, to help them get an apartment on Seventieth Street near Central Park just five blocks from Tina and me. As soon as they took possession they changed the locks on the door, installed new bolts, and I'd hazard a guess that rent payments were erratic at best.

The parties there were boisterous and often punctuated by empty wine bottles smashing against the outside of the door—thrown by a downstairs neighbor who, we were convinced, was an abortionist. The cops, too, paid regular visits to our soirees. A hypnotist friend of Danny's explained the technique of hypnotizing someone to me at one of these wild gatherings. "Concentration! That's the whole secret. Get the subject to concentrate, on a coin, a watch, anything that will focus the mind for more than four seconds, which is the maximum time that a person can keep a single image in the mind's camera. If you can keep them focused for longer than that, they'll enter a hypnotic state. But they must want to do it. They can't be forced. And a word of warning: never, never lose control of them. Use your voice as a leash. If they get off that leash, you never know what'll happen."

Tina was a perfect subject. She trusted me not to make her do anything foolish. She had very highly tuned powers of concentration. The first time I hypnotized her, which took an hour or more, I planted a posthypnotic suggestion that she'd go "zonk" on cue. From then on I could get her to go under by just saying, "Tina, go to sleep."

But Tina was a very special person. She had intuitive depths that I could only look at from a distance and marvel at.

It was at a similar party that we started the "Box." It began as a silly game. Someone at the party got the idea of everyone writing a word or words on little pieces of cardboard. Everyone did so and put them in a big brown paper shopping bag. We took turns at pulling out words and stringing them together. Sometimes they made funny sentences. One of the first ones to come out that made any sense was "I rode red mother like first boat ride."

Eben, Dan, Tina, and I, along with Yoshi, an artist friend from Boston, took the Box game much further. After a month or so we had transferred all the word cutouts to a real box, which Eben had decorated with symbols made of tin. Every time Tina called for an answer, a coherent sentence emerged. I watched her very carefully. She'd shuffle thousands of words and in answer to a question pull out the most extraordinary, most articulate replies. I particularly remember one night when Eben, full of curiosity about painters, asked who the Box liked as an artist. I saw Tina, eyes closed, put her hand into the jumble of words and out came, in sequence, the words "We like the Greek." El Greco was one of Eben's favorite painters.

The episode with the Box was not a one-night wonder. It lasted for more than two years. It obsessed us to the point that none of us would leave the house until the bloody thing had been consulted. At this point Tina and I had been evicted from Seventy-fifth Street by the landlady, who had "found us out," and we had moved in with Eben and Dan. The Box began to take over our lives.

One night the answers that Tina produced before our eyes were so directly related to the questions that we started to become scared, and when Eben asked the direct question "Is there a presence that is answering us?" the word Tina pulled out was "Yes." Our next question was "Where are you?" The words said "Among you now." We started to get very scared.

Eventually we got bored with asking questions of the Box, so we asked for a poem. What we got, over the next year, was a volume of poetry, poetry with such intense imagery that it really did frighten me. We asked for a child's poem and it came out with: "I have three teeth. How many have you?" It went on, "The fairies took them away for building blocks."

Perhaps the most frightening piece of poetry, and the main reason why we destroyed the Box, came toward the end of our psychic adventures:

> That night out there I saw your face
> Where I knew it could not be.
> And then I knew
> That the thin threads
> That hold the mind together had been worn through.
> Will your wild face drive me to such insanity
> That I go planting scarlet flowers
> In the furrows of the sea?

The apartment on Seventieth Street was in the rear of the building and had a three-sided bay window overlooking the enclosure that passed for a garden one floor below. We could look right in the window of the front apartment, which was occupied by two girls who became good neighbors. They'd come through our window, the sills were touching, to our parties or to borrow sugar or whatever. They loved to go naked when they got home from work. They obviously got a kick out of the thought of us peeking through the windows at them parading around in the nude. However, at that time, Eben was at the college of art on Fifty-seventh Street and spent eight to ten hours a day drawing and painting nude models; Yoshi, likewise, on his frequent visits from Cambridge. Danny and I spent many hours with Eben at the art college. Tina and I were lovers. Nudity was hardly a novelty or titillation to us, but if the girls next door were getting a kick out of it, what the hell. So we blacked out our window with cardboard, then cut a large keyhole in it, through which we used to peep at them for a laugh.

The girls were generous with their phone. We couldn't afford one, so we'd climb through to their apartment and use theirs. It was strictly on the honor system, local calls and emergencies only. We paid them back whenever we could. The scheme fell apart when they confronted us one day with an enormous bill from the phone company. The calls were mostly to Tokyo. I mentioned Yoshi, who was like the iceman who cometh. He brought us great joy as well as huge shrimps for tempura and, a rare luxury, sake! While we were enjoying the delicious meals he used to conjure up from nothing, Yoshi would get drunk on hot sake. While the rest of us waxed lyrical with the drink, he would get homesick and have to call his mother in Tokyo. He'd sneak off and make long calls. Long, long calls. It beats me how he didn't kill himself crawling from our window to the girls' window, with a hell of a drop to the cement garden below. Of course, we'd never even missed him. There were lofty and passionate things to be discussed by young bohemians full of hot sake!

When the album *Come Fill Your Glass with Us* was released, the calls started coming in from various people trying to book us as a singing group. Paddy's friend Lou Gordon, the union organizer, talked us into doing a benefit at a church out on Long Island. We talked about it and wondered how we could possibly put together forty-five minutes of songs. And what could we say between songs? It seemed a formidable task.

But we did it and realized at the end of the show that people liked us. The applause is like a drug. A curtain call is a curtain call, like in the theater. We became hungry for more songs and more audiences.

One day we were rehearsing at the Tradition Records office when a call came in from Chicago from a man named Alan Ribback, who had a club called The Gate of Horn. Tommy had played there as a solo. Alan wanted the group he'd heard on the drinking songs album. At first we said no, we're actors, must keep our integrity. When he offered us enough money, we said yes, we'd give it a try. We were all, except Paddy, out of work at the time.

"I need a name to put on the billboard. What are you going to call yourselves?" The thought had never occurred to us, a name for the group. Yes. We needed a name.

"Why don't we each make out a list and see what we come up with?"

The lists read like a who's who of all the ballad groups that ever came down the line. The Moonshiners, the Jolly Tinkers, the Druids, the Chieftains, you name it.

Eventually the day came to fly to Chicago. In those days you had to tag your own bags with the name of your destination. Knowing Paddy's spelling abilities, which were a bit of an in-joke with us, I said, "Paddy, would you like me to write up your bag tag?"

"Fuck off!" He wrote the tag himself. Before they could take the bag away, I checked it. The tag read "Chigeco." Paddy never lived that one down. It would be years before anyone heard of dyslexia.

We still hadn't been able to agree on a name by the time we got to Chicago. When we arrived at the club, the decision had been made for us. The marquee simply had on it, "The Clancy Brothers and Tommy Makem." Just like that.

Our next problem was what to wear by way of stage costume. The Kingston Trio, very much our role models, wore short-sleeved striped shirts. We considered tweed suits. We really didn't have a clue. Browsing through Marshall Field's department store, we found just the bargain we were looking for: tweed suits on sale for twenty-five dollars. For one dollar more, they threw in a second suit. What a bargain! We bought eight suits!

I don't think the jackets were that bad. It was the pants that let us down. Once you sat down in them, they never stood up again. Even walking down the street it looked like you were sitting.

The reviewer for the *Chicago Sun-Times* commented the day after we opened: "Three of the worst haircuts in show business opened at The Gate of Horn last night, The Clancy Brothers. Their partner Tommy Makem seems to have a better barber." He went on to give us a great review, then concluded: "That reminds me, I must get my tweed suit pressed."

Our opening song was "O'Donnell Abu," a raucous, ballsy rebel song. This, we figured, would knock 'em dead, all twenty people in the audience. We were choked up with neckties and the sweat pouring off of us. But we stood up there manfully and I struck a chord on the guitar. "O'Donnell Abu" was supposed to be in the key of A. I had the capo on the wrong fret. I hit a D. Suddenly we were four sopranos. I was going to try to bluff it out but Tom let us down. He stopped after the first line and turned to me. What a look! We all stopped.

"You can keep goin' if you like but I'm not goin' to castrate myself singing in that fuckin' key!"

That was the first, and last, attempt we ever made at formality. Off came the coats. Up went the sleeves. Off came the ties, never again to go on. The audience fell about laughing, all except the group of very serious men who sat together and never clapped. Someone sent up drinks. We suddenly realized how ridiculous it was trying to be serious and proceeded to re-create the atmosphere of the White Horse.

Every night the crowd grew. Every night our confidence grew. Bit by bit the show came together. We started to take delight in it. It dawned on us that what we saw as boundaries to our performance in the beginning were all the time being pushed back, that there was no end to what we could do up there onstage. We were free of the straitjacket of a playwright's lines. Here was something we could make our own.

Every night for a week the silent men would come and sit ominously in the audience, no clap, no smile, no sing-along. Eventually they came to us in the bar after the show and said they had to talk to us privately out on the sidewalk. We went outside with them.

"We're from the North Side chapter of the Irish Republican Movement. We've been checking you lads out. We've come to a decision. You're all right. We have our annual social dance coming up soon and we had to make sure you guys were our kind before we could let you play at it. There's no money involved, of course. It's all for the cause."

Over the month of that Chicago run we made friends with an amazing cross section of people. Irish, folkies, Jewish liberals, doctors and lawyers and politicians, and girls, lots of girls. There's no place on earth that has girls like the Chicago girls. We were having a ball. Little did we know at the time that this was only the beginning. In a couple of years we'd be playing the Playboy Clubs and feeling totally at home in Hugh Hefner's mansion. But that's another story. Right now we had a couple of madcap customers who were strippers from a club down on State Street. One of them, the little fat one, only about nineteen or twenty, fell in love with Tom, or at least his stage persona. "The little bull," she used to call him.

After hours, back in the bar, she'd do a strip for us, part of the common bond of entertainers. She could make her copious breasts twirl in different directions, then she'd get her left buttock churning in a counterclockwise direction while her right buttock set up a clockwise momentum until a harmonious equilibrium was reached. When she'd finish, dress, and come to the bar for another drink, she'd announce to Tom, loud enough for all to hear, "Ev'ytime you sing that song 'The Rising of the Moon,' I have an *organism*." Her friend was more sedate, with short-cropped hair and a bad stammer. When you pressed her as to what she did, she'd say, "D-d-dancer."

"Like your friend?"

"No, no, sta-sta-stately!"

"What does that mean?"

"I only strip to B-Bach and B-B-Beethoven."

In May 1959, Paddy and I headed back to Ireland along with Mick, a Carrick man who worked as a bartender at the White Horse.

It took forever to cross the Atlantic at that time. The old Constellations couldn't get above the weather, so the flights could be bumpy, to say the least. We hit an air pocket at one stage and the coffee the hostess was trying to pour levitated from the pot, drenching and burning her and everyone around.

Generally, though, there was a party mood. Aer Lingus was young and personal. Passengers weren't as blasé as they are today. The excitement of going home was spiced with the fear of flying. The drink was flowing. It was a heady mixture. Mick and Paddy were into the whiskey, and the stories got more and more outrageous.

My ulcer was bad at the time. All I could drink was milk. I swear it was the ulcer that kept me from becoming an alcoholic.

On the long, calm haul that usually came an hour or so out of Gander, the stewardesses had little to do except ferry drink to the nonsleepers, so I'd get out the guitar and find a bit of floor space down by the galley and a gang of us would sit on the floor, me with my bottle of milk, and sing our way across the Atlantic.

I spent some time in Dublin. On the street one day I met Frank O'Connor. We stopped into Davy Byrne's for a whiskey and had a long talk. I had a copy of his latest book, *Kings, Lords & Commons,* under my arm. I had just bought it. He saw it and growled, "Well? Aren't you going to ask me to sign it?"

He talked about the begrudgery that still thrived in Ireland, the small-mindedness of the politicians, and the wall of official hypocrisy that was only now slowly beginning to crumble.

Angela was now working and living in Dublin. I somehow found her, and we rekindled whatever flame we'd had, and started going out on dates. But things couldn't be the same. I had lost my innocence. I told her about Tina.

One night we went to a dance at the Metropole Ballroom, which had a bar. Angela didn't drink. I got very high. We later went back to her flat. Her roommate was away for the weekend. She showed no indication of wanting me to go, so I stayed late, the two of us just sitting and hugging each other on a couch in front of a gas fire, with no need for words. I wanted to stay with her that night, but when I asked her if I could, she was horrified. "God, I wouldn't let any fella stay the night here," she said.

I finally did stay by telling her it was impossible to get into the hotel at that hour. She insisted, though, that I sleep in the other bed and remain fully clothed, which I did. When I awoke in the gray, cold dawn, she wasn't in the room. I found her down in the kitchen, with her coat on, looking miserable and pathetic. I felt a stab of guilt. I knew that I had ruined the lovely, innocent passion that had been part of our youth.

A couple of years later, when the Clancy Brothers and Tommy Makem were all over the airwaves and the newspapers of Ireland, I met Angela at a social function in Limerick. She was engaged to be married, she told me. I wished her happiness and long life. I never saw her again. Recently I got a call from an old friend to tell me that Angela had died. I cried like a child.

When I left Dublin, I took a train to Thurles, where a *fleadh ceoil,* a festival of traditional Irish music, was being held. It was to be my first exposure to the new phenomenon that would sweep the country, and me with it, off our collective feet. I met Paddy, Bobby, and Bobby's girlfriend, Breda, there. Apart from an awful lot of fiddle scraping, there was some potent music. My old friend Paddy Tunney, from our long-ago outing in Letterkenny with the Makems, was there, and a young teacher from the west who sang a funny song about Daniel O'Connell and his plan for making "babies by steam." The pipers were making music like I'd never heard before and a very funny fellow named Robby McMahon lilted hilarious mouth music. The dancing in the streets was the best part, and I danced for most of the night with a lovely girl I met standing on the bumper of a car.

Bobby and I took a trip to Kerry the next day and spent a night of old-time singing with a schoolmate of mine, one of the McGettigan brothers, Tony, at a little pub in a remote part of the Dingle peninsula. I began to rediscover on that trip an Ireland I'd nearly forgotten about, an Ireland, I realized to my surprise, that I deeply loved.

My mother, of course, cried as I was leaving.

"No need to be sad now," I said. "Paddy is still here and Tom just arrived."

"Oh, I know that, boy, but ye all mean something special to me and there's no compensation when ye go."

Before Tom's arrival, Diane had bought the cottage outside Carrick that she was renovating. Since I was about to leave for New York and Bermuda, she may have had a premonition that this would be the last chance to get a portrait of the family in its completeness, at least as complete an entity as I (or Diane) had known it. Whatever it was, she was very insistent that we pose for that picture. She was right, it was to be the last family portrait. In it you can see death in my father's face.

Diane had been using Carrick as her base a lot. Before I left she threw a great hooley in what used to be the barn. She had drawn out and fostered the singing of a lot of the old songs that the family and neighbors had forgotten, or hidden, out of shame, songs that were buried because they were associated with the bad times of poverty, hunger, and oppression. I had never heard Annie Daniel, our kind of second mother, sing "The Bonny Bunch of Roses" or "Hi for the Beggarman." I'd never heard my mother sing "The Bonny Boy," and only rarely before had "Me Grandfather Died" and "The Heights of Alma" been given an airing.

In a way I found myself impatient to get back to the new life I was making in America, and yet I felt the tug of the old genes. Especially in the lamplight of the barn I felt the safety of the clan, the earth-pull of blood, the safe and warm feeling of timelessness. The security of the herd.

Thinking back on it now, and thinking of the patronage of an Deigh Bhean in Cill Cais, who may have guided the other Willim Clancy, two hundred years before, I begin to see the parallel with Diane and the Clancy clan. I was getting closer to my namesake.

Tina met me in New York, and two days later I flew to Bermuda to do another production of *The Tempest.* Basil Langton was directing again. He seemed to be making a career out of the play. This production was to be a lavish, outdoor affair paid for with government money.

Basil and his daughter Jessica met the New York contingent of actors at the airport in Hamilton, with the photographers. We were driven to a mansion called Belair, an old stately house that had belonged to a rich lady who lived now in the States. They told us she used to entertain the governor in her heyday and the cars would be lined up all the way down to the Inverurie Hotel, two miles away on the waterfront. Two cars could pass each other on the staircase, like something out of a swashbuckling film. Most rooms even had four-poster beds. Three servants kept house. We were living like gentry.

On our first night, there was a big party at a house belonging to John Kaufman, the designer: a young bearded character, bright but with a big ego. All the ladies were there, of course. Tranquillity was the name of the house. I felt very quiet and out of place at first, but I started drinking late in the party and relaxed. I had never drunk rum and Coke before and it went down too easily. I soon found myself scraping the nail polish off a girl's toenails. Later I found myself alone with Cyndy—the rest of the party gone, me drunk, and Cyndy most uncooperative. All my friends were gone, including my ride home. Cyndy's boyfriend was coming late to pick her up.

Her boyfriend turned out to be Pat Dunch, a wonderful fellow who would become a close friend. He had a radio show on which I'd later become a regular. He arrived with Bob, a policeman. Fortunately Bob had a motorcycle so I got a ride home. He dropped me near Belair and rode on. It was very late and very deserted by then and I was very drunk and very lost. I remembered hearing that a murder had recently been committed on Cobb's Hill Road, the road Belair was on, and the thought sobered me up rather fast. Finally I found my bearings from a map in a phone booth nearby.

Next day we all went into Hamilton to pick up our mopeds, mobilettes they called them in Bermuda, and started off to see the island.

Bermuda in my memory now is aglow with pink and excitement, long-legged girls in short shorts, horny toads and land crabs by the million with claws erect on warm dark sands at night. It's full of the exhilaration of youth, flying around narrow coral-walled roads on mobilettes. There were girls with perfect little bottoms. Girls painting scenery. Girls making costumes, girls doing makeup. Girls' legs underwater in lighted swimming pools after the show. Girls plunging hand in hand with me into the black waters of Harrington Sound—straight off a grassy lawn. It was a time of screaming hormones and greasepaint sticks and the smell of pinewood mixed with velvet and starched ruffs of stage costumes.

Pat Dunch, Cyndy's boyfriend, took me to the policemen's club one Sunday afternoon where the beer and laughs were flowing. This was a strictly male domain, a macho place. Someone switched the lights off and turned on the projector. The film hadn't been rewound since last night's debacle. The images were upside down and backward. Nobody was sober enough to try fixing it. I saw my first porno flick with my head scrunched as close to upside down as possible—the film starting at a screaming sexual climax, slowing to a backward foreplay, to a frumpy-looking girl rising from the bed naked and getting dressed wrong way round, and then walking backward out a door. No wonder every young white male wanted to join the police force. They had it made.

The island was also a place where one had to be careful. One day a lone walker hailed me on an otherwise deserted beach of pink, powdery sand and stopped me from plunging into a shoal of barracuda cruising along the spindrift. Another day I went to Horseshoe Beach to find a great commotion. A young navy cadet, or what was left of him, had just been pulled from the water, torn in half by a shark in spite of the supposed safety of a shark barrier.

Racial trouble was brewing at that time. On our night off, out of sheer ignorance of the situation, I went into the wrong part of the segregated cinema in Hamilton. No word was said but the hostility around me was palpable.

But what I mostly remember was the play and the theater and the whole atmosphere of what comes back to me now as an almost magical time.

There is a line in *The Tempest* referring to "the still-vex't Bermoothes." Based on the premise that Shakespeare, in his play, was referring to the newly discovered islands in the Atlantic, a celebration of the 350th anniversary of the founding of the colony of Bermuda was planned by the government, with a theatrical production called *This Island's Mine* as its focal point. Basil Langton was starring and directing.

Once again Basil had come through for me and cast me, again, as Ferdinand, the romantic lead.

Langton was a strange man, dark and distant, never up-front friendly, yet he had some kind of unspoken admiration for me.

So here we were in Bermuda, guests of the government and living in the lap of luxury, sleeping in four-poster beds, waited on by maids, vied over every night by the island elite wanting to entertain the New York "actowhs," provided with transport by the government (and chits that got us free petrol anywhere on the island), invites every night after rehearsals/performances to partake of the bounty of the wealthy and the would-be-arty set.

Instead of the customary two weeks' rehearsal, Basil had bargained with the powers-that-be and conned them into four weeks of rehearsal, claiming the difficulties of outdoor staging, the scale of production, the costumes, the stress on his actors, and so on. The run itself was scheduled for two weeks, which gave us six memorable weeks, not only acting but living like the lords, the revered bards, we always knew we should have been.

The costumes had to be authentic; that meant silk next to the skin, linen undergarments, and velvet, heavy hot velvet, on the outside. To make it complete, there was a ruff around my neck and a velvet hat. It took an hour or more for dress and makeup. The heat was stifling in those costumes, but at least it kept me trim—for the girls.

But having come from a less-than-affluent life in New York had its advantages. Being a motor scooter owner in New York City gave me an edge when it came to the mobilettes. Of the twelve professional actors imported to the island I was the only one who came through the adventure unscathed. Two had to be hospitalized, one sent back to New York.

Outside Hamilton, Bermuda's capital, is a wooded hill with a craggy outjutting feature. With a few trees cut down and some earth flattened, this was surrounded by a stage-set village cleverly designed to create the impression partly of Shakespeare's London and partly of the Globe Theatre itself. This was to be our magic-making place for the duration of the production.

. . .

She was so beautiful. Marion was her name. She was seventeen and soft-warm-pretty-sophisticated-sensual and, alas, unattainable. She was painting sets when I first saw her. She sidled up to me after rehearsal and said that "they" were going swimming, would I like to come? It was all quite intriguing.

That night we kissed and cuddled. The following night when I asked her to go swimming with me, she said yes. Yes! She said yes!!

"But I have to pick up my bathing suit at home. It's on the way. I'll take my mobilette and you follow me."

I would have followed that mobilette and its wondrous cargo to hell. We followed the winding Bermudan roads for three or four miles. She turned off at an entrance, with huge ornate gates, to some kind of estate, up a long avenue to a massive house. I thought, she's a maid. We're sneaking around to the servant's quarters to pick up her bikini. Great! We may not even go swimming at all.

She didn't go round the back of the big house. She pulled right up on the gravel by the steps of the front entrance.

"Come in and meet Mummy and Daddy," she chirped. "They said they'd love to meet some of the actors." I went into Governor Woodall's residence and stood in the imperial entrance hall under huge portraits of Her Majesty Queen Elizabeth on one side and himself, the Greek, Prince Philip, on the other, while Marion went off to fetch Mummy and Daddy to see the funny prize she'd brought back from the theater.

"We saw your performance on opening night. Such a romantic! You won't keep our Marion out past one, will you? Charmed to meet you."

"Yes, yes, good show. Very good, old chap. Marion, one o'clock, no later. Have fun, young people."

"Good night, Daddy. Don't worry. He'll have me home by one."

And I did. I did.

"This island's mine, by Sycorax, my mother," roars Caliban as he crashes through the woods bearing a great balk of timber. In that production he came gorilla-like out of the real woods. Ariel perched on a

real crag. Prospero/Shakespeare, at the end, commanded a real "globe" as he gave his famous speech—a speech I loved so much that, each night, I waited for it and listened to it. To this day, I end every performance with "Our revels now are ended."

But I was tired of repeats. Twice I had done *The Tempest,* and a couple of months after my Bermuda adventures I was in a revival of *Shadow and Substance* back in New York, again with the Irish Players. This time Malachy McCourt and I were playing the two curates Tommy Makem and I had played in the previous production.

I had been spending day after day pacing around the apartment on Seventieth Street indulging in imaginary conversations with millionairesses who loved the theater and had suddenly discovered this young Irishman with a dream. My dream was to produce a trilogy of Yeats plays. I was on fire with the idea of doing the plays of Yeats as they should be done.

The perception of Ireland by Americans, particularly American producers, disgusted me, and I was determined that, come Saint Patrick's Day, I would put on a production of Yeats's plays at the Poetry Center in New York, where Dylan Thomas had recorded *Under Milk Wood.* The Poetry Center was located in the Young Men's Hebrew Association building on Lexington Avenue and Ninety-second Street, a perfect venue in which to make a statement that would counteract the green beer and plastic shamrock image of Saint Patrick's Day.

I contacted producer after producer, trying to persuade them that Yeats was the greatest dramatist since the ancient Greeks, but an awkward youth trying to fire up New York producers was like holding a blowtorch to a sheet of asbestos.

One night I thought of Frank O'Connor. Before I picked up the phone I rehearsed a little speech. I was trembling with excitement and apprehension. He answered the phone himself with that gruff, aggressive voice of his: "Yes?"

I forgot what I'd rehearsed, of course. "Hello? Ah—ah, Mr. O'Connor, this is Liam Clancy and ah—"

"Yes?"

"I was in your play *Guests of the Nation.* Remember we met in Dublin back in June—on the street. You signed a copy of *Kings, Lords & Commons* I'd just bought?"

"Yes, yes—I know all that, but what is it you're calling about?"

"Well, I'm trying to produce Yeats plays in New York for Saint Patrick's Day and I was wondering if you could help me."

"Do you realize, boy, that it's Christmastime? I have enough to do without being bothered in my own home by every young dreamer over from Ireland." I had forgotten it was Christmastime; these petty things mean nothing when you're inspired by something greater.

"Where the hell are you, anyway?" he asked me.

"On Seventieth Street."

"Well, I'm in Brooklyn Heights. You obviously know where I live. I'm a fool when it comes to giving my address and phone number to every Tom, Dick, and Harry. It'll take you about half an hour to get here. I'll see you then."

Ecstasy. I don't remember the subway trip. I do remember describing my ideas to him over a Christmas drink and I do remember his reply after my long and idealistic treatise. He analyzed my ideas in one word.

"Crap!"

I withered.

That must have been 11 P.M. By three in the morning he was animated and he had a concept. He theorized that when Yeats wrote about Cuchullain he was writing his own autobiography. He proposed editing the Cuchullain cycle of plays in a way that would illustrate the point. In telling the story of Cuchullain and Emer he was giving a heroic telling of his passion for Maud Gonne and his marriage to Georgie Hyde-Lees.

In mid-January the Cuchullain cycle of Yeats plays was in production. With the help of O'Connor's name the Poetry Center enthusiastically agreed to stage it. His wife, Harriet, wouldn't let him get too involved in it because the heart wasn't good even at that time. After the cast was assembled—consisting mostly of Paddy, Tom, Tommy, and myself—he would come to rehearsal every few days. He mustn't get too excited, his wife kept telling me. But excited he was, excited and intense. Full of emphatic opinions and a gruffness that covered up a basic shyness. I cannot imagine another man in his position putting up with a young upstart like me. But he did. Under his tough exterior he was a sensitive, shy, and honest man. He'd come to a reading of *The Only Jealousy of Emer.* I'd ask him what he thought.

"Crap! You haven't a clue, boy, what it's about. Now, I was at the Abbey Theatre with Yeats and this is what he was saying in that play." He'd explain to me how the plot paralleled what was happening in Yeats's life. I'd go back and redirect the actors. When next he'd come in, he'd say, "That's it!"

Watching us act out *On Baile's Strand,* he'd suddenly exclaim, "By God you've got it! Where did you get it, boy? That's exactly it!"

And all the time I knew his motivation was love, love of Yeats, of the theater, love of life, love of just pure excitement for its own sake, the excitement of being in the thick of the action.

Often he would look in on rehearsal and give directions, then say, "Don't dare expect me to show up on the night of the performance. I'm too old and sick for that sort of thing."

On March 16, 1960, at the Poetry Center of the YMHA, Frank O'Connor was there an hour before the curtain went up—pacing and pacing.

"But don't dare expect me to get on that stage. My heart couldn't take that."

Needless to say, we couldn't hold him back. He spoke for nearly an hour. He had it all prepared. Here's some of what he said: "Every man's life is an allegory. God knows it, the saints live it, the poets write it. . . .

"William Butler Yeats was a good son, a good husband, and a good father, and that doesn't matter. What matters is that all the time he saw himself as a man who perhaps never lived, an ancient Irish hero called Cuchullain. . . . He says that in all of us there are two men—the clever man and the hero—and when the clever man comes on top, it is just as though we had killed our children. He says even more than that. He says that each of us is both a blind man and a fool, and if the hero in us is a bit of a fool, the clever man is always blind."

For those who were in the audience that night at the YMHA, Saint Patrick's Day would never again carry the cursed connotations of plastic shamrocks and green beer.

20

To Lucy
To Lucy
To my love, Lucy.

Poem after poem, handwritten poems by Eben Given to his passionate love, Lucy. As well as being a painter, Eben was a poet and a hopeless romantic. He had been alone all weekend in our Seventieth Street apartment while Tina and I were away in Cambridge. When we arrived back we had difficulty getting into the apartment, what with all the broken glass piled up against the inside of the door. We eventually forced it back and stood in amazement at the sight. Sheaves of pages were strewn all around. Mounds of broken glass were piled up in each corner. Shards of broken bottles covered the floor and filled the marble fireplace. This was the sight that greeted us. Broken glass was everywhere: in the toilet, the bathtub, in the cupboards. And in the midst of the wreckage, Eben, with a sliver of a shattered Pernod bottle in his right hand, was slowly and deliberately carving the name "Lucy" on his left forearm.

With horror we watched Eben carving his arm, then reach for the remains of yet another bottle of Pernod, finish it, and throw the empty bottle haphazardly over his shoulder. Tina went to get cloth and water to clean the wounds. I pried the glass shard from his hand and tried to talk to him. He just pointed at the mantelpiece. I could see nothing but broken glass. He kept pointing, saying nothing. Under the mess I found a note. It said, "Eben, please don't contact me again. I'm in love with a guy. It's over. Face it! Lucy."

We nursed Eben back to health as best we could and tried to get him over the Lucy episode. But a week or so later Tina and I came back from a movie to find both Dan and Eben drinking Pernod and talking a stream of bull. Their arms were bleeding from where they had gashed themselves—both of them this time. They were becoming blood brothers, they said, to seal a decision to go to Europe the next year. They were on fire with the idea of living in Paris, having seen a movie called *The Cousins,* a film about "supersophisticated" people living a hedonist existence in a garish and rich apartment in Paris.

Never have I seen two people work so hard at being artists. Eben had a definite talent, but Dan seemed to me to have more drive than talent. Who knows, maybe he went on to great things that I never heard about. I recall him saying one night, "I firmly believe that all three people in this room will make their mark on this generation" (he ignored Tina). He was getting a thousand dollars from his parents in January, he told us, and that was going to keep Eben and him in Paris until they both became great artists and lived like the people in the movie and died before their time, great but starving. The world wouldn't realize their greatness, of course, until they were dead.

The situation was becoming impossible. There was a film released at the time called *The Horse's Mouth,* about an eccentric artist in London who was obsessed with painting huge murals of massive feet. Our relations with the landlord and the neighbors were bad enough already, but when Tina and I got back to the apartment one night to find the floor strewn with cans of paint and Pernod bottles and the walls covered in paintings of *feet,* we knew the game was up.

Our little commune was disintegrating. About that time Tina broke the news that she was pregnant.

We moved into the only place we could afford, an illegal, subterranean apartment in Greenwich Village that had been used by various orphans of the White Horse in times of destitution. It was underground at number 10 Bank Street, behind the furnace. It cost ten dollars a month.

We were descending straight into hell. Try as I may, I cannot inject a grain of humor into this phase of my life, and most of it I have blotted out, erased, or chosen to forget. I do remember the rats. We had to keep the windows closed to keep them out, even when the heat was unbearable. There was a hot stench from the furnace and the fuel that fed it. Diesel oil wasn't used at the time for central heating; instead they used coke, a derivative of coal. We had to clamber over mounds of this volcanic-like rubble to get to the slapped-up wood-frame hovel in which we now made our home. Tina had to hide her pregnancy from the landlord in case he'd evict us.

In spite of our plight, Tina was happy. She was pregnant with a baby she wanted. She'd have something permanent and valued out of our relationship. She accepted, in herself, that I was not ready—and would not be ready for a long time—to make a mature commitment to wife, family, home, the whole nine yards, as the New York expression would have it.

But I wasn't happy. There was no way I could write home and tell them the reality of what had happened in my life, what a mess I'd made of it. I was living in one world, my family at home in another. The truth could not be told. It would have destroyed my mother.

I was as trapped as the rats in the underground dump we were living in. I was feeling as filthy and rotten as the vile place in which we lay down, where I daren't look under the sink or the legs of the ancient bathtub in the long, thin space called the bathroom, in which there was an abundance of unknown "things." The faucets in the sink gave plenty of scalding-hot water but only a tiny dribble of cold. The bathtub took up the meager width of the bathroom. To bathe you had to take off your shoes, kick at the cockroaches, climb into the rusty tub, and turn on the cold water first thing in the morning. By evening you might have enough cold water to be able to run the hot water and have your bath. It was only when we were preparing to leave the apartment the following August, when our daughter, Anya, was born, that I discovered a cold water stopcock under the sink among the roaches. When I twisted the damn thing I got a gush of cold water that would knock the arse out of a bucket.

I wasn't present at my daughter's birth. Fathers weren't supposed to be present at their child's birth at that time. I was in the White Horse when she was born. I heard the news from a nurse on the pay phone over the clamor of bar-jabber. After I'd gone to the hospital to see my first-born, I went back to the White Horse, and, in line with the macho ethic of the time, I got roaring drunk. When I woke up the following day, there was a buzzing in my ear. Slowly coming to consciousness, I realized that I was holding a telephone I didn't remember picking up, its dial tone still humming. I phoned Tina at the hospital and her first words were, "Thank God it's you! You're alive! I phoned you earlier and all I got were gurgling, snorting sounds. I thought you were dying."

More and more the White Horse Tavern became my escape. More and more the nights of gigging in Gerde's Folk City became the bursts of joy in my life. I had an insatiable hunger for the fulfillment of all the wild dreams I'd had in the loneliness of the garret back in Carrick.

Oh, how I loved little Anya and how I loved Tina, but I was only two years into my liberation, and not all of heaven's horses could drag me back into the enclosure of conformity. Even while I took care of my little family I rampaged through the females of Greenwich Village. Monogamy was a concept I seemed to have left behind back home in William Street.

However, there was no way I could have taken the chance of having a newborn baby in the illegal subterranean pad. I made a frantic search for another apartment. The White Horse network went to work and sure enough our old friend Sybil Weinberger came through. She had a *real* apartment on Perry Street around the corner which she moved out of, God bless her, just so Anya could be brought up in a decent place.

Tina put up with my philandering and late nights until Anya was about four years old. When she could take no more, they moved to Colorado Springs and, later, to Florida. We remained friends and I would jump on a plane and visit them every so often. Many years later, when I had a wife and four children and was living in Ireland, Anya got married. My wife, Kim, and my four kids flew out to Florida for the wedding. Anya cried as I walked her up the aisle to give away the girl that I'd never really been a father to.

Greenwich Village was an island to which people escaped from repressed backgrounds. It was first an Italian ghetto, but at some point it took on a bohemian cargo of artists, sculptors, poets, musicians; not to mention would-be artists, would-be sculptors, and real and would-be-real human beings. Two things we all had in common: we were all escaping something, and we were all finding something else. A new herd was born. The survivors of repression—the Catholic repression of Ireland, the artistic repression of Hibbing—it was all the same. We had to escape from the straitjacket imposed on us by the generations of people who had gone under, the people who had believed in what they were fed by so-called authority figures, the people we loved, like our parents, who had swallowed the directive to be inferior, to know your place, to kowtow to "royalty," "hierarchy," and all the other nonsense.

In the Village we were all refugees, escapees from our own private jails, trying to remake our souls on our own terms.

Drugs may well have been a part of it, especially later on, but in the late fifties and early sixties, the freedom itself was the drug. The euphoria made me want to sing, and I never stopped, onstage or off, except to eat, sleep, and make love—for thirty years, when the sheer exhaustion of constant touring started to take the good out of it.

For us, the White Horse Tavern was the poetic, singing center of the Village. In 1953, Dylan Thomas had taken his last drink there, or rather his last thirty-six drinks. Legend has it that the Welsh poet, overwhelmed by fame, took refuge in the longshoreman's bar on Hudson Street. The doctors told him that even one more whiskey would do in his liver, so he set up a pyramid of thirty-six shot glasses of whiskey on the counter of the White Horse bar. He looked a long time at the pyramid, contemplating. Then he took the top shot glass off the pile, downed it, and with suicidal certainty drank glass after glass until the pyramid was demolished.

He was rushed to St. Vincent's Hospital a few blocks away but never recovered consciousness. In the end he *did* go gentle into that good night.

Crowds of students would come on weekends to worship at the shrine. We, the locals, resented the invasion. This was our sanctuary: the back room was our singing place, the place where sea shanties, rebel songs, and raw love songs were exposed. This was where Theo Bikel could cry over the beauty of his Old Testament recitals, where Richard Farina could hold forth with snatches of his novel in progress, where Jimmy Baldwin could flaunt his homosexual intellectualism and snort scornfully at our ballsy shanties, and where the old bawd, sleeping at the next table, could rise from her stupor—tangle-haired and bleary-eyed—and demand, "What the fuck goes on here?"

One night she woke up when a stampede of students was taking over the back room. I was at the table beside her.

"What the fuck are all these fuckin' kids doin' here?"

I said, "They're here to pay their respects to Dylan Thomas."

"Who the fuck's that?"

"You know—the Welsh poet Dylan Thomas. Used to drink here. That's his picture there over your head."

Bleary-eyed, she looked up and tried to focus. "That son of a bitch," she said as she recognized the picture. She put her head down again on the table. "He was a lousy lay!"

Hamburgers were two bits, twenty-five cents. Beers were fifteen cents. When I was finally able to pay up, my tab was over five hundred dollars. And never once did old Ernie demand payment. For all his gruff exterior we were his nestlings—his care.

Dylan Thomas permeated the paneled walls and was ever-present in our minds as we pretended to be poets and intellectuals and drunks. The cast of characters was as off-the-wall as the graffiti on the wall. Students from NYU would come over to study the toilet scriptures.

Apart from the singers, actors, and poets, there were characters, like Greg Zilbourg, who had played the doctor in the film we'd made, *The Return*. Then there was Marshall Allen, who had lent his Spanish pad to Dick Bagley. Marshall, the intellectual appendage to a foot-long cigarette holder, with a superior snicker to match every topic of conversation that came up, was the one who had crossed my brother Bobby one night—to his peril. Bobby, one of the most basic of men, made some point or other. Marshall responded by drawing a long pull on his cigarette holder, snickering, and declaring, "I happen to have a Ph.D. in that particular subject and you are a buffoon." It took several of us to drag Bobby off him. The look in Bobby's eyes scared even me, who knew that his quick tempers faded as fast as they flared. Marshall, who was used to the to-and-fro of debate with Paddy, Tom, and me—a kind of chess game we played—had to be revived with several cognacs.

Then there were the girls who cared for us all, the nurses of the tormented male minds. One night, as a rather bad practical joke, some lout came in and announced that Dr. So-and-So (an abortionist in New Jersey) had died, and a gasp of dismay and disbelief went up from the entire female company.

Bridget Murnihan, the poet, would rage at us each night. Kelsey Marechal, who had come to sing with us on the drinking song album (even though he couldn't sing), would sit quietly sipping a perpetual brandy and smiling like a Cheshire cat. Writer Delmore Schwartz could be heard defending his paranoia to the barman—"Even paranoiacs get mugged ya know!"

The piss was flowing out under the door of the men's room toilet. Theo Bikel was singing Russian songs in the back room. The woman in the apartment above was pounding the floor over our heads as usual. The old porcelain White Horse steins were overflowing. Old Ernie was abusive—and generous as ever.

"You can't sing here," he was announcing.

"What does he mean we can't sing here?" Theo was demanding.

"I wouldn't mind if he said, 'You *shouldn't* sing here.' But we *can't* sing here? We *can* sing! Listen! Ernie, we *are* singing!"

Off we'd go again.

And by God did we sing! We reveled in the first flush of madness. Nobody had ever done this before. It was all spanking new—wild and new!

It was Kelsey Marechal who moved us into the club scene in New York. Kelsey came from money. He bought One Sheridan Square, previously home to the famous Café Society, where Billie Holiday had once sent shivers through a stunned audience with a song called "Strange Fruit." There he reopened the basement nightclub under its new name. After the Gate of Horn success and the high profile of the Poetry Center's Yeats production, we were ready to take on anything. We weren't exactly cocky but we were excited about having a go. Kelsey asked us to be the opening act for Josh White for his two-week run at One Sheridan Square. For Josh it was much more like home than the Festival Hall in London! For me it was a dream come true, performing with the man himself.

A problem arose which was hard for us to comprehend: America was going through a puritanical-fascist stage at the time. To perform in a nightclub, we had to go down to police headquarters and be photographed and fingerprinted like criminals. The land of the free and the home of the brave was afraid that folksingers like us might destroy its way of life. Hypocrisy went hand in glove with corruption. But then— what's new?

Josh White was a phenomenon. His command of an audience bordered on the hypnotic. His manipulation of his audience, especially young white females, was a skill to be awed by and envious of. He packed the club every night, and when he turned up the heat, there wasn't a dry seat in the house. We, rank amateurs, tried to compete with him, to his great amusement and delight.

Being new to the game, we had no idea of the parameters of performance standards. One night, as the mood struck us, we could be brilliant; the next night, pathetic. We hadn't found a way of dominating either our own performance or the audience. We were tentative and all the time seeking approval before delivering the goods. If audience approval came, we soared. If it didn't, we wilted under the rejection. Our forays onstage were like sexual advances, full of juvenile bravado when we were successful, flaccid confusion when rejected.

Josh could demolish us every night with his professionalism and command. On the night we were winning, we'd come off the stage to thunderous applause.

"Top that, Josh!"

He'd step onstage, while our applause was still hot, throw one leg over a chair, and look the audience, row by row, in the eyes until he had complete silence. Then he'd stroke the guitar strings, just like he stroked my guitar that first night at Diane's party, and start: "I gave my love a cherry." The hook was set. He had them.

The following night we'd belt out our set only to get a rubber-handed applause—no encore—and come offstage with our tails between our legs. There Josh would be with his evil chuckle: "You want me to top that, boys?"

That's when he'd grab the guitar neck way up near the body and unleash a stinging blues riff, finishing off with a walk up and down the bass string with his thumb, blowing us out of existence.

I learned more about stagecraft from that man than I'd learned from all the theatrical people I'd ever encountered. I learned the art of taking delight in what I did.

Josh White's managers, Marty Erlichman and Lenny Rosenfeld, saw the potential in what we were doing. We first met them backstage at One Sheridan Square after the opening-night show and we all went for a drink at the White Horse. They seemed to find us highly amusing. I remember Marty in particular sizing us up with a kind of amused perplexity. Marty and Lenny could have almost been a comedy act themselves. Lenny was the straight man to Marty's nonstop jokes. Marty was shortish, plumpish with thick glasses, while Lenny seemed to feel awkward about his height and went around with a stoop, trying to look the same length as everyone else.

We got together nearly every night after that, and real bonds of friendship had developed by the end of the two-week run. What a sight we must have looked in the bars and restaurants we went to: four white-white Irish guys, two sallow-looking Jews, and one bald black blues singer, deep in a huddle of conversation or conspiratorial laughter. Of course, in Greenwich Village nobody noticed.

Marty and Lenny offered us a management contract and we agreed.

"Why don't we take a rehearsal hall—we'll pay for it—and take a look at your material." Marty was more the spokesman. "We'd like to hear all the songs and poetry, stories, stuff, whatever."

For three days, eight hours a day, we sang and recited and basically unloaded all the cargo we had to offer. It was a fascinating exercise for us as well as for them. Between us we discovered the universal within the parochial. Songs we thought were purely local they thought were exciting. Songs we thought were great, they'd say, "Scrap it. Nobody'll understand it."

You could see how they were trying to tap this raw ethnic energy that radiated from these four greenhorns and make it into a salable commodity. That's how we worked together—using each other to reach a common goal: Jewish-Irish synergy. Gaelic schmaltz and Yiddish blarney—great team! Our goal was success and together we managed to achieve it.

Those sessions had some wonderful moments. After we belted out the Gaelic words of an old song, *"Oro se do bheatha bhaile,"* Marty said, "I love it. Keep it in. What the fuck's it all about?" And when we sang "Bold O'Donohue" with the line "Perhaps now she might think of me as a rather heavy *dew"* (pronounced *Jew* in the Irish dialect), Marty shouted, "Now wait a minute. Let's not get personal about this fuckin' thing." When Tom recited from Joyce's *Finnegans Wake,* "Bygmester Finnegan, of the Stuttering Hand, freemen's maurer, lived in the broadest way immarginable in his rushlit toofarback for messuages before joshuan judges had given us numbers or Helviticus committed deuteronomy"—Marty's amazement was a delight to behold.

"Who made this shit up?"

"James Joyce, the great Irish writer."

"This we got to use! This guy Joyce. Is he goin' to give us any trouble about doin' this?"

"He's dead," said Tom.

"Good!" said Marty.

Marty and Lenny were professionals. They had a kind of genius that opened doors where no one knew doors existed. They forced us to focus on performing a repertoire of songs we had chosen together as a team, and, under their direction, we were gaining a mix of confidence and flamboyance with every show. Soon we were performing at the Village Vanguard and the Village Gate on a regular basis. The Vanguard had been *the* jazz club of New York City. But jazz was on the wane, and folk was on the rise. Jazzmen like Stan Getz opened the show for *us*. I took no delight in that. Here were great musicians, playing second fiddle, so to speak, to a bunch of ballsy ballad-singing bluffers passing themselves off as first fiddle players to packed houses. And that was the crux. We could pack the house every night. Before we arrived on the scene, business was dying. Max Gordon, the Vanguard's owner and a great lover of jazz, knew that in order to keep the music alive you also had to keep the venue alive. Arses on seats.

The Vanguard was packed one night with a party of off-duty New York City cops and their wives, all Irish-American, needless to say. The unfortunate Stan Getz was trying to reach them with his brand of music. No one likes to play his heart out to a wall of uninterested conversation, and on that night my heart went out to a fellow musician who was fighting an uphill battle. Fighting bravely and failing, Stan resorted to leading his band into a jazzy version of "When Irish Eyes Are Smiling." He got instant attention and a boisterous ovation for the duration of the novelty piece and then loud ignorant babble when he reverted to his own music.

Bill Evans, on the other hand, cared nought about nought. Watching him one night, through a haze of smoke, a hunched figure over a keyboard, haloed in a magenta spotlight, I listened to his meanderings on the piano. I heard a chord, an impossible chord, which even a Bill Evans shouldn't dare touch. I suddenly realized that he had fallen asleep at the keyboard, and his head, gently drooping onto the keys, had produced the lost (thank God!) chord.

Lenny did most of the office work. Marty was with us day and night. We had a ball together, telling stories, playing games, traveling together in cars to gigs, going out to lunch at Sardi's, the famous theatrical restaurant on Broadway, where Marty would be paged every five minutes. That really impressed us. "Would Mr. Erlichman come to the phone, please. Mr. Marty Erlichman, please." We actually started to believe his big-shot story until he confided in us one day: "What the hell. My mother; she's got nothing else to do. I get her to have me paged every five minutes. People hear your name. It's good for the image." Marty always talked about his mother, a subject near and dear to every Jewish/Irish boy's heart.

"By the way, I just got you some really nice gigs. The Unicorn in Boston—Sonny Terry and Brownie McGee on the same bill—a coffee shop. No! Hold it! A really classy place. And in Providence. Hey! These are places where you can really learn your trade and polish up your repertoire! I talked to Max Gordon of the Village Vanguard, you know Max. But do you know that Max is a partner of Ernest Jacoby? Jacoby runs the *Blue Angel!* You got to be good to play the Blue Angel. The Blue Angel is the place that's going to make you guys famous! Big stars!

"I also got you a two-week stint in the Village Gate, Art D'Lugoff's place. Very prestigious! Meantime, play Gerde's, what the hell. Pick up some cash, pick up some broads. It's all experience, right?"

It was at Gerde's Folk City that I met Kathy. She was wearing skintight white pants and I was instantly in lust. We had a long and often stormy relationship.

That was about the time the young Bob Dylan showed up in town. Everywhere you went in the Village this young, restless, fidgeting kid seemed to be there: Gerde's, the White Horse, Izzy Young's. We got to like him and we started hanging out together at the Village pad parties. John Hammond of Columbia Records was producing an album of Carolyn Hester and he phoned my brother Paddy at Tradition Records to see if he could recommend a good harmonica player. Paddy suggested the new kid on the block, Bob Dylan, who ended up signing a contract with Columbia.

One night at the bar in Folk City, Dylan said to me, "Hey, Lem! Man, my records are sellin', man! I'm goin' ta be as big as the Clancy

Brothers, man!" He laughed his little-kid-caught-in-the-act laugh. We used to have a lot of fun together. Shortly after that he took off into the firmament.

I have a feeling that Dylan's success affected a lot of his contemporaries. One of the gang had suddenly broken loose. Paul Clayton, for one (he's referred to as Pablo in Dylan biographies), was so devastated that they say he committed suicide by pulling an electric heater into the bathtub. Phil Ochs hanged himself about the same time, and Peter La Farge, another singer/songwriter in the circle, slit his wrists in what had been my girlfriend Kathy's shower.

There was a lot of inbreeding in that Village folk scene of the late fifties and early sixties. Dylan was sharing the affections of Kathy with me when I was out of town on tour, without my knowing it, of course. He told me much later, as in recently. "Well, yeah, man, she was kinda lonesome, ya know. She missed you, man, and you weren't there. I was there, man."

George Papadopoulos, who owned the Unicorn coffeehouse in Boston, wanted us to shoot some publicity pictures on the Boston Common with a real unicorn. Somewhere or other he got a little white pony and stuck a papier-mâché horn on its forehead. I must say it looked very real. It certainly fooled two old ladies who were passing by. I heard one say to the other, "Martha, did you see that? My goodness, I thought they were extinct!"

Sonny Terry and Brownie McGee were, in my opinion, the best blues duo of all time. Brownie was lame, Sonny was blind. They would hobble onstage, anywhere, and when they cut loose with the music, the space around them became electrically, joyously, charged. Serendipity seemed to hover about them. The secret of their fascination for any audience was mainly the talent that bubbled up from a deep, deep well of tradition. There was also an awareness of the suffering from which they'd emerged, a suffering that contained not a whiff of self-pity. In their time, to be black was tough enough, but to be black and crippled in a hostile white America demanded a leather-skinned survival instinct, full of an arsenal of weapons—not the least of which was humor.

Before every show Brownie would drink a whole bottle of cough medicine. "Need it for the throat, man."

"Must be good stuff," said Paddy. "Can I have a look at the bottle?" He read the ingredients.

"Jesus, Brownie, this stuff is mostly codeine. This stuff is addictive as hell."

"Couldn't be, man. I bin takin' that shit for forty years an' I ain' addic'ed yet."

Sonny Terry across the room rolled his blind eyes around and went "hee-hee-hee" in his high-pitched whinny.

The Unicorn, let it be stressed, was a *coffee*house—no booze. That was all right for Tommy Makem, who was a teetotaler, but Paddy, Tom, and I liked a little come-to-life tipple before the show. Shame, shame on Brownie for taking codeine, but God knows there's no harm in a drop of whiskey to warm the larynx. One or other of the brothers brought a bottle of Jameson, secreted in a brown paper bag (which might as well have had *WHISKEY* printed on the front of it), backstage at the Unicorn—in the kitchen, in other words. Tom, in his endless inventiveness, acquired a violin case which, when opened up, revealed, not a fiddle, but a well-stocked bar replete with glasses, cocktail shaker, ice holder, corkscrew, and, of course, booze.

Sonny and Brownie *loved* the coffee at the Unicorn. It consisted of one-quarter cup of coffee as you like it and three-quarters of a cup of Jameson whiskey. We had us one hell of a gig, three glorious weeks of it.

We toured the Midwest with Al Hirt. We became regulars at the Village Vanguard. We opened for Thelonious Monk at the Village Gate. We were in the business of singing in earnest. And we had an ever-growing group of fans that followed us wherever we went. We were on the scene and about to hit it big.

21

Lenny Bruce was the headliner at the New Gate of Horn in Chicago and we were the opening act. I went upstairs to the performance room to see this man in action that I'd heard so much about. I didn't comprehend the social impact of his humor. There was an awful lot of the Carrick lad in me still. It would be a while later before I would get to know the side of American society against which this man was ranting. To me he sounded like a vulgarian trying to shock his audience with dirty words, but, judging by Paddy's sense of awe at listening to Bruce's tirade, I got the impression that his savage humor was aimed at challenging the mind-set of thinking Americans who were now flocking to theaters and folk clubs.

It was probably at the Gate of Horn that our group really came into its own. We were in Chicago for the long haul, six or even eight weeks at a time. We had semipermanent lodgings at 14 West Elm, an apartment-hotel. That's where all the creative work got done. Tommy and I shared one apartment, Paddy and Tom another. Greenwich Village was known as the wild spot, but for us, Chicago had it all.

The songs we worked on during the day we'd bring onstage that night, and since it was only a temporary fling to us anyway, we brought so much fun and infectious hilarity with us onto the stage that the audiences responded both in numbers and in enthusiasm. We began to see well-known faces in the audience. Mayor Daly showed up one night with Ben Briscoe, the Jewish lord mayor of Dublin, in tow. We sang "Moses Ri Tooral I Ay" for him, to his great amusement.

Sharing the bill with Lenny Bruce was an enlightening experience. When he left, an exotic group from Israel took his place. What a knock-out fun show that was, combining Irish and Israeli music. And what a complete contrast: our don't-give-a-fiddlers-fart-belt-'em-out-songs and the Middle Eastern sensuousness of the great Star of Israel, Shoshana Damari, with her troupe of musicians playing wailing, whining strings and talking tablas.

And she *was* a star—dear God was she ever sexy. On her opening night Paddy, Tom, Tommy, and I went upstairs to see her sing and gyrate and seduce. Our eyes were out like organstops. What really impressed us, too, was that Danny Kaye, a big movie star at the time, came back to her dressing room for a long talk after her show. They were obviously old friends.

Shoshana took a shine to me. She emerged from her dressing room one night and walked straight up to the bar where the waitresses and I were having a confab. I can still see the look of shock on their faces when she planted herself between us and said right out, "Come with me, my boy. The driver is waiting. I want you tonight." Zombielike, I followed her to her limo and got in. As we drove away, I looked out the back window and couldn't contain a laugh at the sight of the little group of waitresses out on the sidewalk watching the departing limo in openmouthed wonder.

Back at her hotel suite the diva made me a drink, disrobed, and lay sensually on the bed. I, zombielike again, dutifully stripped. But—try as I may—no hint of an erection would emerge. She purred to me, she stroked me, she whispered sweet Israeli nothings in my ear. Nothing is exactly what happened.

"Perhaps I'm too old for you? Maybe your young waitress would make you excited?"

"No, no," I said. "It's not that. It's just that I'm a little in awe of you."

"That's all right, my boy. Just lay your head on my breast and relax."

Zorba the Greek said, "There is only one sin that God will not forgive—if a woman calls you to her bed and you refuse."

I sinned not. Not that night at least.

Tommy Makem was a gentleman. By his own definition, a gentleman is a fellow who can play the bagpipes, but won't. Tommy was a piper.

The first time we played the "hungry i" nightclub in San Francisco, Tommy had not yet learned to become a gentleman. He insisted on playing his bloody warpipes. I have nothing against bagpipers as long as they play their hellish instruments on a mountaintop in the Highlands of Scotland while I'm clutching a Highland malt whisky in a comfortable hotel in the Lowlands. But the Highland pipes played indoors at close range are an abomination and a health hazard. I know that from firsthand experience because our old cousin Margaret Power kept a budgie in her antique pub near Carrick. It lived a healthy and a happy life for years and was very fond of music until one night a bagpiper came in and struck up a strident wail under the budgie's cage. The poor bird dropped dead on the spot.

The hungry i, on the edge of Chinatown in San Francisco, was one of the most high-profile clubs in America in the sixties. The owner, Enrico Banducci, was one of the "characters" of the period. His highly public battles, mostly psychological, with the great comedian Professor Irwin Corey were of mythical proportions. They were a great double act.

The Clancy Brothers and Tommy Makem came to San Francisco as the opening act for Corey (as he was affectionately known). Perhaps there was a dressing room, I can't remember, but if there was, it was for the star, and we had to be content to change and tune up in a dark corner behind the stage or else in the back alley among the garbage cans and under the windows of the Chinese tenements overhead. When Tommy tuned the pipes, the blast would deafen us for the next hour or so and set our tuning completely awry. I couldn't hear the nylon string guitar well enough to tune it properly, and Paddy and Tom couldn't find a note to start on. It was pure torture. That only went on for the first night or two—then Tommy became a gentleman.

Most of the audience on our opening night was there to see Corey. We were little-knowns; he was a very famous, very funny man (he billed himself as "Professor Irwin Corey—The World's Foremost Authority," he didn't specify on what). Unless you classify Marcel Marceau as a comedian rather than a mime artist, Corey is the only comedian I've ever seen who dared to open his act with ten minutes of silence, pretending to read an imaginary document, front, back, and edges, picking off objectionable bits as if they were little bits of snot and hopelessly trying to rid himself of them. His first word, after this long ordeal, was "However!"

But not everyone in the audience was there to see Corey. Back in the shadows on our opening show (we did three shows a night) was a group of seven or eight men, very subdued, very silent, and very obvious in their attempt to be inconspicuous. They were all dressed in black. As we came offstage after our set, Paddy was saying, "They have to be the local IRA. Remember the time in Chicago? Same thing."

On my way to the men's room, after Corey had started his show, I found myself surrounded and backed into a corner by the mysterious group. I must admit that I was a little bit frightened. A man with a beefy red face, covered in a shy smile, said conspiratorially in my ear, "We're all priests." I must have gasped because he said, "No, it's all right. We were afraid some of our parishioners might be here, but the coast is clear. We can have a bit of fun now for the next two shows." He introduced the group: "I'm Father Moher and this is Father Cuchullain Moriarty and his brother Father Oisin Moriarty, and this is the only one of us who doesn't have to worry about his parishioners finding him in a nightclub, Father Mullin, the chaplain at San Quentin prison. And this is . . ." He went on through the group of conspirators.

The second show was somewhat livelier than the first, and the last show was downright raucous. During Corey's show we all gathered at the bar. Paddy said, "You can all relax now. Let's have a drink."

We got so relaxed that the volume of sound would rise to a high pitch, then everyone would all go "shhhhh" together. The doorman had to gently hush us several times. He seemed to think we were a very funny group, for white guys. The priests in mufti all wanted to hear their favorite songs from the records and were getting more vocal and demanding with every whiskey.

In the midst of all this a stranger came up to me and says, "Could I have a word with you?"

"Are you a priest?"

He laughed. "No, I'm a songwriter and I don't know if you're going to punch me out or buy me a drink." He had my attention.

"I'm the guy who wrote the song 'Clancy Lowered the Boom.' "

I called Paddy and Tom over and said, "This is the guy who wrote 'Clancy Lowered the Boom.' He wants to know if we should buy him a beer or belt him."

So after we picked him up off the floor we bought him a drink. That damned song had tortured my youth. It was a huge hit in Ireland—America, too—but what a teasing I took over it. My schoolmates used me cruelly as only teenagers can. I could hear it in my dreams: "Oh the Clancy. Oh the Clancy. Whenever he got his Irish up, Clancy lowered the boom-boom-boom-boom."

Later we all went out into the back alley to sing the priests' requests. We belted out "Brennan on the Moor" and "Whistling Gypsy" among the trash cans until the doorman appeared again to try and quiet us down. By now he was laughing and slapping his leg. He was a big jovial guy. "Man, what I heard about the Irish is true." He laughed. "You Irish love three things—drinkin', fuckin', and fightin'!" At this point a shower of rice rained down on us from the tenement windows above, a gentle Chinese protest at our disturbances. Father Moher gave the doorman a look of shock and horror. "Well, may God forgive you," he said, then whispered in my ear, "sure we're good for two of them, anyway."

A reviewer for the *San Francisco Chronicle,* whose name I conveniently forget, was up the hill from the hungry i a few nights later at Enrico's

Restaurant. He was a heavy drinker and had an open-ended tab at Banducci's place. When we arrived in the company of Irwin Corey, he looked up briefly from the snooze he was having in his plate of spaghetti, and, focusing on Corey, mumbled a stream of unfathomable profanity.

The Professor proceeded to order the most expensive meals and wines for all of us—most uncharacteristic of Corey—and generally act as the genial and exhibitionistic host. He did an outrageous show around the tables of the restaurant, throwing everything into an uproar, and inviting the patrons, who were having a marvelous time, to drink up and have fun. The drinks were on him. He even sent drinks to the comatose newspaperman. It wasn't difficult to smell the rat—watching the game being played out was the fascinating bit.

We had a lavish meal, something our group wasn't used to. Corey demanded the bill, which had to be quite enormous, and with the waiter's napkin drooped over his arm, he proceeded to the table reserved for the *Chronicle* reviewer. After much shaking and grumbling the poor sot aroused himself and, by dint of years of practice, managed to sign his name for the "waiter." Corey looked at the signed bill, examined it for a moment, shook the unfortunate reviewer once more, and demanded "Tip, tip, tip!" He got a cheer from the assembled company. The owner, Enrico Banducci, was not present, alas, to witness the gesture.

On our closing night at the hungry i, Corey and ourselves collected our paychecks from Enrico. The following morning, Corey, knowing Banducci's penchant for putting "stop payment" on the Professor's checks, was at the bank and had his check cashed before Banducci was out of his bed. Corey invited us to lunch at Enrico's and he actually paid in cash. Just as we finished lunch, Enrico came storming into the restaurant.

"You mean, cheap, cheating, Jewish son of a bitch! You couldn't fucking wait, could you? Straight to the fucking bank! Fucking shyster! You'll never—never, play my club again!" He turned on his heel and walked out. Corey looked at us with the satisfied smile of an evil Cheshire cat and said:

"A little game we play. I manage to get the fucker every time."

. . .

In April 1960 we opened at the Village Gate, Art D'Lugoff's new and hugely successful club on West Fourth Street. The club was at the cutting edge of jazz and folk music. The clientele was the elite of New York's musical aristocracy at the time. Thelonious Monk was a regular. The father of rock and roll lighting, Chip Monk, was making us all look great onstage. The line of customers trying to get in snaked around the block. In the middle of one set, during "Roddy McCorley" or "The Rising of the Moon," I heard a commotion in the audience. Shielding my eyes against the light, I looked out. There were Sidney Poitier and Harry Belafonte, in a celebratory mood I'd say, marching up and down the aisles to the passion of the rebel songs.

It was heady stuff. We did three shows that night. D'Lugoff rushed backstage to know how soon he could book us again. As we were toweling the sweat off, Paddy, who had been subdued all night, called Tom and me aside. He apologized to Tommy.

"Something has come up. Sorry. I have to talk to Tom and Willie in the kitchen."

There, amid the clang and clatter of a kitchen full of shouting Chinese staff, Paddy broke the news about Daddy Clancy. "I got a phone call from Ireland today. He has cancer. He could go anytime. I think we should fly home straightaway."

He was talking, but my mind was not comprehending. Death came to others. Not to me. Not to my father or mother. Not to my family.

"We'll go tomorrow," I said.

"First thing in the morning," Paddy said. "Down to the tax office for clearance." Practical, urgent things would have to keep the vacuum filled.

"I've already booked the flight. I didn't want to tell ye until after the last show."

"What about the concerts next week?" I asked Paddy.

Tom shouted, "Fuck the concerts! This is our father we're talking about. This is Daddy Clancy! You're worried about fucking concerts?"

"I'm not worried about fucking concerts. I just want to know what—"

"Shh—listen," Paddy said, using his hands to hold us down. "Listen. I've called Marty. It's all worked out. Okay? He's talking to the people. Now look! It's easy to get worked up at a time like this. It's going to be rough. We need all the cool we can muster. First things first. We get home and see how the land lies. I want to talk to that doctor. We don't have the whole picture. They may be panicking at home. There may be something that can be done. I don't think we should give up on this thing yet."

That straw of hope was the one I clung to as I drifted into sleep that night.

When we arrived back in Carrick, it was obvious that hope was fading. The cancer had advanced. Daddy Clancy had been moved to the infirmary in Waterford, a depressing old building of gray stone, gray mood, gray everything. After the long flight across the Atlantic we needed a couple of hours' sleep. We went straight to Petie Lawlor's for a nightcap. Petie's was our local pub, a few doors from our house.

At home the tension was tangible. The girls had red eyes from crying bouts and lack of sleep. In hushed tones they overprotected Mammy Clancy: "Let her sleep. Oh, let her sleep. She'll need it now." They fussed about food, about beds—all to keep from thinking. Then the trip to Waterford and the dread of what we would see. They told us to expect the worst.

He was like a skeleton. His mind was gone most of the time. There were sudden lucid patches, and in one of these he grabbed my hand and said, "There's a lovely well near Bessborough, outside the wall, near the Bog Road. Oh, the loveliest water I ever tasted. If I could get a drink from that well, I know it would cure me. This bloomin' thing, if I could only get it up or down. It's like a green apple I swallowed and it's stuck there. And I know that one drink from that well would shift it."

My sister Leish said, "Daddy, I'll find that well. I'll bring some water from it." By the fire in her eyes I knew she meant it. She was beautifully naive. The rest of us around the bed knew he was looking for the well we all seek, the well of life, the well of youth. To my own dying day I will love Leish for that gush of childlike belief.

Then he would drift. He tried to get out of bed.

"Where are you going, Daddy?" Tom asked.

"Oh God, I have to get out quick, boy. I have to get out of the orchard. They're coming over the wall!"

We took watches: Tom and Paddy, then Bobby and I. The girls were coming and going constantly, on compulsion. But he refused to die. The doctor said, "It's gone all through his stomach. There's no hope." But he went on. The neighbors said the Clancy boys were mad. "There they are kicking football on the street when their father is dying in hospital."

And we were mad. That May and into June we tried to keep from going completely mad. We *did* play football on the street. We also drove around the countryside on pub crawls. Diane's cottage was used as a base by Paddy, Tom, and me. Bobby slept at home. Some of the girls moved back into William Street as well to be near the Mother.

I was in constant pain from the stomach ulcer. Milk was my main diet. Paddy and Tom were on the whiskey. I would have been, too, if I could take it.

One night at Petie's pub on New Street they got deep into the booze. The tensions and frustrations were taking their toll. Tom said, "Look at cute-ah, Willie, drinkin' milk." He could never stand it when he was drinking and I wasn't. "Pure and holy Willie, criticizin' us."

After pub closing we went out to Diane's cottage, where I was sleeping in the back room. Paddy and Tom were in the kitchen by the fire. They'd brought back a bottle of whiskey. For some reason I still can't remember, I was in bed naked, something I wasn't in the habit of doing. Naked and sober. Tom and Paddy were talking by the fire in the kitchen, getting louder and more personal—and more abusive. I remember laughing at their foolishness as I lay there trying to sleep, thinking of tomorrow's ordeal at the hospital. "I bet he made her get up and say the rosary with him after he fucked her," I heard coming from the room. They started in on a rowdy rant about Diane and me rutting in the back room of this very cottage.

I remember laughing, and thinking, "I won't let the jealous, ugly taunting of my two drunken brothers get to me." What could they know about Diane and me, the strange intercourse, the psychological mindplay, and the almost fatal consequences of our non-love affair?

Something snapped in my brain. Suddenly I was out in the middle of the floor and I had the hatchet in my hand—not the little hatchet for cutting kindling, but the big heavy chopping one—standing naked, confronting the two brothers. I wanted to kill them! Fortunately they ran out into the night when they saw the sight of a naked apparition with an upraised hatchet, and I stood there in the doorway, impotent as my dying father, naked and crying, shouting at the dark, "I'll kill ye! I'll fucking kill ye!"

Two days after the summer solstice my father died. Paddy and Tom were with him all the night. I spent the night in William Street since Bobby and I were to take over in the morning, but the call came with the dawn. I awakened to urgency in the house. There was no shouting or crying, just Peg saying, "Daddy's dead. Get up quick."

We all gathered around the magnet then, Mammie Clancy. She was holding the family together. She was amazing, giving orders, making jokes and puns, holding back the tidal wave of grief with the power of a woman who had battled all her life with sickness and death—and even with God.

"Bobby, go down quick for the barber—get Ned Driscoll—he'll have to be shaved. Willie—get his brown habit from the top shelf of the wardrobe. That's the one thing he said to me, 'I want to be buried in the habit of the Third Order of St. Francis.' "

Bobby was throwing up. I went for Ned Driscoll; "Poor Bob," was all he said. He got together his towels and razor, lather and brush. He talked all the way to Waterford. Everyday talk.

In retrospect, I feel it was a very good thing that the family, not the hospital people, took care of the dead. When we got to the infirmary, he had been moved to the mortuary chapel. He was laid on a bier and covered only with a sheet. It was up to the family to do the rest. Rigor mortis had set in. Bobby went green again. Ned Driscoll shaved what was left of my father's face, *hum-thum-thumming* all the time. We unfolded the habit and somehow maneuvered him into it. There was nothing left of him. He had been eaten away. It was like dressing a large, stiff doll.

Clean-shaven, habit on, hands folded on his chest, holding his rosary beads, we could now let my mother and the girls in. The undertaker had kept them out on the sidewalk until the ritual was finished.

The girls fell on him screaming, kissing his mouth, moving away to a wall, coming back, then away again, like waves on the shore. My mother, almost calm compared to the girls, just looked at him. "Oh sure, Bob boy, Bob boy," was all she said before the great breaths of anguish racked her body. Her entire being seemed to leave her. Yet even I knew that this was not her first grief.

The funeral procession back to Carrick was an extraordinary revelation to me. In 1960, Ireland was still in the fierce grip of Catholicism. But this was more. This was something primitive, something very deep and very old. As we followed the hearse along the quay in Waterford city, the people along the sidewalks went down like corn before the reaper. Cyclists stopped to bless themselves. Cars pulled over while drivers removed their hats. Women covered their heads and went down on bended knee. All the way to Carrick, sixteen miles, this great obeisance to Lord Death was repeated. Through Mooncoin, Fiddown, Piltown, the village of his birth, past the Three Bridges, down by the monastery, under the railway bridge, where the crowd was gathered by the local hospital, opposite Ash Park. There the hearse slowed to walking pace, and the people of Carrick fell in behind the coffin of my father.

His four strong sons carried him to his grave. When we put him down, my mother said, "I have to wait eight years before I can be buried in the same grave. I'll wait, Bob boy, I'll wait."

That was the 23rd of June 1960. In September of 1968 my mother was buried with the man she had loved, hated, fought with, cursed, made eleven children with, and ultimately had to be united with, truly, flesh of one flesh.

22

Life is never the same after such an experience. There's a big emptiness. You have to take time to grieve of course, but mourning too long will sap the life force out of you. Better to get back in harness and get on with living. After the funeral we flew back to New York and picked up the pieces of our own lives.

I got a call from the casting agency. *Little Moon of Alban* was to be repeated on television. Did I want my part again? It was just the kind of healing work that I needed. I said yes, of course.

Julie Harris was playing the lead again. It was her vehicle. Dirk Bogarde replaced Christopher Plummer, and George

Peppard, who had gone on to stardom, was replaced by another star in the making, Robert Redford. Once again *Little Moon of Alban* was a great television success. The cast changes freshened it all up. Dirk Bogarde hadn't let stardom go to his head. With that slightly confused half smile of his, that so characterized his "Carry On" film parts, he was charming and so easygoing to work with. Robert Redford was newer to the game and seemed a bit nervous at the beginning, like the rest of us, but he soon showed his professional mettle. He was one of the boys.

After my father's death all of this playacting lost some of its luster for me. Maybe my father was right—we were all just acting the goat.

But we had to make a living. My father was dead. My father had lost his father and grieved, his father in turn had suffered the grief of the ages. "The generations break like waves upon the shore." It wasn't long before I was drawn into the excitement again of being part of a hectic television production.

Everything happened very fast after that. Marty Erlichman took on the role of our booking agent. He had us playing all the colleges in the New York/New England area. How I wished then that I'd been able to go to college in America. The girls, in their miniskirts at the time, seemed so—accessible. After a death, life wants to assert itself.

We went back to the Gate of Horn in Chicago. We had an opening act named Maya Angelou. Black, beautiful, and tall, she reminded me of the old song called "Dink's Song," which goes, "She moves her body like a cannon ball." She had the body, she had the words, she had the presence. Sometimes she was a little wobbly on the pitch, but who cared? She was majesty itself. Her followers loved us; our followers loved her. In her autobiography she wrote about our common experience.

In her book *The Heart of a Woman,* she describes arriving at the Gate of Horn for the gig we were doing together. She remembered, very accurately, Tom's boisterous sound-check and the passionate, revolutionary words of the songs we sang. Odetta, whom we considered an old friend by this time, showed up on opening night along with Oscar Brown Jr. and Amanda Ambrose.

We really hit it off together and the whole run of the gig was memorable. On our wild closing night we all got drunk together (except Tommy Makem, of course) and toasted our common cause.

Describing our plane trip back to New York, she wrote:

> The trip was riotous. Many passengers were incensed that four white men and a black woman were laughing and drinking together, and their displeasure pushed us toward silliness. I asked Liam to translate a Gaelic song that I had heard him sing a capella. He said he'd sing it first.
>
> His clear tenor floated up over the heads of the already-irate passengers. The haunting beauty of the melody must have quelled some of the irritation, because no one asked Liam to shut up.

The song that I sang for her on the plane was "Buachaill on Eirne." It's a love song.

The black thread of the civil rights movement was pushing through the fabric of the American flag. A different nation was struggling to be born. Just as in recent Irish history, the underdog of America was asserting itself. No more second-class citizenship. We, the blacks and the Irish, both oppressed peoples, were taking delight in our own cultures, our *sean nos,* their soul singing, set dancing, and slang like "Dig, man?" which sounds so much like *"A dtigeann tu?"* meaning "Ya get it?" It was all so similar and all with the same purpose: to confuse the common enemy in the hive—the wasp!

A Broadway production of Little Moon of Alban was in the planning, and I was asked to join the cast once again. Tom was in a play at the time and Tommy was doing a solo gig. We hadn't yet committed ourselves to giving up acting to become full-time singers.

The script for *Little Moon* was rewritten (and padded out, always a bad idea) and a new director appointed. I don't even remember his name, another bad sign. Julie Harris, of course, was a fixed star. Robert Redford stayed on as the young IRA man. John Justin (from *The Thief of Baghdad)* was the new male lead. Stefan Gerach, Jamie Ross, Norman Barrs, Helena Carroll, and a handful of others, including myself, stayed on as the second-string players.

TV was so simple compared to mounting a Broadway production. The unions, such as the stagehands' and the musicians' unions, had become very strong—so strong that, to my mind, they usurped the role of management as the exploiters. Such are the pendulum swings. Left to right, right to left. Because I played harmonica at the opening and close of the play, the musicians' local declared the play to be a musical. I got up on stage every night and did my bit for $75 a week on the road and $175 on Broadway while fifteen idlers from the union played poker every night in a room under the stage—at $250 a week each!

Not only was featherbedding rampant in the theater business; residual McCarthyism was crucifying us when we sang in the clubs and coffeehouses. Every entertainer was considered a "commie." Every night either the cop thugs or the union thugs would call at the club you were playing to demand something or other. It was a real case of right meets left. They were all fascists when the circle closed.

The deal for pre-Broadway tryouts was two weeks in Philadelphia, then two weeks in Washington before hitting Broadway. The idea was to fine-tune the play using the country bumpkin audiences before letting New York sophisticates see it, and, of course, the critics.

Over the years a tradition of accommodations for the actors had built up. Stars and producers stayed in one level of accommodation, the rest of us stayed in the local fleabag.

Robert Redford had started out like the rest of us, but as time went by it became clear that he was being groomed for stardom by the powers-that-be. Politics replaced art. Of Robert Redford I must say that none of this seemed to change him. He remained a most likable fellow and a pleasure to work with. But isn't that what makes a star?

Hotel Fleabag in Philadelphia wasn't quite as bad as the Kilkenny louse house I'd once stayed in—but close. It stank to high heaven. Communal bathroom down the hall, walls made of wallpaper, doors with peepholes made by voyeurs between rooms. Paper-and-spit plugs in some of the peepholes. Privacy for body functions or lust—out of the question. The place was also a firetrap.

One good thing about being on the road with the show up and running was that most of the days were free. I would spend all day walking around Philly, which wasn't nearly as bad as W. C. Fields made it out to be. The museum was nearly always my first destination, for a soul cleansing, then on through the park, along by the river, a wonderful meditative time. My thoughts much of that time were on my father, and the worth—or worthlessness—of life and death.

Washington was a shock to me. The hotel was better and the sights impressive, but the slums that started at the bottom of the steps of Capitol Hill had to make you think. If the men of power can't see, or refuse to see, the poverty on their own doorstep, what hope is there for the rest of the good old U.S. of A.? I started working on a song about Capitol Hill, comparing it with the ruins of the Rock of Cashel in Tipperary, the seat of power for so many centuries, a place I had just visited shortly before:

> In Washington one day
> Through your Capitol I wandered.
> And beneath the great white dome
> I stood awhile and pondered—
> If the wind one day will blow
> Through these columns and these hallways,
> If this greatness has to pass,
> As greatness passes, always;
> If the powerful ones who rule
> O'er this country that you cherish,
> Know that arrogance of power
> Is the rock on which you perish.

I thought that was a great phrase I'd coined, "arrogance of power." Before I could finish the song I walked into a bookstore one day and saw a huge display for the new best-seller *The Arrogance of Power* by Senator William Fulbright. I was so pissed off I scrapped the song.

The Broadway opening was a multiple disaster. The internal political infighting that had infected the faceless production people had cast
a pall on our whole troupe. There was an air of gloom at the traditional
after-show party at Sardi's as we waited for the reviews in the early edi-
tions of the newspapers. We were panned big-time by the critics. The
play closed after ten days.

But for me, worst of all, on the night of my first decent paycheck—
the check on which I was depending so heavily to pay my bills—my
dressing room was burglarized while I was onstage. We had been given
our pay before the show in cash in little brown envelopes. I left mine—
plus my wallet, watch, and whatever small change I had, in the dressing room while I did the first scene. I came back after the scene via the
under-stage passage (where the union musicians were playing poker,
the bastards!), and when I opened the dressing room door, the window
to the fire escape was wide open, my watch, wallet, and pay packet gone!

The word spread during intermission. I made a plea to the management—what desperate circumstances this left me in, etc., but I got a
deaf ear. The whole cast was shocked and angry.

We finished the play as it had started, with me playing my harmonica under the Dublin streetlamp. That was a forlorn sound that
night. We took our curtain calls and went to remove our makeup and
costumes.

Back in my dressing room on the table was an envelope. In it was a
note from Julie Harris with a check for my full wages inside.

When I stormed down and knocked on the door with the star on it,
a firm voice from inside said, "If that's Liam, the answer is no! I'm not
taking back the check!"

Well, as an actress she'd always made me melt, since first I saw her
in *East of Eden* torn between James Dean and Richard Davalos, but her
kindness that night to a bit player gave me a glow that dispelled even
the gloom of our sorry *Little Moon.*

Maybe, after all, there was more to the people of the footlights than
just acting the goat.

. . .

Shortly after the play closed, the Clancy Brothers and Tommy Makem made their debut opening at the very grand, very uptown nightclub the Blue Angel. All the front tables were reserved by the cast of *Little Moon of Alban.*

The Blue Angel was the most prestigious club in Manhattan at the time. Marty Erlichman somehow managed to book us in there, probably because we regularly played its sister club in the Village, the Village Vanguard. Some of our followers in the Village cried "sellout." But mostly our friends were delighted that some of the Village misfits had made it. They came up in troops that first opening night even though it was snowing heavily, but the snobby bar was so alien to our usual environment that the Village crowd gravitated en masse to Jimmy Glennen's pub around the corner.

Jimmy Glennon was a Mayo man, west-of-Ireland madness in every bone in his body. A thoroughly professional publican, he was also an alcoholic. But he had the timing of his drinking bouts down to an exact science. On the opening night of our three-week run at the Blue Angel he told us that he had booked out the entire club for himself, his friends, and most of his staff for the closing night. Jimmy always planned his mad bouts well ahead of time.

I was in his company the night he was telling his staff what the sequence of events would be when we all came back to his place for the closing-night party.

"Now, I'm going to come back drunk. The Clancys will be with me. You'll give three rounds of drinks. Then you will cut me off. I'll get into a fury and fire you all on the spot—tell you all that you're sons of whores. Understood? Keep serving the Clancys, *but*—throw me in a cab, pay the fare, and send me home. Now, this is the way it's going to happen and I know it. Now that I'm stone-cold sober, I can tell you that any one of you who, on the night, doesn't do just what I told you is fired."

And that's exactly the way it happened.

. . .

That was our first outing in the Blue Angel. There were to be several more before the night Marty and Lenny got the *Ed Sullivan* talent scouts in.

Moving uptown had been a major culture shock. The bar of the Blue Angel had Bobby Short playing and singing show tunes. He was the closest that New York could come at the time to Sam of *Casablanca*. The walls were padded. The waiters, even the American ones, spoke broken English. In our first week there, Ava Gardner came by. Edward and Mrs. Simpson, the star-crossed royal English lovers, also showed up one night, but hearing Irish rebel songs coming from the main room, they never got beyond the bar.

Jack E. Leonard was the headliner on that particular stint. He got totally pissed off at us. We were the opening act and we should have known our place in the pecking order. We upstaged him by getting out onstage and singing "Sam Hall," getting the audience to sing along with us on the chorus, "Damn your eyes—Blast your soul—Bloody Hell—Shit!" which they did with a right goodwill.

Irwin Corey would have loved that, but Jack E. Leonard came up to our dressing room after the performance.

"You know what? You fucking guys are too fucking much. I'm the fucking *star*. I call *the shots*. You come here and you get the audience to say 'Shit!' How can I top that? Am I going to go out there and tell them to say 'Fuck!'? You guys are fucking ruining me. Fuck you! I'll never descend to that level. So—fuck you." He pretended to be joking.

Ernest Jacoby was manager and co-owner of the Blue Angel with Max Gordon. Jacoby reminded me of de Gaulle. He had that aristocratic look: the aquiline nose, the arrogant air. His club was impeccably run. He treated us with the courtesy he would have given to the jazz players from the Blue Angel's sister club, the Village Vanguard, or to Ava Gardner or to an abdicated king. Somehow, suddenly, we were big names. The scouts from *The Ed Sullivan Show* duly came to the Blue Angel, as Marty said they would, and after the show, invited us for drinks.

"Guys, that was class. We'd love to have you on *The Ed Sullivan Show.*"

We weren't that impressed. We were arrogant. Young and arrogant. As they say in Ireland, we didn't give a tinker's damn. But we accepted.

But then one night Marty came to us and said, "I've found her! You've got to do me a favor. Cut ten minutes out of your show tonight."

"Who have you found, Marty?"

"I found the next Judy Garland." He paused for effect. "I found her singing in a review in the Village. She's sleepin' in a hallway, on a mattress, for Chrissake! She's great. Swear to God! If I can get her to have a nose job, she'll be the next Judy Garland."

The following night she showed up: big nose, big personality, big bundle of nerves.

"Hi, guys. I'm Barbra. Oh God, I'm scared shitless."

Tommy Makem says to her, "I bet you're wearing red knickers."

"How'd you know?"

She pulls up her skirt in front of God and Bobby Short and everyone and displays red pantaloons almost to the knee.

"Jeez, guys, I'm nervous. What am I goin' to sing? Marty wants me to do my interpretation of 'Happy Days Are Here Again'—I do it with a kind of ironic edge to it. I don't know. I'm so nervous I can't think straight."

"Try an Irish Mist," I said.

"What's that?"

"It's a liqueur—kills butterflies."

"Yeah? I'll have a double."

That night Barbra Streisand became a star—even without the nose job. The *Ed Sullivan* scouts were there. Marty made a deal. A funny girl was born.

Marty was frantically trying to find a costume of some kind for us to wear on *The Ed Sullivan Show*. My mother, who knew how cold American winters could be, had sent four Aran sweaters for us. The letter she wrote at the time tells the whole story of the Aran sweaters. I found it recently after all these years.

Dec 13th 1960

That's a grand letter we got this morning. And the paper cutting and write-up! I'm wondering how did I produce such sons and daughters, I being so thick. Anyway looking at your picture I'd say you're "handed down" from Da McGrath (R.I.P.). The write-up and letter brought him back so clearly to my mind that I'm praying for him all day. I wanted to get four pullovers {Aran sweaters} made so ye'd have them for Christmas, but the woman codded me and made only one. Then I got Peggy Drohan {first cousin} to make two and the lads {the girls} to make Tommy's. I sent them off two days ago. They are all different sizes so ye can swap. I just got a rib on the necks (Bobby's idea) and I think it's a good one. Everything is going fine in the insurance business—only that empty chair—I'm tired now Willie, I get shaky when I'm tired. God bless you boy. Love and good wishes from all.

Mammie

On a night in January 1961 we did *The Ed Sullivan Show.* We had rehearsed two songs for it. On the particular night, the starring act got sick. The producer came to us in a panic.

"We've got a problem. Could you guys improvise three extra songs?" That would leave us with about fifteen minutes out of a one-hour show!

"Sure. That's not a problem."

Standing in the wings, I was frantically trying to clear my nose—I had a miserable cold—when I burst a blood vessel. A fountain of blood came gushing from my nose. In the darkness of the wings I was bent over trying to keep the blood off the white sweater when the stage manager came to us.

"One minute to show time." He didn't see my predicament in the dark.

"Be good, gentlemen. Remember—there's eighty million people watching you!" My nosebleed stopped instantly. Cut off by sheer terror.

The night after *The Ed Sullivan Show* we went to the White Horse.

We were heroes. Even old Ernie smiled. Young Ernie set up a round on the house for us. He was laughing.

"Ya know that old broad lives upstairs? The one who's been callin' the cops and makin' such a fuss all these years when you guys were singin' in the back room? Well, she calls in here today. 'I saw some guys on *The Ed Sullivan Show* last night and, jeez, they sounded just like the guys that are always singin' down here.' I said, 'They *are* the guys who are always singin' down here.' And she says, 'Jeez, and to think I been beatin' my broom handle on the floor all this time trying to get them to shut up. Now they're on *The Sullivan Show*. Guess I'll never do that again. I'm bein' serenaded by famous people—for free!' That's what the old broad says. Here, guys, let me get you another."

A few days later we were walking down State Street in Chicago. We were opening that night in the New Gate of Horn. A passerby stopped us on the street.

"Hey! I saw you guys on *The Ed Sullivan Show.* Fantastic! You guys were fabulous! Can I have your autographs? Martha! Look who we got here. The Clancy Brothers!"

"And Tommy Makem," Tommy added.

"The Clancy Brothers!" another passerby shouted.

Soon we were surrounded by a mob—signing autographs as fast as we could scribble.

Writing furiously, Tom looked over his shoulder.

"Hey!" he said. "We're fuckin' famous!"

Afterword at Petie's

When the hectic days of the March tour were behind us; the big highs of Carnegie Hall and *The Ed Sullivan Show;* the tense tours of the New England college circuit; in terrifying little six-seater planes, the time would come to gather in our local pub, like birds on a wire, in the Lion's Head, ready for migration. Ahead of us were the long, lovely summers in Ireland.

On one such occasion, on a spring day in the nineteen-sixties, Paddy, Tom, and I met up as usual in the pub before hailing a cab to the airport. Outside the street-level window of the Lion's Head bar, the Greenwich Village rites of spring were underway. We downed cold steins of beer and watched the passing carnival as the poet, Joel Oppenheimer, told us about the acting part he had been offered in a new avant-garde film. He was saying, "Marty, the director, says to me, 'Hey, Joel, you want to play a part in my new film? It's set in a nuthouse.' I says to him, 'What part do you want me to play?' He says, 'The chicken-fucker, it's a small part. You see, we're dollying down this hallway looking at what's happening in each of the cells as we pass by, and in one of them there's this guy fucking a chicken. You look just right for the part. We can keep your name off the credits if you want.' 'Hell no,' I said to him, 'I'll play your chicken-fucker, but I gotta get my name up there—in big letters.' "

Meantime outside the window two lovesick gays stopped for a long, passionate kiss. Across the street a drunk was making his way along the iron railings of Sheridan Square. Just opposite the Head he stopped, shouting, "Fuck the sodomites!" (Few steps.) "Fuck the Jews!" (On again.) "Fuck the Catholics! Fuck the niggers!" Then, pausing for a good breath, he threw himself against the metal railings, his arms wide like Christ on the cross, and shouted, "I hate everyone irrespective of class, creed, or color!" Tom says, "Jesus, look at that." I thought he meant the drunk or possibly the gays, but no, there was a flash of color and we all took our beers outside to watch a character pass by on an old-fashioned "penny-farthing" bicycle. He was dressed in a pink tutu complete with pink tights, ballet slippers, and pink plumage as headgear.

Yes, the annual Village outpouring of individual expression was in full swing along Christopher Street and down past Gay Street. The ordinary folks who lived in the old red sandstone buildings, mostly long-established Italian families, loudly protested the homosexual gatherings on the stoops (that's what they call the steps up to those buildings for some reason). So they devised a clever solution. Each morning, the old mamas, shouting Italian obscenities at the gays, would install what became known locally as "de-faggoters" on the fire escapes over the stoops. These devices were cheap galvanized bathtubs punched with pinprick holes and filled with water in the morning. They dripped all day, keeping the steps wet. That solved the problem. "Piles, my dear, hemorrhoids," I overheard one exotic creature say to another.

As we watched, the penny-farthing bicycle came back down Christopher Street from another direction, except this time a beautiful harlequin in black and white and gold diamond shapes was riding it. Moments later the bicycle turned at the intersection of Gay Street and came back again with the ballerina flashing pink tights and tutu. It was the same guy, one-half ballerina/one-half harlequin, going up and down Christopher Street in the spring sunshine, displaying his plumage. Tom said, "Thank God we're going back to the sanity of Ireland tonight."

As usual on our early-morning arrival in Ireland for the summer recess, we had a ritualistic celebration of homecoming. We threw the suitcases into the house on William Street, kissed everyone hello, then went to our local, Petie's, for a nightcap before going to bed for the day. Well, after all, we had been flying all night.

Petie Lawlor lived with his old mother over the pub that had been in the family since Bianconi had started his stagecoach business in Ireland in 1815, and nothing much of the old establishment had changed.

Petie was not well when we came in for our nightcap that morning. He was thumping his chest and taking frequent sips from what looked like a glass of water under the counter.

"Oh God, hello, lads, welcome back." (*Thump, thump* on the chest.) "How are ye? Jesus, ye're more famous than ever." (*Thump, thump.*) "Ye're never off the feckin' radio." (*Thump.*)

"What's wrong with the chest, Petie?" Tom asked.

"It's not the chest, Tom boy, it's the heart. I'm tryin' to get the feckin' thing started."

"Well, that fuckin' water won't help," says Tom (words from the wise). "Try a drop of brandy and port."

"Oh Jesus, no! I could never drink in the daytime, never!"

I smelled his glass. "What's that you're drinking now, Petie?" I asked.

"Oh sure, Liam, that's only oul' gin. When I'm drinking I drink only the best—top shelf—Redbreast whiskey. That's my drink."

"Give us a taste of what you're drinking there," says I. It smelled like straight gin.

"How many of those have you had today, Petie?"

"I won't tell you a word of a lie, Liam, that's number seven." (*Thump, thump.*)

Just then in came Tommy Carney. "Hello, lads. Did ye hear the explosion last night? The wind blew up the river! A good one, isn't it? D'ye get it? The wind blew up the river."

Tommy was a wit in his own mind and had started a local publication called the *Carrick Opinion.* But inside, Tommy must have been a troubled man. Like many an overpious, misguided Irishman, Tommy had gone to Spain with General O'Duffy to fight for Franco and Holy Mother Church in the Spanish Civil War. Although he never got to fire a shot in Spain, in his old age he was haunted by the memory of the atrocities he'd seen. As we talked to Petie (*thump, thump*), we could hear Tommy in the corner: "Holy Mary Mother of God—." Large bottle, rosary beads, and sudden ejaculations of bits of the Hail Mary and Glory Be.

In comes Kevin Driscoll, all stammer and underbite and gums and smiles. Kevin was a longtime friend. We shared many adventures. "Aw janey! Hello, lads. Wa-welcome home. I lost me teeth! Meself and Bobby went off last ni-night to Thurles—a little pub for a session. I had only half a crown so I thought I'd be cute and get a small bottle. Ba-Bobby bought a whiskey. He had only a half a crown, too, but he-he knew the woman of the house had a heavy ha-and. She thought a glass of whiskey was—ya know—a big glass—full of whiskey. When I saw the way she was pouring I said, 'Ch-change my small bottle for a glass of whiskey, please ma'am.' Jay we got awful drunk, I was throwing up on the street. When I woke up this mo-morning I had a mouth full of no teeth. I called Bobby and he told me where we were, so I fa-phoned the woman in the pub and asked her if she found any ta-teeth. She said yes, there was a shower of rain last night, she said, and when she went out to sweep the sidewalk this morning, weren't the set of teeth la-laughing up at her from the gutter. She put them in a package and they're arriving on the three o'clock bus. We're having a coming home party in the pub at the bus stop. Can ye come?"

I looked at Tom—he looked at me—I looked at Paddy—and he looked at Petie.

"Another, lads?" (*Thump, thump.*)

"Ah, I think we'd better go to bed, Petie," said Paddy, thinking more of escape than bed.

"We'll have one for the bed," says Tom.

Just then in comes Johnny Walsh, the young athlete now slightly over the top, full of briskness, rubbing his hands. I think to myself, "Thank God there's one sane person left in Carrick, anyway."

"Small bottle, Petie," says Johnny. "Well, hello, lads, how are ye? My God, I can hardly speak to such famous people. Saw ye on the television at the National Stadium. By God, ye're puttin' Carrick on the map. We're all proud of ye. Can I buy ye—?" He stopped in midquestion. His eyes glazed. He looked off into the corner of the bar, not the one where Tommy Carney was going "Holy Mary," but across from there under a table. There was horror and fixation on his face. He crouched, held out his clenching hands, and started to sneak up on something under the table. He stops, straightens up, walks back to the counter, and picks up the conversation quite normally. "Anyway, lads, it's great to see ye. I suppose ye'd see a lot of changes in Carrick now. It's probably lookin' very small to—" He stops again. Down he gets on all fours and starts creeping stealthily toward the table.

"What the hell is wrong with him?" Tom asked Petie.

"Don't mind him," says Petie. "The poor hoore was hypnotized ten years ago at a variety concert in the cinema and he's looking for the leprechauns ever since. Poor"—*thump*—"fucker!"

So there we were, drinking at Petie's at eleven o'clock in the morning, just off the plane from New York, our best athlete looking for fairies under a table, our local wit saying prayers to save his troubled soul, our neighbor waiting for his tee-teeth to come off a bus, and our publican thumping his chest trying to get the feckin' heart started.

Tom turned and says, "What time is the next flight back to New York and the sanity of Greenwich Village?"

Index